Symbols, Abbreviations, and Contents

Commonly Used Abbreviations and Symbols

Help Yourself

A Guide to Writing and Rewriting

THIRD EDITION

Help Yourself

A Guide to Writing and Rewriting

THIRD EDITION

Marylu Mattson
Sonoma State University

Sophia Leshing

Elaine Levi

Charles E. Merrill Publishing Company
A Bell & Howell Company
Columbus   Toronto   London   Sydney

Cover art by M. C. Escher, courtesy of Vorpal Gallery
Cover design by Tony Faiola

Published by Charles E. Merrill Publishing Company
A Bell & Howell Company
Columbus, Ohio 43216

International Standard Book Number: 0-675-20027-X
Library of Congress Catalog Card Number: 82-61432
Printed in the United States of America
8 9—91 90 89

Words, like glasses, obscure everything they do not make clear.

Joseph Joubert

Our thanks to Helen Jaskoski for her help on this project.

To the Instructor

If papers turned in to you include errors in mechanics, grammar, and/or organization, and if you find time inadequate for individual tutoring or repeated review, *Help Yourself, A Guide to Writing and Rewriting* may provide the kind of help you and your students need.

The intent here is to furnish a guide that students can use without an instructor's help in both writing and revising their papers. This guide works without complex rules, technical language, or linguistic theories about English—an intent that should become evident through the following explanation of organization and content.

Help Yourself contains two frames of reference for locating materials. The table of Contents contains chapter titles; Symbols, Abbreviations, and Contents contains an alphabetical list of major items discussed. Both listings are keyed to commonly used correctional symbols and abbreviations.

The organization and content of the book are such that the students can understand any chapter they turn to and can understand it without reference to any other chapter. Material is self-explanatory, and almost all terms used in a chapter are explained in that chapter. In revising papers, students will be using your marginal notations as stepping-stones to the kind of help you might give if you were more than one person. These steps will be—

1. moving from your marginal symbol or abbreviation to the same symbol or abbreviation in the table of Contents;
2. moving from the table of Contents to the chapter indicated;
3. reading the rule and studying the explanations and examples in that chapter;
4. taking the Quick Quizzes and studying the answers;
5. doing the exercises in Review and Practice and studying the answers;
6. taking the Chapter Test and studying the answers;
7. following the step-by-step Procedure for Recognizing and Correcting Errors (a procedure that can be used at any time in the process of writing or revising a paper).

In addition to its use as a student's self-help guide in writing and revising papers, *Help Yourself* lends itself to—

1. classroom teaching of grammar, mechanics, and elementary composition;
2. specific and general review;
3. individual assignments based on needs of specific students;
4. help for the inexperienced student in organizing and writing essays.

We recognize that problems in teaching English are manifold, and that the basic goal of college composition classes—to lead students to critical thinking and then to conveying their meaning via the written word—encompasses much more than mechanics, grammar, and organization. We have, however, limited ourselves to what, in our experience, seem to be the most common compositional errors of college students.

That *Help Yourself* is appearing in a third edition testifies to a widespread need among students for a review of basic points of English grammar—a situation we can all regret. Those of you who are familiar with the text will find a reordering of the book's sections and a sharpening of some parts, based on useful criticism we have received. If those of you using the text for the first time find it helpful in speeding the arduous process whereby students become competent, confident writers, the book has done its job.

We hope *Help Yourself* advances your students' learning and eases your teaching task.

To the Student

"I know you believe you understand what you think I said, but I am not sure you realize that what you heard is not what I meant."

Anon.

This statement suggests a certain communication gap, and communication is what language is all about. Effective communication means knowing what you want to say and saying it precisely and without ambiguity. You have your whole life experience to draw from in finding what you want to say and a whole language to draw from in finding how to say it. *Help Yourself* should help you solve many of the difficulties you may have with one language—English. *Help Yourself* does not cover everything; it covers only those things that are most commonly confusing. Such things as writing style and grammar theory are not discussed.

This is a do-it-yourself book. You will find every chapter self-explanatory—understandable by itself. Every problem discussed is explained simply and is illustrated with many examples.

You will find explanations, exercises, and tests with answers for checking your progress. On pages xiii-xxix you will find a pretest that should help you identify your problems. To help you find what you are looking for, *Help Yourself* has two frames of reference for locating materials. The regular Contents on page xi lists topics by chapter, together with the kinds of correctional abbreviations and symbols that may appear in the margin of a paper returned to you by your instructor. Symbols, Abbreviations, and Contents appears inside the front cover. It lists topics alphabetically and also includes correctional abbreviations and symbols.

Here is an illustration of how *Help Yourself* might be used in revising a paper. Let us assume that you are enrolled in an English course the object of which is to teach you to write logical, clear, grammatically acceptable papers. Your topic has been assigned, and you turn in a paper entitled "Experimental High Altitude Farming." Upon getting it back and noticing the marks in the margin, you may feel panic—a feeling that should be dispelled with the aid of this book.

Understand that those marks in the margin are your instructor's coded message to you. Your first job is to decode them. For example, you may find the abbreviation *dang*. You see that *dang* appears opposite a sentence that reads, "While milking a cow, the stool broke." (Do stools milk cows?) *Dang* is not a mild obscenity voiced by your professor and thus should not be taken personally. Prove this by looking on the left side of the table of contents and noting that *dang* is an abbreviation for *dangling modifier*. To the right of *dangling modifier* is a page number that guides you to an explanation of what a *dangling modifier* is and of how to know one when you see one. Doing the exercises should help you learn to undangle any *dangling modifier* you may run across in the future.

As you read through a chapter, you may come upon a star such as the star at the end of this sentence.* This star refers to a note in bold type immediately following the item and explains a special term—such as *verb*, for example. Read the explanations. Each special term is explained in every chapter in which it is used.

Just as with *dang*, you can decode other marginal marks and learn to remedy—and then to avoid—the errors they call to your attention. Thus, it is conceivable that by the time you have read the explanations and done the exercises in *Help Yourself*, you will be able to save your panic for some other course.

Since few professors can discuss each paper with each student, they speak to their students through marginal notations. Many of these notations are either abbreviations or symbols, both of which are a kind of **shorthand for the names of common errors.** These notations are shown both on the inside covers and in the Contents. You will need to know only one notation for each chapter, except for punctuation, for which you will need to learn several notations. In each case, you will need to know the notations your professor chooses.

By reading chapter titles and notations together, you should be able to guess the meaning of most abbreviations. A few notations are not immediately obvious, such as the following:

inc = incomplete sentence See chapter 2
ag = agreement See chapter 4 and chapter 5
ambig = ambiguous, or unclear See chapter 6
MM, mm = misplaced modifier; *dm* = dangling modifier;
sq = squinting modifier See chapter 10
/ /, *prl, para* = parallelism See chapter 11
K, k, awk = awkward See chapter 12

We also want to call your attention to the appendixes and glossary at the end of the book—items usually not high on a student's list of things to read. Possibly helpful material dealing with commonly confused words and with some technical aspects of various parts of speech is gathered in the appendixes. The glossary explains many of the unfamiliar terms you may encounter during your writing classes.

Whatever your present level of writing proficiency, we hope you will decide that *Help Yourself* has been a help to you.

Contents

Commonly Used Abbreviations and Symbols

k/k/awk
v. voice
wdy/wordy
chop/choppy
stringy str/string
¶

PRETEST

INSTRUCTIONS

The purpose of these pretests is to help you identify some of your writing problems and to direct you to the chapters that can help you solve those problems. Each section of the pretest covers material from one section of the book. For example, items 1–21 are from chapter 1; items 22–43 are from chapter 2. In addition, in parentheses following each item is the page on which you can find an explanation of the items, followed by the section number for that item within the chapter.

If you decide to test yourself on pronoun-antecedent agreement, for example, do items 65–74 of the pretest, check your answers with the answers on page xxviii, and then turn to chapter 5 to study whatever you feel you need to work on. On the other hand, you may decide to do all of the pretest items (1–220) at one sitting for a general survey of what you should plan to study.

If you have neither missed nor guessed at the answers for a particular chapter, the chances are good that you need little work on the material in that chapter.

If you have missed none, or few, of the items, but were unsure of some, you might want to skip the chapter, but test yourself by taking the chapter test and studying the answers.

If you have missed or guessed at many of the items from a chapter, you need to study the entire chapter thoroughly.

Chapter 1, Parts of Speech: items 1–21 (pages 1–27)

Under *Answers, write* the part of speech of each underlined word (or group of words). Check ***Sure*** if you are sure of your answer; check ***Unsure*** if you guessed at your answer.

	Answers	Sure	Unsure
Model: An atom is not the smallest unit of matter. (p. 2; A–1)	noun	______	✓
1. Men club the newborn seals to death in a bloody orgy. (p. 2; A–1)	______	______	______
2. Duke Ellington played frequently at Carnegie Hall. (p. 3; A–1)	______	______	______
3. Your morality may be my *obscenity.* (p. 5; A–1)	______	______	______
4. Few have crossed *no-man's-land.* (p. 6; A–1)	______	______	______
5. The hiker *reached* his destination. (p. 7; A–2)	______	______	______
6. The teachings of the Old and New Testaments *are called* the Judeo-Christian ethic. (p. 8; A–2)	______	______	______

	Answers	Sure	Unsure
7. *It* is a complex form of government. (p. 10; A–3)			
8. *Whoever* wants the stale candy can have it. (p. 10; A–3)			
9. *Green* hair looked out of place, since the others had purple hair. (p. 10; A–4)			
10. His 98-year-old, *hard-of-hearing*, nearly blind grandmother just scaled Mount Everest. (p. 10; A–4)			
11. The children, *underfed* and pot-bellied, ought to concern everyone. (p. 11; A–4)			
12. He goes *quickly.* (p. 11; A–5)			
13. It is *vitally* important that this message go through. (p. 12; A–5)			
14. It is entirely *too* important a commodity for one person to control its manufacture. (p. 13; A–5)			
15. He sat *by* the door. (p. 14; A–6)			
16. We gave it *to* them. (p. 14; A–6)			
17. Whales *and* dolphins are both marine mammals. (p. 14; A–7)			
18. Will she give a report on cytogenetics *or* nerve regeneration? (p. 14; A–7)			
19. *Although* dogs bark at night, a baby's cry is far more disturbing. (p. 15; A–7)			
20. *Because* the night has a thousand eyes, there must be many peeping Toms. (p. 15; A–7)			
21. *Ouch!* (p. 16; A–8)			

Chapter 2, The Sentence and the Sentence Fragment: items 22–43 (pages 29–50)

Some of the following groups of words are sentences; some are not. Under *Answers*, *write* ***S*** if the item is a sentence; *write* ***frag*** if the item is not a sentence. *Check* ***Sure*** if you are sure of your answer; *check* ***Unsure*** if you guessed at your answer.

	Answers	Sure	Unsure
Model: Annette speaks.	S		✓
22. The clues were obvious, but the conclusion eluded us. (p. 30; A–1)			

	Answers	Sure	Unsure
23. Did Linda tear along the dotted line? (p. 30; A–1)	______	______	______
24. Before you enter. (p. 32; A–2)	______	______	______
25. The man who came to dinner. (p. 33; A–2)	______	______	______
26. Slowly but surely, is choking itself to death. (p. 34; B–1)	______	______	______
27. After a long night, the dawn. (p. 34; B–1)	______	______	______
28. The writer beginning his novel. (p. 34; B–1)	______	______	______
29. To think is important. (p. 35; B–2)	______	______	______
30. The economist suggested. (p. 36; B–2)	______	______	______
31. I expect it. (p. 35; B–2)	______	______	______
32. Since the speech has ended. (p. 36; B–2)	______	______	______
33. I did not know. (p. 36; B–2)	______	______	______
34. That Beethoven composed nine symphonies. (p. 36; B–2)	______	______	______
35. The area that contained the mineral deposits. (p. 36; B–2)	______	______	______
36. She fainted. (p. 30; A–1)	______	______	______
37. Should John fly. (p. 35; B–2)	______	______	______
38. To be seen. (p. 35; B–2)	______	______	______
39. On time. (p. 34; B–1)	______	______	______
40. He is mining. (p. 30; A–1)	______	______	______
41. Who that was. (p. 35; B–2)	______	______	______
42. Most visitors to the city like. (p. 36; B–2)	______	______	______
43. Unless we receive the payment within a week. (p. 35; B–2)	______	______	______

Chapter 3, Verbs: items 44–50 (pages 51–75)

Some of the sentences are correct; some contain *unnecessary tense shifts.* Under *Answers, write* ***C*** if the sentences are correct; *write* ***shift*** if the sentences contain any unnecessary tense shifts. *Check* ***Sure*** if you are sure of your answer; *check* ***Unsure*** if you guessed at your answer.

	Answers	Sure	Unsure
Model: The baby was born last spring; he will be a year old next week.	C	______	✓

	Answers	Sure	Unsure
44. Yesterday Yorick celebrated his birthday and wash his car. (p. 68; B–1)	______	______	______
45. The plane will land tonight, and Glinka will meet it. (p. 69; B–2)	______	______	______
46. Yesterday I was sick, today I am well, and tomorrow I will return to work. (p. 69; B–3)	______	______	______
47. Yesterday I borrowed a lawnmower and mow our lawn. (p. 68; B–2)	______	______	______
48. I have called the plumber twice; according to his answering service, he will call me tomorrow. (p. 69; B–3)	______	______	______
49. I have finish the "Unfinished Symphony." (p. 54; A–2)	______	______	______
50. By the time you reach home, we will have decided where to spend the weekend. (p. 57)	______	______	______

Chapter 4, Subject-Verb Agreement: items 51–64 (pages 77–94)

Some of the following sentences are correct; some are not. Under *Answers, write* ***C*** if the sentence is correct; *write* ***inc*** if the sentence is incorrect. *Check* ***Sure*** if you are sure of your answer; *check* ***Unsure*** if you guessed at your answer.

	Answers	Sure	Unsure
Model: Halloween come once a year.	inc	✓	______
51. Joan lives alone. (p. 78; A–1)	______	______	______
52. Members of the football team need vitamins. (p. 79; A–2)	______	______	______
53. Both needs dentures. (p. 79; A–2)	______	______	______
54. Just one error in all those numbers throws the total off. (p. 80; B–1)	______	______	______
55. The early bird, despite his rewards, lose sleep. (p. 80; B–1)	______	______	______
56. The team refuses to eat at Bar F Ranch. (p. 81; B–2)	______	______	______
57. The string quartet plays tonight. (p. 81; B–2)	______	______	______
58. Each of us create his own hell. (p. 82; B–3)	______	______	______
59. Everything under the sun, moon, and stars has a reason. (p. 82; B–3)	______	______	______

	Answers	Sure	Unsure
60. Neither a borrower nor a lender are involved. (p. 84; B–5)	______	______	______
61. Either libraries or museums are open tomorrow. (p. 84; B–5)	______	______	______
62. Either they or I are to drive. (p. 84; B–5)	______	______	______
63. Robin, with Nora and Della, is trying organic farming. (p. 84; B–6)	______	______	______
64. There are several inert gases. (p. 85; B–7)	______	______	______

Chapter 5, Pronoun-Antecedent Agreement: items 65–74 (pages 95–112)

Some of the following sentences are correct; some are not. Under *Answers, write* ***C*** if the sentence is correct; *write* ***inc*** if the sentence is incorrect. *Check* ***Sure*** if you are sure of your answer; *check* ***Unsure*** if you guessed at your answer.

	Answers	Sure	Unsure
Model: Water seeks its own level.	C	______	✓
65. An army marches on its stomach. (p. 96; A–1)	______	______	______
66. Neither knew their mother's birthday. (p. 97; A–1)	______	______	______
67. One of the senators continued his argument after the meeting's adjournment. (p. 98; A–3).	______	______	______
68. Each of the women has their reasons for being here. (p. 98; A–3)	______	______	______
69. Neither the play nor the novel has their characters well defined. (p. 98; A–3)	______	______	______
70. The flock of pheasants left its nest. (p. 99; A–4)	______	______	______
71. Wise people keep their own counsel. (p. 100; B–1)	______	______	______
72. The mass immunization program was planned by the physicians through their medical society. (p. 102; B–3)	______	______	______
73. Either the interview or the films will have its place on the program. (p. 102; B–3)	______	______	______
74. Several councils were negotiating among themselves. (p. 102; B–4)	______	______	______

Chapter 6, Pronoun Reference: items 75–80 (pages 113–125)

Some of the following sentences are correct and clear in their meaning; others are not. Under *Answers, write* ***C*** if the sentence is correct and clear; *write* ***unc*** if the sentence is unclear. *Check* ***Sure*** if you are sure of your answer; *check* ***Unsure*** if you guessed at your answer.

	Answers	Sure	Unsure
Model: Hugh and Edmund talked together and then he left town.	unc	✓	______
75. The opponents made their reasons clear. (p. 114; A–2)	______	______	______
76. Each filed their own income tax report. (p. 114; A–1)	______	______	______
77. As Fernanda adjusted the dial and rotated the antenna, it broke. (p. 116; B–1)	______	______	______
78. Iris asked Thea to be her traveling companion because Thea understood Iris. (p. 116; B–2)	______	______	______
79. The overweight fighter ate less and exercised more; this helped him to lose weight. (p. 117; B–3)	______	______	______
80. Keith used the desk for his typewriter and the table for his record player. Jonathan did not appreciate this. (p. 117; B–3)	______	______	______

Chapter 7, Pronoun Case: items 81–104 (pages 127–163)

Some of the following sentences are correct; others are not. Under *Answers, write* ***C*** if the sentence is correct; *write* ***inc*** if the sentence is incorrect. *Check* ***Sure*** if you are sure of your answer; *check* ***Unsure*** if you guessed at your answer.

	Answers	Sure	Unsure
Model: It was he.	C	______	✓
81. You tell whoever asks that I am out. (p. 131; A–1)	______	______	______
82. You and me fight all the time. (p. 128; A–1)	______	______	______
83. Who came after she finished singing? (p. 129; A–1)	______	______	______
84. My friend saw as much as I. (p. 130; A–1)	______	______	______

	Answers	Sure	Unsure
85. Pablo gave a picture to whoever visited his studio. (p. 131; A–1)	_______	_______	_______
86. The finalists were they and I. (p. 133; A–2)	_______	_______	_______
87. My roommate will be who? (p. 133; A–2)	_______	_______	_______
88. Impulse led him into the debate. (p. 136; B–1)	_______	_______	_______
89. Glenda remembered to call them. (p. 137; B–1)	_______	_______	_______
90. Annette turned to answer she. (p. 137; B–1)	_______	_______	_______
91. The referee knew no one but I. (p. 140; B–1)	_______	_______	_______
92. That reporter questioned everyone except her and them. (p. 140; B–1)	_______	_______	_______
93. The diet helped Marvin more than me. (p. 139; B–1)	_______	_______	_______
94. He is the one whom I nominated. (p. 140; B–1)	_______	_______	_______
95. Stephanie gave him the book. (p. 141; B–2)	_______	_______	_______
96. Nobody told she the truth. (p. 141; B–2)	_______	_______	_______
97. Giving he the book was a nuisance. (p. 142; B–2)	_______	_______	_______
98. The druggist brought I the prescription. (p. 142; B–2)	_______	_______	_______
99. The tax assessor's office sent me, as well as he, a refund. (p. 143; B–2)	_______	_______	_______
100. They ran from him. (p. 144; B–3)	_______	_______	_______
101. Our house is on fire. (p. 150; C–2)	_______	_______	_______
102. Her leaving by plane coincided with me coming by train. (p. 150; C–2)	_______	_______	_______
103. The car with the dead battery is mine. (p. 148; C–1)	_______	_______	_______
104. Who's has no brakes? (p. 148; C–1)	_______	_______	_______

Chapter 8, Run-on Sentences: items 105–110 (pages 165–182)

Some of the sentences are correct; some are *run-on sentences.* Under *Answers, write* ***C*** if the sentence is correct; *write* ***RO*** if the sentence is incorrect. *Check* ***Sure*** if you are sure of your answer; *check* ***Unsure*** if you guessed at your answer.

	Answers	Sure	Unsure
Model: This sentence is incorrect it is a run-on.	R.O.		✓
105. Most of the children were playing together, Marcia was alone. (p. 167; A–1, A–2)			
106. Marriage is a game for two, it should be played without kibitzers. (p. 167; A–1, A–2)			
107. When did he get to town, and when will he come over? (p. 167; A–1)			
108. A recession may be unnoticed by the employed person but it is a disaster to the unemployed. (p. 169; B–1, B–2)			
109. Jim forgot it was Thursday; therefore, he failed to keep his dental appointment. (p. 169; B–1, B–2)			
110. I cooked the egg for two minutes the white was still nearly raw. (p. 171; C–1, C–2)			

Chapter 9, Punctuation: items 111–175 (pages 183–242)

Some of the sentences are correct; others are incorrectly *punctuated.* Under *Answers, write* ***C*** if the sentence is correct; *write* ***punc*** if the sentence is incorrect. *Check* ***Sure*** if you are sure of your answer; *check* ***Unsure*** if you guessed at your answer.

	Answers	Sure	Unsure
Model: Is Joe here.	punc	✓	
111. He came to the rehearsal carrying his cello on his back. (p. 185; A–1)			
112. She got her BA. (p. 185; A–2)			
113. Who invented the electric ice cream freezer. (p. 186; B)			
114. Help! (p. 186; C)			
115. It's five o'clock. (p. 188; D)			
116. John wouldn't go there if you paid him. (p. 188; D–1)			
117. The day's end finally arrived. (p. 190; D–2)			
118. Where is the womens' dressing room? (p. 190; D–2)			
119. The club of the mother's-in-laws has just opened. (p. 190; D–2)			

	Answers	Sure	Unsure
120. The lives of Lewis's and Clark's were different. (p. 191; D–2)			
121. The fish's scales were luminescent. (p. 191; D–2)			
122. What is the president-elect's name? (p. 191; D–2)			
123. Here are two 5's and two 10s'. (p. 192; D–3)			
124. Most of the '49ers didn't find gold. (p. 192; D–3)			
125. The dog chased its tail. (p. 193; D–4)			
126. Who's slide rule did he use? (p. 193; D–4)			
127. The soloist sang off-key, and the audience walked out. (p. 196; E–1)			
128. We visited Italy France, and England. (p. 196; E–1)			
129. A delicate, gray, metal, mobile won first prize. (p. 196; E–1)			
130. He became a respected, versatile painter. (p. 198; E–1)			
131. After all eclipses are not daily occurrences. (p. 198; E–1)			
132. Our tax bill having been paid, we started a budget for the next year. (p. 199; E–1)			
133. He needs money, not sympathy. (p. 199; E–1)			
134. If he thinks that he is wrong. (p. 200; E–1)			
135. Rembrandt, the painter, etched. (p. 201; E–2)			
136. Your plane, Doctor Frankenstein, will leave at midnight. (p. 201; E–2)			
137. What, after all threatens them? (p. 202; E–2)			
138. The vernal equinox, which occurs in March, is the first day of spring. (p. 202; E–2)			
139. "She screamed" get off my toes!" (p. 203; E–2)			
140. Jesse was born January 3, 1970. (p. 204; E–2)			
141. He lives at 1234 Lanir Street Boston, Massachusetts. (p. 204; E–2)			

	Answers	Sure	Unsure
142. World War I ended November 11, 1918. (p. 204; E–2)			
143. Phyl was the only nurse; the surgeon needed her. (p. 208; F–1)			
144. As the sun had set; lights came on in all the houses. (p. 208; F–1)			
145. He overhauled the engine, repaired the dent, and replaced the tires, and when he had finished, he sold the car. (p. 208; F–2)			
146. Children are basically honest people, therefore, it is unfortunate when adults teach them, by example, to lie. (p. 209; F–3)			
147. Styles in music change; consequently, today's top ten harmonies will be tomorrow's lost chords. (p. 209; F–3)			
148. Maud, the violinist; Herbert, the flutist; and Grace, the noted harpist, were waiting for their instruments to arrive. (p. 210; F–4)			
149. Snyder spoke to Jones—a hard man to please—about the assignment in Boston. (p. 212; G)			
150. The candidate—I should have introduced you to him—was very impressive. (p. 212; G)			
151. Epictetus encouraged individuality in one of his writings: "As bad performers cannot sing alone, but in a chorus, so some persons cannot walk alone." (p. 214; H–1)			
152. We will find the promised: "city overrun with vipers." (p. 215; H–1)			
153. The recipe calls for a variety of fish: sardines, anchovies, halibut, and herring. (p. 215; H–2)			
154. They knew he was: a writer, an actor, and a director. (p. 215; H–2)			
155. You will need to supply two things for the trip: You will certainly need a sleeping bag. You will probably need an air mattress. (p. 216; H–3)			
156. We like both playwrights, Molière arouses our admiration and O'Neill our sympathy. (p. 216; H–4)			
157. He felt un- comfortable. (p. 218; I–1)			

	Answers	Sure	Unsure
158. On that date, the a-doption proceedings began. (p. 219; I–1)	______	______	______
159. You have the stre-ngth to go on. (p. 219; I–1)	______	______	______
160. Send the sergeant-at-arms here. (p. 220; I–2)	______	______	______
161. He is going to re-cover those chairs. (p. 220; I–3)	______	______	______
162. Coleridge started his poem, "In Xanadu did Kubla Khan/A stately pleasure-dome decree." (p. 222; J–1)	______	______	______
163. The first chapter of *The Mother Tongue* is entitled "Our Hybrid Heritage." (p. 223; J–2)	______	______	______
164. Everyone was surprised when the soprano sang the tenor aria *The Flower Song* in last Saturday's performance of "Carmen." (p. 223; J–2)	______	______	______
165. The reviewer of this book says, "Mr. Jerry Mander's collection of political essays opens with a provocative proposal entitled 'You Draw Your Line; I'll Draw Mine.' " (p. 223; J–2)	______	______	______
166. Her friends called her "Verny." (p. 224; J–3)	______	______	______
167. "On your left, Rich replied." (p. 225; J–4)	______	______	______
168. "How do we get back to the highway?" she asked. (p. 226; J–4)	______	______	______
169. Bake the cake in a moderate oven (350°) for 30 minutes. (p. 227; K)	______	______	______
170. The rust remover cleans in eight seconds. (At least that is what the ad claims). (p. 228; K)	______	______	______
171. "The significance of this discovery [made in 1892] was that it opened the entire area for further exploration." (p. 228; L)	______	______	______
172. "The director of the company . . . has resigned." (p. 229; M)	______	______	______
173. ". . . John Jones has resigned." (p. 229; M)	______	______	______
174. "The salinity of several bodies of water . . . has increased. . . ." (p. 229; M)	______	______	______
175. "Are there any great men alive today. . . ?" (p. 229; M)	______	______	______

Chapter 10, Dangling, Squinting, and Other Misplaced Modifiers: items 176–190 (pages 243–264)

Some of the sentences are correct; some contain *misplaced modifiers.* Under *Answers, write* ***C*** if the sentence is correct; *write* ***MM*** if the sentence contains a misplaced modifier. *Check* ***Sure*** if you are sure of your answer; *check* ***Unsure*** if you guessed at your answer.

	Answers	Sure	Unsure
Model: Like the robin, I enjoy painting the swan.	mm	______	✓
176. Running to the bus, Steven broke his glasses. (p. 245; A–2)	______	______	______
177. Shuffling the cards, an ace slipped to the floor. (p. 247; A–2)	______	______	______
178. While doing the dishes, an ambulance raced down our street. (p. 249; A)	______	______	______
179. To be able to type for long periods of time without tiring, your seat should be comfortable. (p. 250; A)	______	______	______
180. Hearing the siren, Orpheus pulled over to the curb. (p. 247; A)	______	______	______
181. The ticket agent told us eventually new schedules would be available. (p. 251; B–1, B–2)	______	______	______
182. The item was added to the budget following the mayor's request and the city council's approval. (p. 251; B–1)	______	______	______
183. Arriving in Boston before the day was over, we found a motel. (p. 251; B–1, B–2)	______	______	______
184. Regularly, Fidelio vowed to wax his car. (p. 254; B)	______	______	______
185. Artemus walked around the apartment absentmindedly brushing his teeth. (p. 255; B)	______	______	______
186. I washed the car along with two friends last night. (p. 258; C)	______	______	______
187. We watched workmen extracting grape juice from the barn roof. (p. 258; C)	______	______	______
188. Entering the museum, we saw the stegosaurus and the mastodon. (p. 258; C)	______	______	______
189. We saw the two-car accident going to work. (p. 258; C)	______	______	______

	Answers	Sure	Unsure
190. The room was large and neatly arranged and held many people. (p. 258; C)			

Chapter 11, Parallel Construction: items 191–196 (pages 265–279)

Some of the sentences are expressed through *parallel construction*; some are not. Under *Answers, write* ***C*** if the sentence is parallel; *write* ***nonpara*** if the sentence is nonparallel. *Check* ***Sure*** if you are sure of your answer; *check* ***Unsure*** if you guessed at your answer.

	Answers	Sure	Unsure
Model: Cows, pigs, and goats wandered through the market place.	C		✓
191. She caught a trout, perch, and an eel. (p. 269; chapter 11)			
192. He chose neither to referee nor playing. (p. 269; chapter 11)			
193. Television is able to close minds, to deaden thought, and to dull feelings. (p. 269; chapter 11)			
194. In the woods, under a tree, a stream alongside, I left the insect repellent. (p. 270; chapter 11)			
195. After removing the egg membranes, the biologist divided the eggs into groups, and he placed them in saline. (p. 272; chapter 11)			
196. Venus's flytrap resembles the orchid, smells unpleasant, and bites the hand that feeds it. (p. 268; chapter 11)			

Chapter 13, Voice: items 197–203 (pages 287–295)

In some of the following sentences the verbs are in the *active voice*; in other sentences the verbs are in the *passive voice*. Under *Answers, write* ***A*** if the verb is in the active voice; *write* ***P*** if the verb is in the passive voice. *Check* ***Sure*** if you are sure of your answer; *check* ***Unsure*** if you guessed at your answer.

	Answers	Sure	Unsure
Model: She offended him.	A	✓	
197. My nephew works hard. (p. 288; A)			

	Answers	Sure	Unsure
198. The village was destroyed by the earthquake. (p. 289; A–2)	______	______	______
199. A package was left in our mailbox. (p. 289; A–2)	______	______	______
200. He was offended by her. (p. 291)	______	______	______
201. The earthquake destroyed the village. (p. 289; A–2)	______	______	______
202. Someone left a package in our mailbox. (p. 289; A–2)	______	______	______
203. The new medical plan was approved by the city council. (p. 289; A–2)	______	______	______

Appendix D, Commonly Confused Words: items 204–220 (pages 349–359)

From the words in parentheses, *select* the one word that correctly completes the meaning of the sentence, and *write* it under *Answers. Check* **Sure** if you are sure of your answer; *check* ***Unsure*** if you guessed at your answer.

	Answers	Sure	Unsure
Model: Yesterday, I (ate, eight) lunch at 1:00.	ate	✓	______
204. They took communion at the (altar, alter). (p. 349; 1)	______	______	______
205. I have (born, borne) this pain too long. (p. 350; 1)	______	______	______
206. He has not one (cent, scent, sent) to his name. (p. 350; 1)	______	______	______
207. She was very (discreet, discrete) about what was told to her confidentially. (p. 351; 1)	______	______	______
208. Their son had (groan, grown) three inches in the last year. (p. 352; 1)	______	______	______
209. Will you (higher, hire) her? (p. 352; 1)	______	______	______
210. He (need, knead, kneed) his opponent as they grappled for the football. (p. 352; 1)	______	______	______
211. (Peace, Piece) is the absence of war. (p. 353; 1)	______	______	______
212. The (son, sun) is central to our solar system. (p. 354; 1)	______	______	______
213. Shall we go (there, they're, their)? (p. 355; 1)	______	______	______

		Answers	Sure	Unsure
214.	What is the (anecdote, antidote) for this poison? (p. 356; 2)			
215.	Totalitarian powers suppress (decent, descent, dissent). (p. 357; 2)			
216.	It was (implicit, explicit) in her statement, though she did not say it in so many words. (p. 357; 2)			
217.	For (instance, instants), a camel is a mammal. (p. 357; 2)			
218.	That noise is driving me mad! Will you please be (quit, quite, quiet)? (p. 358; 2)			
219.	This (receipt, recipe) calls for dry mustard. (p. 358; 2)			
220.	The clinical trials showed that 83% of the patients treated with this medicine were cured. The medicine was, therefore, (effective, powerful). (p. 358; 2)			

Answers: Pretests

1. noun or common noun
2. proper noun or noun
3. noun or abstract noun
4. noun or compound noun
5. verb
6. verb or verb phrase
7. pronoun
8. pronoun
9. adjective
10. adjective or compound adjective
11. adjective
12. adverb
13. adverb
14. adverb
15. preposition
16. preposition
17. conjunction
18. conjunction
19. conjunction or subordinating conjunction
20. conjunction or subordinating conjunction
21. interjection or exclamation

22. S
23. S
24. frag
25. frag
26. frag
27. frag
28. frag
29. S
30. frag
31. S
32. frag
33. S
34. frag
35. frag
36. S
37. frag
38. frag
39. frag
40. S
41. frag
42. frag
43. frag

44. shift
45. C
46. C
47. shift
48. C
49. shift
50. C

51. C
52. C
53. inc
54. C
55. inc
56. C
57. C
58. inc
59. C
60. inc
61. C
62. inc
63. C
64. C

65. C
66. inc
67. C
68. inc
69. inc
70. C
71. C
72. C
73. inc
74. C

75. C
76. unc
77. unc
78. C
79. unc
80. unc

81. C
82. inc
83. C
84. C
85. C
86. C
87. C
88. C
89. C
90. inc
91. inc
92. C
93. C
94. C
95. C
96. inc
97. inc
98. inc
99. inc
100. C
101. C
102. inc
103. C
104. inc

105. RO
106. RO
107. C
108. RO
109. C
110. RO

111. C
112. punc
113. punc
114. C
115. C
116. C
117. C
118. punc
119. punc
120. punc
121. C
122. C
123. punc
124. C
125. C
126. punc
127. C
128. punc
129. punc
130. C
131. punc
132. C
133. C
134. punc
135. C
136. C
137. punc
138. C

139. punc	140. C	141. punc	142. C
143. C	144. punc	145. punc	146. punc
147. C	148. C	149. C	150. C
151. C	152. punc	153. C	154. punc
155. C	156. punc	157. C	158. punc
159. punc	160. C	161. C	162. C
163. C	164. punc	165. C	166. C
167. punc	168. C	169. C	170. punc
171. C	172. C	173. C	174. C
175. C			

176. C	177. MM	178. MM	179. MM
180. C	181. MM	182. C	183. C
184. C	185. MM	186. MM	187. MM
188. C	189. MM	190. C	

191. nonpara	192. nonpara	193. C	194. nonpara
195. C	196. C		

197. A	198. P	199. P	200. P
201. A	202. A	203. P	

204. altar	205. borne	206. cent	207. discreet
208. grown	209. hire	210. kneed	211. Peace
212. sun	213. there	214. antidote	215. dissent
216. implicit	217. instance	218. quiet	219. recipe
220. effective			

Help Yourself
A Guide to Writing and Rewriting
THIRD EDITION

CHAPTER 1

Parts of Speech

- **Items 1–21 in the Pretest refer to this chapter.**

Chapter Contents

RULE: | Use parts of speech correctly.

The way a word is used in a sentence determines what part of speech it is: noun, verb, pronoun, adjective, adverb, preposition, conjunction, or interjection. A group of words working together as a unit—a phrase or a clause—can also function as a part of speech in a sentence. Knowing what the parts of speech do will help you understand the English sentence better.

A Single Words as Parts of Speech

A-1 Noun (n.)

A *noun* is a word that names something: *locomotive, artist, peace, atom, Ruth Sanger, Stanley, United States of America* are nouns.
Every noun is either a *common* noun or a *proper* noun.

Common noun (com. n.)

A *common noun* is the **general** name for a person, place, or thing.

Examples

a. My *brother* (com. n.) is at *home* (com. n.).

b. The *woman* (com. n.) is a brilliant *actress* (com. n.).

c. The *team* (com. n.) is playing in another *city* (com. n.).

d. The *ship* (com. n.) sank after hitting an *iceberg* (com. n.).

e. An *atom* (com. n.) is the smallest *unit* (com. n.) of *matter* (com. n.).

Quick Quiz: A

Underline each common noun.

Model: The dog barks.

1. The book is too heavy to carry.
2. The sun, the moon, and the stars cannot all be seen at once.
3. The physician and her husband went to the beach.
4. The sailors would not go near the water.

Answers to Quick Quiz A are on page 25.

Proper noun (prop. n.)

A *proper noun* names a ***specific*** person, place, or thing and is capitalized. Your own name is a proper noun.

Examples:

a. *Peter* (prop. n.) came home.

b. *Glenda Jackson* (prop. n.) is a brilliant actress.

c. The *Yankees* (prop. n.) are playing in *Pittsburgh* (prop. n.).

d. The *Titanic* (prop. n.) sank after hitting an iceberg.

e. Did you call me, *Mother* (prop. n.)? (*Mother, father, aunt, grandfather,* etc., are proper nouns when they are *used as titles.*)

Quick Quiz: B

Underline each proper noun.

Model: Maria Callas died in 1977.

1. Duke Ellington played frequently at Carnegie Hall.
2. Yesterday, Ophelia left; today, Uncle Calvin arrived.
3. The *Monitor* and the *Merrimack* were early iron-clad ships.

Answers to Quick Quiz B are on page 25.

Proper nouns, *special cases*

A common noun, when used as a **title** or part of a title, becomes a proper noun.

Examples

a. *Doctor Julius Pepper* (prop. n.) is not the doctor I asked to see.

NOTE: *Doctor* as part of the title is capitalized, but *doctor* as a common noun is not.

b. *Saint Joan* (prop. n.) was canonized in 1920.

c. The judge who heard the case was *Judge Blanche Bay* (prop. n.).

d. *Doctor John Watson* (prop. n.) was associated with *Sherlock Holmes* (prop. n.).

NOTE: Frequently, a title is abbreviated: **Dr.** *John Watson*

e. *Mr. Spock* (prop. n.) of the starship *Enterprise* (prop. n.) has become a folk hero.

f. How long will *The Force* (prop. n.) be with us, *Father?* (prop. n.)

g. *Sir Francis Drake* (prop. n.) helped to establish English sea power.

NOTE: Expressions such as *sir, madam, queen, pope,* etc. are **not** capitalized unless they are part of a title.
Yes, *madam,* you are correct.
But, *sir,* that is not your coat.
The *queen* left on her spring tour.

Quick Quiz: C

Underline each proper noun.

Model: Ms. Smith and Mr. Aston play basketball.

1. Who was The Wizard of Oz?
2. Chicago is called The Windy City, and New York, The Big Apple.
3. The problem was that King Kong was not understood.
4. Professor Rosen is being considered for the Nobel Prize.

Answers to Quick Quiz C are on page 25.

Concrete noun (conc. n.)

A concrete noun—it can be common or proper—names something that can be **detected through the senses** (sight, hearing, touch, smell, taste) or that has been proven to exist.

Examples

a. The phonograph *record* (conc. n.) was worn out.

b. Have you seen *The White House?* (conc. n.)

c. The *gears* (conc. n.) never meshed very well.

d. *Zara,* (conc. n.) *Ernani,* (conc. n.) and the *dog* (conc. n.) were at the *lake.* (conc. n.)

NOTE: Zara and Ernani are both proper nouns, while dog and lake are common nouns; all however, are concrete nouns.

e. How many *protons* (conc. n.) does that *atom* (conc. n.) have?
(Although most single protons and atoms have not been seen, their existence has been scientifically proven.)

Quick Quiz: D

Underline each concrete noun.

Model: The lilac smelled sweet.

1. This is not your property.
2. Who is buried in this tomb?
3. The museum displays her sculpture annually.
4. Albert and Agatha built the motor for their car.

Answers to Quick Quiz D are on page 25.

Abstract noun (abs. n.)

An abstract noun—it can be common or proper—names something that lacks physical qualities, but that **expresses an idea, a feeling, a thought.** *Idea, feeling, thought, happiness, sadness, ecstasy, hatred, passion, Mr. Big, concern* are all abstract nouns.

Examples

a. *Terror* (abs. n.) was endless.

b. Who among you always experiences *happiness?* (abs. n.)

c. Your *morality* (abs. n.) may be my *obscenity.* (abs. n.)

d. The *choice* (abs. n.) is not always ours.

e. The *Catch-22* (abs. n.) is that you cannot get there from here.

Quick Quiz: E

Underline each abstract noun.

Model: Love is difficult to define.

1. Do you think we can define beauty?
2. Where is the tranquility I once felt?
3. Truth and reason generally go together.
4. John Bull and Uncle Sam symbolize Great Britain and the United States.
5. Ronald and Jennie had never known such ecstasy before.

Answers to Quick Quiz E are on page 25.

Compound noun (comp. n.)

A compound noun—it can be either common or proper—consists of two or more words (1) fused into one word, (2) hyphenated, or (3) neither fused nor hyphenated.

Compound nouns as single words

Examples

a. She is a *daredevil* [comp. n.]. (*dare* + *devil*)

b. His *jawbone* [comp. n.] was wired together in two places. (*jaw* + *bone*)

c. Did you see the huge *iceberg* [comp. n.]? (*ice* + *berg*)

Compound nouns as hyphenated words

Examples

a. The *attorney-general* [comp. n.] is to speak tonight.

b. His *mother-in-law* [comp. n.] is a licensed pilot.

c. Few have crossed *no-man's-land* [comp. n.].

d. Fort Dix was the scene of the *court-martial* [comp. n.].

NOTE: To pluralize (make more than one) most **hyphenated** compound nouns, add **s** to the **first** word in the compound. Three *attorneys*-general ran for governor of Rhode Island.

Compound nouns that are neither fused nor hyphenated

Some compound nouns stand as separate words.

Examples

a. The *secretary bird* [comp. n.] has a powerful beak.

b. Do you know where the *fire escape* [comp. n.] is?

c. The champions of the *Big Ten* [comp. n.] and the *Pac Ten* [comp. n.] generally meet each *New Year's Day* [comp. n.].

d. No one can eat that much *ice cream* [comp. n.]!

e. To what church does the *praying mantis* [comp. n.] go?

NOTE: When in doubt about how a compound noun should be written, consult a current dictionary.

Quick Quiz: F

Underline each compound noun.

Model: The bedrock was reached at twelve feet.

1. Who are their fathers-in-law?

2. Women who have not had German measles should be immunized against them before becoming pregnant.

3. I would have given my eyeteeth to have seen his reaction.

4. The blast-off will occur soon.

Answers to Quick Quiz F are on page 25.

A-2 Verb (vb.)

A *verb* is a word (or group of words) that tells (1) what the subject of a sentence **does,** (2) what the subject ***is,*** or (3) what *action* the subject ***receives.***

What the subject *does, did,* or *will do*

Verbs that tell what the subject *does, did,* or *will do* are sometimes called "action" verbs because they name an action.

Examples

subj. vb.
a. The hiker *reached* his destination.

subj. vb.
b. The thought *troubled* him deeply.

subj. vb.
c. By tomorrow, she *will have driven* her first 10,000 miles.

subj. vb.
d. They *did* not *leave* until the next day. (*Not* is ***not*** part of the verb; it is an adverb.)

Action verbs in the sentences above are *reached, troubled, will have driven, did . . . leave.*

What the subject *is, was,* or *will be*

Verbs that tell what the subject *is, was,* or *will be* belong to a class of verbs called "linking verbs" (or "copulas"). These verbs "link" the subject of the sentence with a word or words (called "subjective complements") which give additional information about the subject.

Examples

subj. vb.
a. We *are* all cowards.

subj. vb.
b. The United States Senate *is* possibly the most important deliberative body in the world.

subj. vb.
c. That *seems* unimportant.

subj. vb.
d. She *must have been* the first to identify the species.

In the examples above, the words that follow the verbs *is, seems,* and *must have been* are subjective complements.

Notice that in each instance the "complement" following the linking verb refers back to the subject:

forms of the verb **be** used as linking verbs	They were unusually quiet. John is tall. Mary and Roy are friends.
verbs about the **senses** used as linking verbs	Roses smell good. The sea looks calm. His voice sounds flat. Burlap feels rough. Vinegar tastes sour.
verbs such as seems used as linking verbs	He seems discouraged. Clowns only appear sad.

What action the subject *receives, received,* or *will receive*

Examples

subj. vb.
a. Marissa *was reported* to the police.

subj. vb.
b. The horse *was cured.*

subj. vb.
c. The teachings of the Old and New Testaments *are called* the Judeo-Christian ethic. (See also chapters 3 and 4 and the Index for more about verbs; see chapter 13 regarding passive voice.)

Quick Quiz: G

Identify the underlined verbs in the following sentences either as action *or as* linking *verbs.*

Models: Tanya listened carefully to the music. ___action___
The forest fire seems to be moving toward the town. ___linking___

1. I am fairly confident. ________
2. Physiology students perform dissections. ________
3. Computer terminals have become familiar sights. ________
4. Peanut shells littered the floor. ________
5. The choir, which hadn't practiced, sounded terrible. ________
6. The messenger sounded the alarm. ________

7. The prospects look good. ____________

8. Boulders smashed the walls. ____________

Answers to Quick Quiz G are on page 25.

Transitive and Intransitive Verbs

- Some action verbs need to be followed by a noun (or nounlike structure) to make a complete thought.

Examples For dinner, Zacha consumed (vb.) two steaks (direct object).

Drea learned (vb.) electronics (direct object).

Scotty delivers (vb.) the evening paper (direct object).

- Action verbs that require direct objects are called *transitive verbs.*

- Some verbs do not need to be followed by a noun (or nounlike structure) to make a complete thought.

Examples Cattle graze (vb.).

The bridge collapsed (vb.).

Our apple trees have bloomed (vb.).

- Verbs that do not require direct objects are called *intransitive* verbs.

- Some verbs are transitive in one sentence but intransitive in another. It simply depends upon whether the verb is followed by a direct object.

Examples Muriel *cheated.* (intransitive)
Stefan *cheated* the customer. (transitive)

The patient *breathed* slowly. (intransitive)
(Note: *Slowly* is an adverb, not a noun.)
The patient *breathed* oxygen. (transitive)

Quick Quiz: H

Label the underlined verbs transitive *or* intransitive.

Model: Jack snores. ——intransitive——
General Motors manufactures cars. ——transitive——

1. He finished the assignment. ____________

2. Travel agents arranged train reservations for us. ____________

3. Phil jogs daily. ____________

4. Birds fly. ____________

5. Pilots fly planes. ____________

Answers to Quick Quiz H are on page 26.

A-3 Pronoun (pron.)

A *pronoun* is a word that **stands** for (or substitutes for) **a noun.**

Examples

a. Joan (noun) is here.

She (pron.) is here. (*She* stands for the noun *Joan.*)

b. Democracy (noun) is a complex form of government.

It (pron.) is a complex form of government. (*It* stands for the noun *democracy.*)

c. Our Humane Societies (noun) annually kill thousands of stray dogs (noun) and cats (noun).

They (pron.) annually kill thousands of *them* (pron.). (They [Humane Societies] annually kill thousands of them [dogs and cats].)

d. *He* (pron.) and *she* (pron.) met with Ulbrecht only twice.

e. *Whoever* (pron.) wants the stale candy can have *it* (pron.).

(See also chapters 5, 6, 7, and Appendix B for more about pronouns.)

A-4 Adjective (adj.)

An *adjective* is a word that **describes or modifies a noun.**

Examples

a. *Red* (adj.) roses (noun) are not sold here.

b. *Green* (adj.) hair (noun) looked out of place, since the others had *purple* (adj.) hair (noun).

c. *The* (adj.) *sophisticated,* (adj.) *athletic,* (adj.) *tall,* (adj.) *robust* gymnast (noun) is no relation to me.

NOTE: *The,* which is called a **definite article,** functions as an adjective, as do the **indefinite articles** *a* and *an.*

d. *His* (adj.) *98-year-old,* (adj.) *hard-of-hearing,* (adj.) nearly *blind* (adj.) grandmother (noun) just scaled Mount Everest.

NOTE: *Hard-of-hearing* and *98-year-old* are each composed of more than one word. Adjectives composed of more than one word are called ***compound adjectives.*** **Notice** that the parts of compound adjectives are hyphenated.

His functions as an adjective, as do other **possessive case pronouns.** See chapter 7.

adj. noun adj. noun
e. She hopes to climb *another* face of Everest *next* year.

noun adj. adj.
f. The children, *underfed* and *pot-bellied,* ought to concern everyone.

NOTE: Adjectives sometimes follow the nouns they modify—usually for emphasis.

Quick Quiz: I

Underline each adjective.

Model: I heard their often-repeated statements.

1. The ever-present danger has not been remedied by his ill-chosen remarks and stupid acts.
2. The patient, feverish and unconscious, died.
3. He was a tall, blond man, and he had one black shoe.
4. The bright, flickering embers hypnotized his 12-year-old brother and her 9-year-old sister.
5. Who can ever forget the spicy aroma of Mona's herb garden?

Answers to Quick Quiz I are on page 26.

A-5 Adverb (adv.)

An *adverb* **describes (or modifies) a verb, an adjective, or another adverb.** An adverb often answers the questions "How?", "Where?", "When?", "To what degree?", "How often?". Adverbs also are used to express affirmation or negation.

An adverb that modifies a verb

An adverb that modifies a verb adds information that is not supplied by the verb alone.

Examples

vb. adv.
a. He goes *quickly.* (*Quickly* answers **"How?"**)

adv.
b. Take the guests *inside.* (*Inside* answers **"Where?"**)

adv.
c. The storm will arrive *tomorrow.* (*Tomorrow* answers **"When?"**)

adv.
d. She calls *frequently.* (*Frequently* answers **"How often?"**)

e. *Certainly* (adv.), Linda is coming. (*Certainly* expresses **affirmation.**)

f. Linda is *not* (adv.) coming. (*Not* expresses **negation.**)

Quick Quiz: J

Underline each adverb.

Model: The people in our neighborhood walk <u>energetically</u>.

1. The crisis will be upon us soon.
2. Ronald and Wanda play endlessly.
3. Dracula and a few friends will be arriving shortly.

Answers to Quick Quiz J are on page 26.

An adverb that modifies an adjective

An adverb that modifies an adjective adds information that is not supplied by the adjective alone.

Examples

a. Chris is *very* (adv.) active (adj.). (*Very* tells *how* active Chris is. He is very active.)

b. Who can ever forget the softly (adv.) spicy (adj.) aroma of the herb garden?

c. The *extremely* (adv.) sophisticated (adj.), *slightly* (adv.) athletic (adj.), *hardly* (adv.) robust (adj.) gymnast is no relation to me.

d. These *cruelly* (adv.) underfed (adj.), *horribly* (adv.) pot-bellied (adj.) children ought to concern everyone.

e. His *barely* (adv.) 98-year-old (adj.), *very* (adv.) hard-of-hearing (adj.), *nearly* (adv.) blind (adj.) grandmother just scaled the *unusually* (adv.) high (adj.) Mount Everest.

Quick Quiz: K

Underline each adverb.

Model: An <u>especially</u> tasty chili relleno is served.

1. *Julia* and *The Turning Point* began the decidedly overdue revival of films in which women play significant roles.
2. He is a slightly bald man.
3. The singularly important papers were found in a shoe box.

Answers to Quick Quiz K are on page 26.

An adverb that modifies another adverb

An adverb that modifies another adverb adds information that is not supplied by the first adverb alone.

Examples

adv. adv.
a. She plays the piano *extremely* beautifully. (*Extremely* modifies *beautifully* and makes a more precise statement.)

adv. adv.
b. Charles learns *fairly* quickly. (Charles does not learn quickly, only *fairly* quickly.)

adv. adv.
c. They *very* suddenly jumped off the roof of the building.

adv. adv.
d. Her donkey does not bray *particularly* loudly.

adv. adv.
e. It is *entirely* too important a commodity for one person to control its manufacture.

NOTE: Many, but not all, adverbs end in ***-ly.***

Quick Quiz: L

Underline each adverb that modifies another adverb.

Model: It rains so often.

1. Very probably, they have returned the money.
2. My reach extends too much longer than his.
3. The play was surprisingly poorly presented.

Answers to Quick Quiz L are on page 26.

A-6 Preposition (prep.)

A *preposition* is a word whose main function is **to relate a noun or a pronoun to another word** in the sentence. A preposition generally refers to *position in time or space.*

above	between	of	through
about	by	off	to
around	for	on	toward
at	from	onto	under
behind	in	out	with
beside	into	over	without

Some **Group Prepositions**

by means of	in place of
by virtue of	in spite of
in front of	with regard to

Examples

a. He sat *by* (prep.) the door.

b. *After* (prep.) the basketball game, she went home.

c. The group went *over* (prep.) the rocks, *behind* (prep.) the shoring, *into* (prep.) the camp.

d. He came *from* (prep.) Alabama *with* (prep.) a banjo *on* (prep.) his knee.

e. We gave it *to* (prep.) them.

Prepositions sometimes help to form verbs.

In English, prepositions also are sometimes added to verbs to produce other verbs. Notice how the addition of prepositions to the verb *come* results in new meanings:

Example verb *come*

come **at**	I'm afraid he will come at me. (attack)
come **about**	How did it come about? (happen)
come **across**	You will come across a clue. (find)
come **around**	The fighter will come around. (regain consciousness)
	Joe will come around to your view. (eventually support)

A-7 Conjunction (conj.)

A *conjunction* is a word that **joins** words or group of words. Conjunctions are either *coordinating* or *subordinating.*

Coordinating Conjunctions (coord. conj.)

A *coordinating conjunction* is a word that joins sentence elements of *equal* form, weight, or function—two ***nouns*** or two ***subject+verb*** units, for example. The coordinating conjunctions are *and, but, for, nor, or, so,* and *yet.*

Examples

a. Whales (noun) *and* (coord. conj.) dolphins (noun) are both marine mammals.

b. He went to the jazz festival, (subject + verb unit) *but* (coord. conj.) she went to the hockey game. (subject + verb unit)

c. "Across the river *and* (coord. conj.) into the woods *but* (coord. conj.) not through the jungle" were the instructions she received.

d. He was hungry, *yet* (coord. conj.) he did not eat.

e. Will she give a report on cytogenetics *or* (coord. conj.) on nerve regeneration?

Quick Quiz: M

Underline coordinating conjunctions.

Model: Press and public are not always informed.

1. It was not that important, yet they did not like the outcome.
2. Blood serum can easily be divided into the albumin and the globulin fractions.
3. Is it the albumin or the globulin fraction that is water soluble?

Answers to Quick Quiz M are on page 26.

Subordinating Conjunction (sub. conj.)

A *subordinating conjunction* is a word that joins and shows a relationship between two elements that are of **unequal** importance in the eyes of the writer. Following are some subordinating conjunctions: *after, although, as, as long as, because, before, how, however, if, since, that, though, unless, until, when, whenever, where, wherever.* The subordinated unit is generally a dependent clause since it lacks a sense of completeness even though it has a subject + verb unit. (See chapter 2, C-3.)

Examples

sub. conj. + (sub. + verb unit) = dep. clause
a. **although** *dogs bark* at night (lacks sense of completeness)

sub. conj. + (sub. + verb unit) = dep. clause
b. **when** *cars were made* better (lacks sense of completeness)

sub. conj. + (sub. + verb unit) = dep. clause
c. **as long as** those *owls hoot*

sub. conj. + (sub. + verb unit) = dep. clause
d. **if** in the beginning *he knows* nothing

sub. conj. + (sub. + verb unit) = dep. clause
e. **because** the *night has* a thousand eyes

Each of the above *subject+verb units* asks for something to complete its meaning. Attaching a subject+verb unit that has a *sense of completeness*—an ***independent clause***—to each of the dependent clauses will complete the sentence.

Examples

dep. clause | indep. clause
a. Although dogs bark at night, we sleep soundly. (The more important part of the sentence is *we sleep soundly,* while *Although dogs bark at night* is subordinate to [less important than] the independent clause that can stand alone as a sentence.)

indep. clause | dep. clause
b. There were few repairs when cars were made in that manner.

dep. clause / indep. clause

c. As long as those owls hoot, he cannot go to sleep.

indep. clause / dep. clause

d. It will take him a long time to learn the subject if he knows nothing in the beginning.

dep. clause / indep. clause

e. Because the night has a thousand eyes, there must be many peeping Toms.

Quick Quiz: N

Circle the subordinating conjunction, *underline once* the **less important** part of the sentence (the dependent clause), and *underline twice* the **more important** part of the sentence.

Model: (Because) she has gone, I no longer speak with her.

1. Provided our balance-of-payments position improves, the stock market should go up.
2. The crime rate will go down when people take more responsibility for their neighbors.
3. We were worried since his plane was three hours late.
4. Because he is always alone, he is miserable.
5. Because he is miserable, he is always alone.

Answers to Quick Quiz N are on page 27.

A-8 Interjection (interj.)

An *interjection* is an **exclamation** expressing strong or sudden emotion. An interjection generally consists of one or very few words and often ends with an exclamation mark.

Examples

a. *Ouch!* (interj.)

b. *No,* (interj.) you cannot get him to change his mind. (*No* is a mild interjection and is generally followed by a comma or a period.)

c. *Whew!* (interj.) I'm exhausted!

d. "*Ah, shucks!* (interj.) She didn't understand me," he moaned.

NOTE: You will have little need for interjections in writing your papers, although you may have need for them when you get those papers back. Interjections are used most commonly in spoken English and in writing dialogue that represents spoken English.

A-9 Verbals

A *verbal* is formed from a verb but **functions as some other part of speech.** *Infinitives, gerunds,* and *participles* are verbals.

Infinitive

An *infinitive* is the **to** form of a *verb. To go, to ride, to think, to report* are examples of infinitives. Infinitives function as *nouns, adjectives,* and *adverbs.*

An *infinitive* can function **as a noun.**

Examples

infin.
a. *To play* is natural for a child.

infin.
b. *To think* takes time and care.

infin.
c. My ambition is *to ski.*

An *infinitive* can function **as an adjective.**

Examples

infin.
a. The plane *to inspect* is over there. (The infinitive *to inspect* modifies the noun *plane.*)

infin.
b. The Dodgers are the team *to beat.* (*To beat* modifies the noun *team.*)

infin.
c. The race *to win* is the Kentucky Derby.

An *infinitive* can function **as an adverb.**

Examples

infin.
a. We were too hurried *to stop.* (The infinitive *to stop* modifies the adjective *hurried.*)

infin.
b. Everyone came *to watch.* (The infinitive *to watch* modifies the verb *came.*)

c. He was too angry *to think, to react,* or *to move.*

NOTE: Do not mistake an infinitive for a prepositional phrase beginning with the preposition *to.*

prep. phrase — infin.
I went *to the river to look.*

A preposition always requires a noun or pronoun as object (river). In an infinitive, the word **to** *is always followed by a verb.*

Gerund

A *gerund* is the **ing** form of a *verb. Climbing, trotting, resting* are examples of gerunds. A *gerund* functions **only as a noun.**

Examples

gerund
a. *Educating* is the function of schools.

gerund
b. You can get here by *driving.*

gerund
c. *Chewing* is difficult without good teeth.

Present participle

A *present participle* is the **ing** form of a *verb.* But while the gerund functions as a noun, the *present participle* functions **as an adjective.**

Examples

pres. part.
a. A *barking* dog can warn of danger. (The present participle *barking* modifies the noun *dog.*)

pres. part.
b. We belong to a *debating* society. (*Debating* is an adjective that modifies the noun *society.*)

pres. part.
c. The *winding* road led nowhere.

Past participle

A *past participle* is the **past form** of a *verb. Walked, laughed, eaten* are examples of past participles. The *past participle functions* **as an adjective.**

Examples

past part.
a. The *excited* boy forgot to give us the message. (The past participle *excited* modifies the noun *boy.*)

past part.
b. She showed us the *broken* flask. (*Broken* is an adjective that modifies the noun *flask.*)

past part. past part.
c. The tools, *rusted* and *bent,* were found in the basement. (The past participles *rusted* and *bent* both modify the noun *tools.*)

Quick Quiz: O

Underline each verbal and *write* the part of speech it functions as in the space given.

Model: Neither of them liked dancing. *noun*

1. The opening selection was played on the tuba. ____________
2. It was too good to lose. ____________
3. The snail to study is new to this part of the country. ____________

4. In the first place, swimming is good exercise. ____________

5. The fortified structure was constructed in 1798. ____________

6. Skiing to the lodge is a more direct way to get there. ____________

Answers to Quick Quiz O are on page 27.

B Phrases as Parts of Speech: Their Forms and Their Functions

A *phrase* is a group of words that functions as a unit. A phrase generally lacks all or part of a subject + verb unit and lacks a sense of completeness.

Phrases travel under various *names*—which you may choose to learn—but the important thing to understand is how they *function* in a sentence: some as *nouns*, some as *adjectives*, and some as *adverbs*. The following material will help you understand how phrases are *built* and how they *act as parts of speech*.

B-1 Prepositional phrase

Form

A prepositional phrase consists of

(a) a preposition
(b) a noun or pronoun, called the *object of the preposition*
(c) modifiers—if any—of the noun or pronoun

Function

A prepositional phrase generally functions as an *adjective* or as an *adverb*.

Prepositional phrases used as **adjectives**

Examples

a. A government *of the people* [prep. phrase] is likely to endure. (*Of the people* modifies the noun *government*.)

b. What does a giraffe *with a sore throat* [prep. phrase] do?

c. "The smell *of smish*," [prep. phrase] they said, "was a mix *of smog and fish*." [prep. phrase]

Prepositional phrases used as **adverbs**

prep. phrase

Examples **a.** *After the ballgame,* we shared a ride to a restaurant. (*After the ballgame* modifies the verb *shared* and answers the question **When?**)

prep. phr. prep. phr.

b. *Over hill, over dale,* we will hit the dusty trail. (*Over hill, over dale,* modify the verb *will hit* and answer the question **Where?**)

prep. phrase

c. The physician reported the test results *with precise detail.* (*With precise detail* modifies the verb *reported* and answers the question **How?**)

B-2 Verb phrase and verbal phrase

NOTE: Because of similarity in the names "verb phrase" and "verbal phrase," it is easy to confuse the two.

A *verb phrase* is simply any verb containing more than one word: *am going, have been gone, will be singing,* etc.

vb. phrase

Examples **a.** We *were eating.*

vb. phrase

b. They *had been driving* all night.

vb. phrase

c. Congress *will have convened* by the time she gets there.

A *verbal phrase,* on the other hand, is built upon a ***verbal***—which is a word derived from a verb but used as some other part of speech. There are three kinds of verbals: infinitives, gerunds, and participles.

Infinitive phrase

An *infinitive* is the **to** form of a verb: *to do, to make, to cry,* etc. An *infinitive phrase* consists of the infinitive form of a verb and any other word or words necessary to its meaning. An infinitive phrase can ***function*** as a ***noun.***

infin. phrase

Examples **a.** *To have them here* is a mixed blessing.

infin. phrase

b. His hope was *to keep the manuscript.*

infin. phrase

c. *To find the truth* was her guiding impulse.

An infinitive phrase can **function** as an ***adjective.***

infin. phrase

Examples **a.** The prize *to be awarded* is not worth much. (modifies noun *prize*)

infin. phrase

b. The task *to be done* is at hand.

infin. phrase

c. She was the person *to do it.*

An infinitive phrase can **function** as an ***adverb.***

infin. phrase

Examples **a.** He brought the car to the shop *to be repaired.* (modifies the verb *brought*)

infin. phrase

b. We rose *to salute the flag.*

infin. phrase

c. She was too headstrong *to consider the consequences.*

Gerund phrase

A *gerund* is the **ing** form of a verb: *doing, making, crying,* etc. A gerund phrase consists of the gerund and any other words necessary to the meaning of the phrase. A gerund or gerund phrase **functions** as a **noun.**

gerund phrase

Examples **a.** He tried *rowing to Australia.*

gerund phrase

b. *Fighting with him* will get you nowhere.

gerund phrase

c. You can get to New York by *going through the Holland Tunnel.*

Participial phrase

Participles assume several forms:

Present participle = **ing** form of a verb: *seeing, doing, liking, crying,* etc.
Past participle = past form of a verb: *saw, did, liked, cried,* etc.
Perfect participle = *have seen, have done, have liked, have cried, have proven,* etc.

A participle can function as an *adjective.*
A phrase that begins with a participle is called a *participial phrase* and can **function** as an **adjective** or as an **adverb**.

part. phrase

Examples **a.** The cow *chewing its cud* is a Holstein.
(*Chewing* is the present participle of *chew.* It is also an adjective modifying *cow.*)

part. phrase

b. *Angered by the experience,* the speaker walked out of the room. (past participle)

part. phrase

c. Antonia, *having come from Ohio,* was surprised by the mild climate. (perfect participle)

part. phrase

d. They returned *looking sheepish.* (present participle; adverb)

NOTE: See chapter 10, "Dangling, Squinting, and other Misplaced Modifiers," regarding misuse of participial phrases.

B-3 Absolute phrase

An *absolute phrase* consists of a *noun* or *pronoun* and a *participle.* An absolute phrase is a grammatically independent part of a sentence. In *meaning,* however, it is logically connected with the main idea in the sentence.

Examples

a. *Rations having been lost,* the climbers became uneasy. [abs. phrase]
(*Rations having been lost* is an absolute phrase. Note, however, that *the climbers became uneasy* can stand alone as a sentence.)

b. *Radames having arrived,* Aida expected a warm reception. [abs. phrase]

c. *The count being completed,* they announced the results. [abs. phrase]

C Clauses as Parts of Speech

The two types of clauses are *dependent* and *independent.* An independent clause can stand as a complete sentence; it does not function as a part of speech. Each **clause** that functions as a single part of speech is a **dependent** clause. A dependent clause can function as a noun, or as an adjective, or as an adverb.

C-1 Noun clause

A dependent clause that is a subject or an object is a *noun clause.* A noun clause is generally introduced by words such as *when, what, that, whatever, who, whoever, how.*

Examples

a. *What she said* was never mentioned. (*What she said* is the subject of the verb *was mentioned.*) [noun clause]

b. *When Alphonzo will get out of the hospital* is still not known. (The noun clause is the subject of the verb *is.*) [noun clause]

c. The rider said *that his car went out of control.* (*That his car went out of control* is the object of the verb *said.*) [noun clause]

C-2 Adjective clause

A dependent clause that modifies a noun or a pronoun is an *adjective clause.* An adjective clause is generally introduced by a word such as *that, who, where, which.*

Examples

a. A physician *who practices bad medicine* is a danger to the community. (*Who practices bad medicine* modifies the noun *physician.*) [adj. clause]

b. One *who has never lied* is rarer than a water buffalo in the Sahara. (*Who has never lied* modifies the pronoun *one.*) [adj. clause]

adj. clause

c. No one needs a car *that will not run.*

adj. clause

d. Pittsburgh, *where he was born,* suffered badly from the storm.

C-3 Adverbial clause

A dependent clause that modifies a verb, an adjective, or another adverb is a clause functioning as an adverb. An adverbial clause may show time, place, cause, effect, and certain other relationships. It is often introduced by a word such as *when, while, before, after, during, where, as, that, than, in order that, if.*

adv. clause

Examples **a.** You may enter *after the house lights dim.* (*After the house lights dim* modifies the verb *may enter* and shows a time relationship.)

adv. clause

b. They camped *where they could see the moon rise.*

adv. clause

c. *While you are dieting,* do not eat a big meal.

adv. clause

d. Alice is older *than he is.*

REVIEW AND PRACTICE

Exercise A *In the space following each underlined word, write the* **part of speech** *of the word.*

Models: The symptoms noun of preposition asthma noun include verb noisy breathing with preposition difficult adjective expiration.

1. Yesterday, __________ we __________ saw a huge __________ crowd at the stadium.

2. To whom __________ did you give the multi-colored __________ scarf?

3. They seem __________ genuinely __________ happy __________ to see us.

4. Dr. Margaret Mead __________ was one of the most __________ famous anthropologists in the world. __________

5. "Fathead!" __________ he shouted.

6. Wayne and __________ his brother reached the top of the mountain, but __________ his __________ brother's __________ friend did not make the climb.

Exercise B In the space provided following each underlined phrase or clause, *write* the **name** of that phrase or clause. If the phrase or clause modifies another word in the sentence, *draw* **an arrow** to that word.

Model: Dr. Strangelove, whom you met yesterday, adj. clause will not be with us long.

1. The seas were so high that the pilings were undermined. ______________
2. They went there so they would not feel alone. ______________
3. That house will have been sold ______________ by Monday.
4. Having formed a plan ______________, they escaped.
5. That she is running for reelection ______________ was announced yesterday.
6. He is always on the phone. ______________
7. The film that you saw ______________ is R-rated.

Answers to Chapter Review and Practice are on page 27.

ANSWERS: CHAPTER 1

Answers to Quick Quiz A

1. book 2. sun, moon, stars 3. physician, husband, beach 4. sailors, water

Answers to Quick Quiz B

1. Duke Ellington, Carnegie Hall 2. Ophelia, Uncle Calvin 3. Monitor, Merrimack

Answers to Quick Quiz C

1. The Wizard of Oz 2. Chicago, The Windy City, New York, The Big Apple 3. King Kong 4. Professor Rosen, the Nobel Prize

Answers to Quick Quiz D

1. property 2. tomb 3. museum, sculpture 4. Albert, Agatha, motor, car

Answers to Quick Quiz E

1. beauty 2. tranquility 3. truth, reason 4. John Bull, Uncle Sam 5. ecstasy

Answers to Quick Quiz F

1. fathers-in-law 2. German measles 3. eyeteeth 4. blast-off

Answers to Quick Quiz G

1. linking 2. action 3. linking 4. action

5. linking (*terrible* refers to choir)
6. action (the messenger performed an action)
7. linking
8. action

Answers to Quick Quiz H

1. transitive
2. transitive
3. intransitive (daily is not a noun)
4. intransitive
5. transitive

Answers to Quick Quiz I

1. The, ever-present, his, ill-chosen, stupid 2. The, feverish, unconscious 3. a, tall, blond, one, black 4. The, bright, flickering, his, 12-year-old, her, 9-year-old 5. the, spicy, Mona's, herb

Answers to Quick Quiz J

1. soon 2. endlessly 3. shortly

Answers to Quick Quiz K

1. decidedly 2. slightly 3. singularly

Answers to Quick Quiz L

1. Very 2. too 3. surprisingly

Answers to Quick Quiz M

1. yet 2. and 3. or

Answers to Quick Quiz N

1. Provided our balance-of-payments position improves, the stock market should go up.
2. The crime rate will go down when people take more responsibility for their neighbors.
3. We were worried since his plane was three hours late.
4. Because he is always alone he is miserable.
5. Because he is miserable, he is always alone.

Answers to Quick Quiz O

1. opening, adjective
2. to lose, adverb
3. to study, adjective
4. swimming, noun
5. fortified, adjective
6. skiing, noun; to get, adjective

Answers to Chapter Review and Practice

Exercise A

1. Yesterday, adverb we pronoun saw a huge adjective crowd at the stadium.
2. To whom pronoun did you give the multi-colored adjective scarf?
3. They seem verb genuinely adverb happy adjective to see us.
4. Dr. Margaret Mead noun or proper noun was one of the most adverb famous anthropologists in the world. noun
5. "Fathead!" noun he shouted.
6. Wayne and coordinating conjunction his brother reached the top of the mountain, but coordinating conjunction his pronoun/adj brother's adjective friend did not make the climb.

Exercise B

1. The seas were so high that the pilings were undermined. adverbial clause
2. They went there so they would not feel alone. adverbial clause
3. That house will have been sold verb phrase by Monday.
4. Having formed a plan participial phrase, they escaped.
5. That she is running for reelection noun clause was announced yesterday.
6. He is always on the phone. prepositional phrase
7. The film that you saw adjective clause is R-rated.

CHAPTER 2

The Sentence and the Sentence Fragment

- **Items 22–43 in the Pretest are from this chapter.**
- **The procedure for recognizing and correcting sentence fragments is on page 33.**

Chapter Contents

RULE: | Every sentence should contain at least one subject+ verb unit and should communicate a sense of completeness.

A The Sentence and Its Essential Elements

A *sentence* is a group of words that contains at least one subject+verb unit and that communicates a sense of completeness. A sentence begins with a capital letter and ends with a period, a question mark, or an exclamation mark. A subject+verb unit and a sense of completeness are the essential sentence elements.

A group of words that lacks all or part of the subject+verb unit or a sense of completeness is a sentence fragment,* an incomplete sentence.

*fragment: Professional writers often use sentence fragments (incomplete sentences) intentionally to heighten the effect of their writing. In general, however, college papers should not contain sentence fragments.

A-1 The subject+verb unit

The subject

The *subject* of a sentence *tells who or what the sentence is about.* Everything else in the sentence helps to make a statement or ask a question about the subject.

Examples

a. *Annette* (subj.) speaks.
(*Annette* names the person whom the sentence is about.)

b. In addition, the *plumber* (subj.) from the Instant Plumbing Company has been fired.
(*Plumber* names the person whom the sentence is about.)

c. Get out!
(This sentence is a command that does not state its subject. Whenever a command or a request does not state its subject, that subject is understood to be the word *you.* Such a subject is an *unexpressed* or *understood* subject.)

d. Did *Linda* (subj.) tear along the dotted line?

e. *I* (subj.) did not go to the lecture.

f. The *clues* (subj.) were obvious, but the *conclusion* (subj.) eluded us.
(*Clues* and *conclusion* name what the sentence is about.)

The verb

The *verb* of a sentence tells *what the subject does, what the subject is,* or *what action the subject receives.*

Examples **a.** Annette *speaks.* (vb.: *speaks*)
(*Speaks* tells what the subject does.)

b. In addition, the plumber from the Instant Plumbing Company *has been fired.* (vb.: *has been fired*)
(*Has been fired* tells what action the subject receives.)

c. *Get* out! (vb.: *Get*)

d. *Did* Linda *tear* along the dotted line? (vb.: *Did … tear*)

e. I *did* not *go* to the lecture. (vb.: *did … go*)

f. The clues *were* obvious, but the conclusion *eluded* us. (vb.: *were*; vb.: *eluded*)
(*Were* tells what the subject *clues* is, and *eluded* tells what the subject *conclusion* does.)

The subject + verb unit

A *subject + verb unit* is the combination of a subject (expressed or unexpressed) and its verb. In sentences that make a statement ("declarative" sentences), the subject generally precedes the verb, although much can come in between.

Examples **a.** *Annette speaks.*
(*Annette* + *speaks* = subject + verb unit)

b. *The plumber* from the Instant Plumbing Company *has been fired.*
(*plumber* + *has been fired* = subject + verb unit)

c. *Get* out!
(*you* (understood subj.) + *get* = subject + verb unit)

d. *Did Linda tear* along the dotted line?
(*Linda* + *did tear* = subject + verb unit)

e. *I did* not *go* to the lecture.
(*I* + *did go* = subject + verb unit)

f. The *clues were* obvious, but the *conclusion eluded* us.
(This sentence is made up of two sentences:
1) The clues were obvious,
2) but the conclusion eluded us.
Each of the two sentences in this **compound sentence** has its own subject + verb unit:
clues + *were* = subject + verb unit 1
conclusion + *eluded* = subject + verb unit 2
See also see section C-2, and for correct punctuation of compound sentences, see chapter 8.)

Quick Quiz: A

Circle subjects, *underline* verbs, and *write* the subject + verb units in the right-hand column.

Subject + Verb Unit

Model: At first, his car led by three laps, but we won the race. car + led / we + won

1. The owner discovered the robbery this morning. ______
2. According to some thinkers, Machiavelli was the first modern political scientist. ______
3. He is demanding a refund, and Alice thinks he will get it. ______ ______
4. Ten top stars of professional football and show business gathered for a salute to the world of sports. ______ ______
5. The oil industry has not accepted its share of the blame for pollution of the harbor. ______

Answers to Quick Quiz A are on page 48.

A-2 The sense of completeness

In addition to having a subject + verb unit, *a sentence communicates a sense of completeness*—a feeling that the writer has completed his or her thought.

Examples In each pair of examples below, **1.** lacks a sense of completeness and is therefore a fragment, while **2.** communicates a sense of completeness and is a sentence.

a. 1. Before you (subj.) enter (vb.). (lacks sense of completeness)

2. Before you (subj.) enter (vb.), you (subj.) must present (vb.) your pass. (sentence)

subj. vb.
b. 1. I like. (lacks sense of completeness)

subj. vb.
2. I like microbiology. (sentence)

subj. vb.
c. 1. The man who came to dinner.

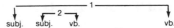

1 (subj. → vb.); 2 (subj. → vb.)
subj. subj. vb. vb.
2. The man who came to dinner stayed for breakfast.
(subject + verb unit 1 = *man + stayed; subject + verb unit 2 = who + came*)

subj. vb.
d. 1. That he wanted to get out of the army.

subj. 1; 2 (subj. → vb.)
subj. vb. vb. 1
2. That he wanted to get out of the army was no secret.
(The entire group of words *That he wanted to get out of the army* is the subject of the verb *was.* Subject + verb unit 1 = *That he wanted to get out of the army + was,* and subject + verb unit 2 = *he + wanted*)

Quick Quiz: B

Write complete in front of each item that has a sense of completeness. *Write incomplete* in front of each item that lacks a sense of completeness.

Model: incomplete In order to convince the public, it seems.

1. ______________ The moratorium has cooled partisanship.

2. ______________ The District of Columbia, which was well planned.

3. ______________ For a time, it seemed that even his gigantic reserve of energy was not enough.

4. ______________ The unwritten code that requires harmony after a debate.

5. ______________ That the Rose Bowl is the best game of the day.

Answers to Quick Quiz B are on page 48.

B The Sentence Fragment and How to Correct It

A *sentence fragment* is a group of words that *lacks all or part of the subject + verb unit, lacks a sense of completeness,* or *lacks both.*

NOTE: A sentence fragment (also called an *incomplete sentence* or a *fragment*) may look like a sentence by starting with a capital letter and ending with a period or other end mark.

B-1 Correcting the sentence fragment that lacks all or part of the subject + verb unit

Correct a sentence fragment that lacks a *subject* by adding a *subject*.

Examples

a. fragment: Stopped again.

sentence: The *motor* (subj.) stopped again.

b. fragment: Will be arriving late.

sentence: *Guests* (subj.) will be arriving late.

c. fragment: Slowly but surely, is choking itself to death.

sentence: Slowly but surely, every urban *area* (subj.) is choking itself to death.

Correct a sentence fragment that lacks a *verb* by adding a *verb*.

Examples

a. fragment: The report, thorough but inconclusive.

sentence: The report *is* (vb.) thorough but inconclusive.

b. fragment: After a long night, the dawn.

sentence: After a long night, the dawn *came* (vb.).

c. fragment: The engineer to design the bridge.

sentence: The engineer *plans* (vb.) to design the bridge.

Quick Quiz C

Each sample below has 1) a subject + verb unit, **or** 2) only a subject, **or** 3) only a verb. *Underline* the item in each sample, and *write* the proper term in the blank provided.

Models: Ann, expecting to be married. ___subject___
The trees blew in the wind. ___s+v unit___

1. You give me doubts. ________

2. The aircraft known as the L-1011. ____________

3. Invested all their resources in stocks and bonds. ____________

4. The time passed far too quickly. ____________

5. Realistic hopes for success. ____________

6. Tries to complete all the tasks. ____________

Answers to Quick Quiz C are on page 48.

B-2 Correcting the sentence fragment that lacks a sense of completeness

A group of words, even though it contains a subject+verb unit, is a sentence fragment if it lacks a sense of completeness.

Examples

a. I expect.

b. The economist suggested.

c. Most visitors to the city like.

d. The speaker had been saying.

e. Since the speech has ended.

f. Unless you make the payment within a week.

g. That Beethoven composed nine symphonies.

h. The man who came to dinner.

i. The area that contained the mineral deposits.

Correct certain sentence fragments that lack a sense of completeness *by adding* one or more words.

Examples

a. fragment: I expect*
sentence: I expect it.

*expect. *Expect* is one of the verbs that need some addition to complete their meaning. See "Transitive Verb" in Chapter 1. Some other verbs of this type are *ask, mean, need, say, see, suggest, like.* I *like* them.

b. fragment: The economist suggested.
sentence: The economist suggested a remedy for inflation.

c. fragment: Most visitors to the city like.
sentence: Most visitors to the city like to be entertained.

d. fragment: The speaker had been saying.
sentence: The speaker had been saying nothing new.

Correct certain sentence fragments that lack a sense of completeness *by removing a word* such as *since.**

*since: *Since* is one of several expressions used to introduce sentences or parts of sentences. Other such introductory expressions are *after, although, as, as long as, because, before, even though, if, provided, that, though, unless, until, what, when, which, who.* These words often introduce *dependent clauses* (subject + verb units that lack a sense of completeness). See also section C-3.

Examples

a. fragment: Since the speech has ended.
sentence: The speech has ended.

b. fragment: Unless you make the payment within a week.
sentence: You make the payment within a week.

c. fragment: That Beethoven composed nine symphonies.
sentence: Beethoven composed nine symphonies.

d. fragment: The man who came to dinner.
sentence: The man came to dinner.

e. fragment: The area that contained the mineral deposits.
sentence: The area contained the mineral deposits.

Correct a sentence fragment that lacks a sense of completeness *by combining* it with an adjoining, related sentence.

Examples

a. adjoining sentence: I can leave.
fragment: Since the speech has ended.
resulting sentence: Since the speech has ended, I can leave.

b. adjoining sentence: We will assume you are dead.
fragment: Unless you make your payment within a week.
resulting sentence: We will assume you are dead unless you make your payment within a week.

c. adjoining sentence: Edward is my colleague.
fragment: The man who came to dinner.
resulting sentence: Edward, the man who came to dinner, is my colleague.

This last method of correcting fragments is probably the most useful to you. In student papers, sentence fragments usually occur because the writer ends one sentence, then incorrectly begins a new one with material that really only completes the thought of the original sentence.

Examples: That night the campground was entirely full. Of tourists from other parts of the state. *frag.*

It will be necessary to restrict admission to the rock concert. Unless adequate provision can be made for public safety. *frag.*

In each example above, the second "sentence" is incomplete and really should be joined to the one preceding it.

Examples: That night the campground was entirely full of tourists from other parts of the state.

It will be necessary to restrict admission to the rock concert unless adequate provision can be made for public safety.

Correct a sentence fragment that lacks a sense of completeness *by rewriting.*

Sometimes simply attaching the fragment to an adjacent sentence is not enough since an awkward, inefficient, or confusing sentence will result. In these instances, rewrite.

Example: The water supply simply was inadequate for the town. Which was provided by two fairly shallow wells.

Rewrite: The water supply, which was provided by two fairly shallow wells, simply was inadequate for the town.

Example: My parents were deprived of educations because each of them had to work to support younger brothers and sisters. Both of whom always regretted their lack of educational advantages.

Rewrite: Because they both had to work to support younger brothers and sisters, my parents, to their regret, were deprived of educational advantages.

Quick Quiz D

a. Which of the following are fragments? (*Circle the numbers.*)
b. Which can be combined to form complete sentences? (*Circle the groups of numbers.*)

Model: 1. The drought ended none too soon. 2. Since the crop yields had been pitifully small for two years.

a. Fragments: (Circle fragments) 1 (2)

b. Combine: (Circle groups that should be combined) (1 2)

1. It is possible for students to earn college credit by working in the community. 2. Or by studying abroad. 3. It is important, however, for those interested in such programs to make the decision early enough. 4. To allow them to consult with their advisors, to discuss what preparations are necessary. 5. And to arrange financial aid. 6. If it will be necessary.

a. Fragments: (Circle fragments) 1 2 3 4 5 6

b. Combine: (Circle groups that should be combined) 1 2 3 4 5 6

Answers to Quick Quiz D are on page 48.

Procedure for Recognizing and Correcting Sentence Fragments

RULE: Every sentence should contain at least one *subject + verb unit* and should communicate *a sense of completeness.*

NOTE: Your instructor's marginal notation generally identifies your error.

frag. In the morning stopped again at the beach.

Step 1: Look for a subject + verb unit. If there is no subject, add one.

In the morning stopped again at the beach contains a verb, *stopped,* but no subject. Therefore, add a subject. Corrected, the sentence might read

In the morning, the tourists stopped again at the beach.

frag. *All in the family at home*

Step 2: Look for a subject + verb unit. If there is no verb to go with the subject, add one.

All in the family at home contains a subject, *all,* but lacks a verb. Therefore, add a verb. Corrected, the sentence might read

All in the family dined at home.

frag. *In May, I expect.*

Check for a sense of completeness.

Step 3: *In May, I expect* lacks a sense of completeness. Therefore, complete the meaning of the sentence. Corrected, the sentence might read

In May, I expect to go to Italy if I have the money.

NOTE: When combining sentences, be sure to adjust punctuation and capitalization as needed.

Step 4: If the fragment is not part of an adjoining sentence, complete the meaning of the fragment by adding one or more words or by removing a word such as *since.* (See p. 36.)

Step 5: Rewrite, if necessary.

If you decide to write a new sentence, be sure it contains a subject + verb unit and a sense of completeness.

C Types of Sentences

In your writing you will use four types of sentences:

the **simple** sentence
the **compound** sentence
the **complex** sentence
the **compound-complex** sentence

Each type has (at least) one subject + verb unit; each has a sense of completeness. They differ from one another 1) in their complexity, and 2) in their ability to express different shades of meaning.

C-1 The Simple Sentence

The *simple sentence* consists of **one subject + verb unit:**

subj. vb.
Examples **a.** Annette speaks.

subj. vb.
b. The plumber has been fired.

subj. vb.
c. The clues were obvious.

NOTE: *Simple* sentences can be long, but each has only one subject + verb unit:

subj. vb.
d. In addition to all the other equipment, he also carried Rick's full pack over the pass to the meadow on the other side of the lake.

The simple sentence, besides being used separately, sometimes also helps to form the other types of sentences. It can also be called an **independent clause** (subject + verb unit with a sense of completeness). The descriptions of the other types of sentences will use that term.

C-2 The Compound Sentence

The *compound sentence* consists of two (or more) simple sentences, that is to say, *two (or more) independent clauses.* Each clause could stand alone as a complete sentence:

Examples

indep. cl. 1 indep cl. 2
a. The clues were obvious, but the conclusion eluded us.

The clues were obvious.
But the conclusion eluded us.

indep. cl. 1 indep cl. 2
b. The plumber has been fired, and the carpenter has quit.

indep. cl. 1 indep cl. 2
c. Existing technology will be used, or new methods will be developed.

indep. cl. 1 indep cl. 2
d. The winter was unusually severe; the spring, however, was mild.

NOTE: In the first three examples, the independent clauses are connected by a comma + a coordinating conjunction (but, and, or). In the last example, the independent clauses are connected by a semicolon. Chapter 8 offers more detail about the punctuation of sentences containing two or more independent clauses.

Quick Quiz E

In the following sentences, *underline each subject + verb unit. Label* each sentence either *simple* or *compound.*

Model: I ran for congress, but my opponent defeated me. *compound*

1. The farmers gathered around the burning barn, and they offered advice to the firefighters. ____________

2. On her way home from the office, Frieda met an old neighbor from Kalamazoo. ____________

3. The new products are well-packaged, but the old ones still sell better. ______________

4. Frieda was on her way home; she met an old friend. ______________

5. The blossom-laden trees lined the roadway between the towns that Sunday morning. ______________

Answers to Quick Quiz E are on page 48.

C-3 The Complex Sentence

The *complex sentence* consists of **one independent clause** and also contains **one (or more) dependent clauses.** While the independent clause of a complex sentence might stand alone as a sentence, the dependent clause never can since it lacks a sense of completeness.

Example [independent clause: The plumber has been fired] [dependent clause: although his work was satisfactory.]

The plumber (subj.) has been fired (vb.). (subject + verb unit; sense of completeness)

Although his work (subj.) was (vb.) satisfactory (subject + verb unit; but lacks sense of completeness)

Recognizing Dependent Clauses

Dependent clauses **begin with subordinating conjunctions** (expressed or unexpressed). These subordinating conjunctions* cause the lack of a sense of completeness. In the following example, various subordinating conjunctions introduce the dependent clauses.

*subordinating conjunctions: (See page 15 for a comparison of coordinating and subordinating conjunctions.)

Example The plumber was fired . . .

. . . **after** he (subj.) broke (vb.) the pipe.

. . . **as** he (subj.) left (vb.) the property.

. . . **because** he (subj.) flooded (vb.) the house.

. . . **before** he (subj.) could explain (vb.).

. . . **since** he (subj.) refused (vb.) to work.

. . . **whenever** he (subj.) started (vb.) a new job.

Each of the dependent clauses in this example lacks a sense of completeness *because* each is introduced by a subordinating conjunction.

Use of Dependent Clauses

Dependent clauses are versatile. They can be used as various parts of the sentence:

- Dependent clause as *subject* of a complex sentence.

independent clause
dep. cl. vb.

Examples **a.** That he is clever is obvious.
(*That he is clever* works together as a unit to form the entire subject of the sentence.)

- Dependent clause as *object* of a complex sentence.

independent clause
dep. cl.

b. I know that the report is due.
(*That the report is due* works together as a unit to form the entire direct object of the verb *know.*)

- Dependent clause as *modifier of a noun* in a complex sentence.

noun dep. cl.

c. The stranger who visited them left early.
(Independent clause: *The stranger . . . left early.*)

- Dependent clause as *modifier of a verb* in a complex sentence.

vb. dep. cl.

d. We will eat when we get there.
(Independent clause: *We will eat. . . .)*

Quick Quiz F

Underline each *dependent clause* in the complex sentences below. *Circle* each *subordinating conjunction.*

Model: I usually know (how) <u>George gets his money.</u>

1. Ask Richard when he will return.
2. Although it's late, let's phone him.
3. I needed the part that he dropped in his pocket.
4. Don't you wonder whether they will remember us?
5. After they bought the property they improved it.

Answers to Quick Quiz F are on page 49.

Coordination and Subordination

Compound sentences give approximately equal importance to each of their independent clauses.

Example

a. Jim studies naval architecture, and he visited the Maritime Museum.

b. The youth park needed new equipment, but there were no funds.

c. The stock market rallied in May; it reached a new high for the year.

Complex sentences, through their use of dependent clauses, emphasize some parts of the sentence (the independent clause) while subordinating other parts (the dependent clause(s)).

Examples

a. [dep. cl.: Since he studies naval architecture,] [indep. cl.: Jim visited the Maritime Museum.]

b. [dep. cl.: Although the youth park needed new equipment,] [indep. cl.: there were no funds.]

c. When the stock market rallied in May, it reached a new high for the year.

Quick Quiz G

Label each of the following sentences as *compound* or *complex.* If the sentence is complex, *underline* the *dependent clause.*

Model: Nero fiddled <u>while Rome burned</u>. complex

1. Silence is golden, but sometimes it's yellow. ____________
2. The poet says that no man is an island. ____________
3. I trust you; you're my friend. ____________
4. I trust you because you're my friend. ____________
5. When summer comes, it will be too late. ____________
6. There are two principles that can be applied. ____________
7. I would join them, but they don't know me. ____________

Answers to Quick Quiz G are on page 49.

C-4 The Compound-Complex Sentence

The compound-complex sentence combines the features of the compound sentence with those of the complex sentence. The compound-complex sentence contains (1) at least two independent clauses and (2) at least one dependent clause.

Examples

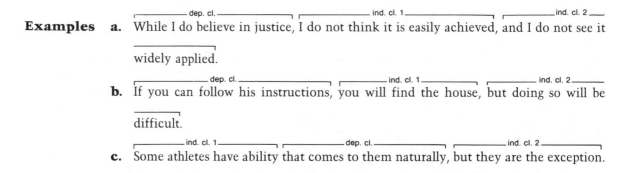

a. [dep. cl. While I do believe in justice,] [ind. cl. 1 I do not think it is easily achieved,] and [ind. cl. 2 I do not see it widely applied.]

b. [dep. cl. If you can follow his instructions,] [ind. cl. 1 you will find the house,] but [ind. cl. 2 doing so will be difficult.]

c. [ind. cl. 1 Some athletes have ability] [dep. cl. that comes to them naturally,] but [ind. cl. 2 they are the exception.]

REVIEW AND PRACTICE

Each of the sections of this Review and Practice is different. Do some exercises in each section, check your answers, then decide which sections—if any—you need to continue to work through. Answers are on pages 49–50.

Exercise A Below are 12 groups of words: some are sentences; some are sentence fragments. Mark the sentences **C;** mark the fragments **frag.**

Models: ___C.___ She forgot.
___frag.___ Going to bed.

1. ______________ On time.

2. ______________ Running to work.

3. ______________ Abner was still running.

4. ______________ Should John fly.

5. ______________ Eager to be seen.

6. ______________ Dante complaining to Beatrice.

7. ______________ Who arranged the display?

8. ______________ Who that was.

9. ______________ The horse that kicked you.

10. ______________ After eating, he slept.

11. ______________ Makes all other cars obsolete.

12. ______________ Stop it!

Exercise B Each item below consists of several word groups printed as sentences. *Underline* all fragments.

Model: They studied the town. <u>From the top of the hill</u>.

1. I don't know what he wants. Until he asks.
2. Not only that. I cannot understand the formula for increasing velocity in falling bodies.
3. He has gone. To interview for the position advertised in last night's paper.
4. Censorship remained. In the hands of parents.
5. Diving makes me sick. Dizzy, mostly. However, I am a good swimmer, although not a fast one.
6. No one can explain what a melody is. Each definition only making the subject more confusing.
7. Nature, as he described it, is violent. With animals devouring each other in their fight for survival.
8. The job was dull, but she took it anyway. It being necessary to eat.
9. The notary public now uses a rubber stamp. Instead of the old seal that embossed a design in the paper. Because so many documents are photographed.
10. At first, the beautician thought that dyeing was fun. In an odd way.

Exercise C Make a sentence by connecting a, b, or c on the left with the fragment on the right.

Model: a. She went ———— for the money.
b. To go
c. Going

1. a. Turning the knob
   b. Turn the knob — to the off position.
   c. After turning the knob

2. a. Provided gloves are worn
   b. Gloves being worn — when working with strong chemical solutions.
   c. Wear gloves

3. a. Pesticides have killed several species
   b. Pesticides that have killed several species — are still on the market.
   c. That pesticides having killed several species

4. a. The board of directors needed time
   b. The board of directors needing time — to consider its choice.
   c. The board of directors, which needed time

5. a. Spanish, French, and Italian being
   b. Spanish, French, and Italian are — Romance languages.
   c. Although Spanish, French, and Italian are

6. a. That he expects
   b. Having expected — trouble.
   c. He expects

7. a. Edna composing
b. Edna is composing — a rock opera.
c. Edna to compose

8. a. The runner to slide
b. The runner is to slide — whenever he can.
c. The runner sliding

9. a. They want
b. Since they want — a new contract.
c. To have wanted

10. a. When the attorney made
b. The attorney made — a summation.
c. The attorney making

Exercise D Change each sentence fragment to a sentence *by crossing out one word.*

Model: The men ~~who~~ captured him.

1. Because the marines have landed.

2. If you can go.

3. The child who was lost.

4. The lecture that is being held.

5. The idea that had been stolen.

Exercise E If an item below is a complete sentence, *write* **correct** in the blank; if it is an incomplete sentence, *write* **frag.** If a fragment simply needs to be attached to the preceding sentence, *write* **frag/attach** in the blank.

1. Those who return to college after an absence of several years may feel a sense of inferiority. 2. And sometimes find it difficult to fit into college life comfortably. 3. Many institutions of higher learning have established "re-entry programs." 4. To assist such students. 5. Who have every right to expect a satisfying college experience. 6. The transition back to college often becomes easier and quicker for mothers who have raised their families. 7. And now have time to study. 8. For older people who look forward to the enrichment education can provide. 9. For individuals who hope to train for jobs in new fields. 10. Simply having the opportunity to come together with others who share their hopes and misgivings seems to reassure these returning students. 11. Since it lets them realize that their feelings of being out of place are unfounded.

1. ________	2. ________	3. ________	4. ________
5. ________	6. ________	7. ________	8. ________
9. ________	10. ________	11. ________	

Answers to Review and Practice are on pages 49–50.

CHAPTER TEST

Below are groups of words written as sentences. Some are sentences and some are sentence fragments. Write **C** *in front of each sentence, and write* **frag** in front of each sentence fragment.

Model: ~~*frag.*~~ At dinner.

1. _______ The tree surgeon from the Senesino Tree Service to come Wednesday.
2. _______ Fill this cup.
3. _______ Frustrated again.
4. _______ Was at work for three days.
5. _______ The husband and the wife.
6. _______ After stapling, you may fold and mutilate this card.
7. _______ The horseman being insecure on his horse.
8. _______ Skiing being thrilling.
9. _______ The congressman to run for the senate.
10. _______ The porpoise began to speak.
11. _______ You said.
12. _______ Until you get over your anxiety.
13. _______ Although you think so.
14. _______ Starting salaries are low.
15. _______ In the morning after only three hours of sleep to be awakened early.
16. _______ The problem that plagued you.
17. _______ Why he played.
18. _______ The garbage, which was not collected.
19. _______ That is your theory.
20. _______ Who asked me that?
21. _______ The area in southern Italy that contained the precious mineral deposits.
22. _______ To think is important.
23. _______ She's ill.
24. _______ The person who wants to understand with some thoroughness the dimensions of the problem.
25. _______ For allowing these conditions to continue without any attempt at correcting them.

Answers to Chapter Test are on page 50.

ANSWERS: CHAPTER 2

Answers to Quick Quiz A

1. owner + discovered 2. Machiavelli + was 3. he + is demanding, Alice + thinks, he + will get 4. stars + gathered 5. industry + has accepted.

Answers to Quick Quiz B

1. complete 2. incomplete 3. complete 4. incomplete
5. incomplete

Answers to Quick Quiz C

1. You give s+v unit
2. aircraft subject
3. Invested verb
4. time passed s+v unit
5. hopes subject
6. Tries verb

Answers to Quick Quiz D

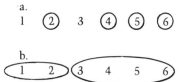

a.
1 (2) 3 (4) (5) (6)

b.
(1 2) (3 4 5 6)

Answers to Quick Quiz E

1. farmers gathered, they offered; compound
2. Frieda met; simple
3. products are, ones sell; compound
4. Frieda was, she met; compound
5. trees lined; simple

Answers to Quick Quiz F

1. when he will return
2. Although it's late
3. that he dropped in his pocket
4. whether they will remember us
5. After they bought the property

Answers to Quick Quiz G

1. compound
2. complex; that no man is an island
3. compound
4. complex; because you're my friend
5. complex; when summer comes
6. complex; that can be applied
7. compound

Answers to Review and Practice

Exercise A	Notice that . . .
1. frag	
2. frag	A word ending in *ing* cannot act as a complete verb.
3. C	
4. frag	This fragment lacks a sense of completeness. With a question mark, this would be a sentence: Should John fly?
5. frag	The *to* form of a verb cannot act as the verb of a sentence.
6. frag	A word ending in *ing* cannot act as a complete verb.
7. C	
8. frag	
9. frag	
10. C	
11. frag	
12. C	*Stop it!* is a command. The unexpressed subject is *you*.

Exercise B

1. Until he asks.
2. Not only that.
3. To interview for the position advertised in last night's paper.

4. In the hands of parents.
5. Dizzy, mostly.
6. Each definition only making the subject more confusing.
7. With animals devouring each other in their fight for survival.
8. It being necessary to eat.
9. Instead of the old seal that embossed a design in the paper. Because so many documents are photographed.
10. In an odd way.

Exercise C

1. b. Turn the knob—to the off position.
2. c. Wear gloves—when working with strong chemical solutions.
3. b. Pesticides that have killed several species—are still on the market.
4. a. The board of directors needed time—to consider its choice.
5. b. Spanish, French, and Italian are—Romance languages.
6. c. He expects—trouble.
7. b. Edna is composing—a rock opera.
8. b. The runner is to slide—whenever he can.
9. a. They want—a new contract.
10. b. The attorney made—a summation.

Exercise D

1. ~~Because~~	The marines have landed.
2. ~~If~~	You can go.
3. ~~who~~	The child was lost.
4. ~~that~~	The lecture is being held.
5. ~~that~~	The idea had been stolen.

Exercise E

1. Correct
2. Frag/attach (lacks subject)
3. Correct
4. Frag/attach (lacks s + v unit)
5. Frag/attach (lacks sense of completeness)
6. Correct
7. Frag/attach (lacks subject)
8. Frag/attach (lacks sense of completeness)
9. Frag/attach (lacks sense of completeness)
10. Correct
11. Frag/attach (lacks sense of completeness)

Answers to Chapter Test

1. frag	6. C	11. frag	16. frag	21. frag
2. C	7. frag	12. frag	17. frag	22. C
3. frag	8. frag	13. frag	18. frag	23. C
4. frag	9. frag	14. C	19. C	24. frag
5. frag	10. C	15. frag	20. C	25. frag

CHAPTER 3

Verbs and Verb Tense Shift

- **Items 44-50 in the Pretest are from this chapter.**
- **The procedure for recognizing and correcting errors in verb tense is on page 70.**

Chapter Contents

RULE: | Use verb tense accurately to show when an action happened.

Almost every sentence is about some action. The part of the sentence that expresses the action is the verb. The *tense* of the verb tells the reader something about the *time* at which the action occurred.

A Verb Tense Forms: What They Mean and How to Use Them Accurately

You do not have to know technical terms to use tenses correctly, but you should know (and probably already do know) these basic terms: past, present, and future. In general,

Past means before now.
Present means now.
Future means after now.

A-1 Past tense

Simple past tense

The *simple past tense* (sometimes called simply the *past tense*) says that the *action started and ended before the present.* Many verbs (called regular or weak verbs*) form the simple past tense by adding **d** or **ed** (use + d = *used,* walk + ed = *walked*). Some verbs (called irregular or strong verbs*) form the simple past tense **in other ways** (run = *ran,* come = *came,* go = *went,* be = *were,* sleep = *slept,* swim = *swam*).

*weak verbs: See page 58.
*strong verbs: See page 60.

Examples

vb.
a. Heather *walked* in the woods.

vb. vb.
b. Mike *left* before you *left.*

vb. vb.
c. Paul *took* these photographs of the guacharo when he *lived* in Trinidad.

Progressive Past Tense

The *progressive past tense* says that *an action started and was continuing (was progressing) before the present.* The progressive past tense is formed by combining the simple past tense of the verb *be** and the *-ing form of the verb** *being used.*

*be: See page 64 for the past tense of the verb *be.*
* the *-ing* form of the verb is called the *present participle:* walk + ing, think + ing, *rowing, planting.* See page 18 for more on the use of the present participle.

Examples **a.** I *was walking*, you *were walking*, and they *were walking* too.

b. Joni and Robert *were leaving* the house.

c. At noon, Kiko *was grinding* lenses.

Past Perfect Tense

The *past perfect tense* says that *the action had been started and completed (perfected) before some specific time or event in the past.* The past perfect tense is formed by combining *had* (the *simple past tense* of the verb *have**) and the *past participle* of the verb being used. Had walked, had eaten, had gone, had been* are in the past perfect tense.

*have: See page 65 for the past tense of the verb *have*.
*The *past participle* of a regular verb is formed by adding *d, ed,* or *t to the simple present tense* of the verb. The past participles of irregular verbs are formed in various ways. See pages 61–63 for the past participles of some common irregular verbs, and see page 18 for more on the use of the past participle.

Examples **a.** Ron *had left* town before his wife's arrival yesterday.
The action—leaving town—had been started and completed before the specific past event—his wife's arrival.

b. The reporter *had finished* her interview an hour before the plane took off.
The action—finishing her interview—had been completed before the plane took off.

c. Our team *had made* only four baskets by the time the half ended.
The action—making the baskets—had been completed before the half ended.

A-2 Present tense

Simple Present Tense

The *simple present tense* (often called simply the *present tense*) can say several things; for instance, the simple present tense can say that *something is true now.*

Examples **a.** They *have* ten projects in ten states.

b. Washington, D.C. *is* our capital.

c. Marion *knows* three languages: English, Swahili, and Italian.

The simple present tense can say that something *happens regularly.*

Examples **a.** It *rains* every November.

b. My uncle *walks* to work daily.

vb.
c. They always *exercise* before breakfast.

The simple present tense can be used to give a sense of the present to things in the past. (This use is often called the *historical present.*) Even though a literary work was written in the past, we often speak about it and about its author's writing in the present tense.

Examples **a.** Shakespeare, Molière, and Pushkin ***are*** great writers.

b. In Charles Dickens' *Hard Times,* Louisa Gradgrind ***is*** clearly the embodiment of the crippling effects of a strict education.

NOTE: We do not use the historical present in speaking of an author's own life.

Examples **a.** Edna St. Vincent Millay, author of "Renascence," *liked* (not likes) solitude.

b. T.S. Eliot, who *lived* in the United States until 1914, says in "Dry Salvages," "Not fare well,/But fare forward, voyagers."

Progressive Present Tense

The *progressive present tense* says that *something has started and is continuing (is progressing) now,* in the present. The progressive present tense is formed by combining the *present tense* of the verb *be* with the *-ing form of the verb being used.*

vb.
Examples **a.** Mickey *is buying* a house.

vb.
b. We *are enjoying* ourselves.

vb.
c. Scientists *are discovering* more and more about the functioning of the human body.

Present Perfect Tense

The *present perfect tense* says that something *has been started and has been completed (perfected) before the present* (the time it is being talked about). The present perfect tense is formed by combining the *present tense* of the verb *have* with the *past participle of the verb being used.*

vb.
Examples **a.** I *have finished* the *Unfinished Symphony.*

vb.
b. John Anonymous *has left* many poems unsigned.

vb.
c. Buck Rogers and Flash Gordon *have* both *been* out of this world for years.

A-3 Future tense

Simple Future Tense

The *simple future tense* (sometimes called simply the *future tense*) says that something *has not started yet, but will start* at some time after the present. The simple future tense is formed by *combining **will** (or shall*) with the verb being used.*

*Traditionally, *will* and *shall* have differed from one another in meaning. Since the distinctions between them are not consistently observed even in serious writing, *will* is generally used in this book in all future tenses.

Examples **a.** An hour after lunch, they *will launch* the ship.

NOTE: The future tense often is also expressed by saying that something **is going to happen.** Thus, they *are going to launch* the ship.

b. The Irish wolfhound *will bark* up any tree.

c. No, Olive *will* not *try* to swim the English Channel.
(Olive *is* not *going to try to swim* the English Channel.)

Progressive Future Tense

The *progressive future tense* says that an action *has not started, yet will start and will be continuing (will be progressing) at some time after the present.* The progressive future tense is formed by *combining **will** (or shall), **be,*** and the ***-ing** form of the verb being used.*

Examples **a.** The pirates *will be walking* the plank.

b. Rollo predicts she *will be running* for mayor.

c. *Will* you *be using* your calculator tonight?

Future Perfect Tense

The *future perfect tense* says that something *will have been completed before some other specific future time or event.* The future perfect tense is formed by *combining* ***will*** *(or* **shall**) and ***have*** *with the* ***past participle*** *of the verb being used.*

Examples **a.** Kip *will have napped* for an hour by the end of the lecture.

b. By eight in the morning, they *will have left* for work.

c. I *will have gained* ten pounds by the time the holidays have ended.

A-4 Formation of tenses

Past Tenses *(before now)*	*Present Tenses* *(now)*	*Future Tenses* *(after now)*
	SIMPLE TENSES	
Simple Past Tense A. Regular (VERB + ED or D) verbs I *walked.* She *skated.* B. Irregular* verbs They *left.* We *ate.*	**Simple Present Tense** (VERB) or (VERB + S) They *walk.* He *leaves.*	**Simple Future Tense** WILL* + (VERB) You *will walk.* She *will leave.*

* See pages 61–63 for the past tenses of commonly used irregular verbs.
* See section A-8 for an explanation of auxiliary verbs such as *will.*

Past Tenses *(before now)*	*Present Tenses* *(now)*	*Future Tenses* *(after now)*
	PROGRESSIVE TENSES	
Progressive Past Tense WAS or WERE + (VERB + ING) She *was walking.* They *were leaving.*	**Progressive Present Tense** AM or IS or ARE + (VERB + ING) I *am walking.* He *is leaving.* You *are eating.*	**Progressive Future Tense** WILL + BE + (VERB + ING) I *will be walking.* He *will be leaving.*
	PERFECT TENSES	
Past Perfect Tense A. Regular verbs HAD + (VERB + D or ED) We *had walked* *They had helped* B. Irregular verbs HAD + past participle* We *had left* He *had eaten*	**Present Perfect Tense** A. Regular verbs HAVE or HAS + (VERB + D or ED) You *have walked* She *has helped* B. Irregular verbs HAVE or HAS + past participle We *have left* He *has eaten*	**Future Perfect Tense** A. Regular verbs WILL + HAVE + (VERB + D or ED) She *will have walked* I *will have helped* B. Irregular verbs WILL + HAVE + past participle We *will have left* You *will have eaten*

*See pages 61–63 for the past participles of some commonly used irregular verbs.

A-5 Meaning of tenses

These tense forms	*convey these meanings*	*and are called:*
	PAST	
1. She *walked* to work.	The action happened before the present time, before now, before this moment.	past or simple past
2. We *were walking* to work.	The action was going on—was progressing—before the present.	progressive past
3. They *had walked* to work many times before the establishment of the bus line.	The action had been completed before some specific past time or event.	past perfect
	PRESENT	
4. a. The days *are* warm. b. I *walk* to work regularly. c. *The Birds of America,* published in 1827, *is* John James Audubon's most famous work.	a. The action is true now. b. The action happens regularly. c. The action is historically true and continues to be true now.	present or simple present (historical present)
5. You *are walking* to work, I see.	The action is going on at present, now.	progressive present
6. He *has walked* five miles this morning.	The action has been completed before the present.	present perfect
	FUTURE	
7. She *will walk* to work tonight.	The action has not yet happened, but will happen sometime after the present.	future or simple future
8. We *will be walking* there later.	The action will be happening sometime after the present.	progressive future
9. *I will have walked* a mile by the end of this hour.	The action will have been completed before some other specific future time or event.	future perfect

A-6 Regular (weak) verbs, their principal parts and conjugations

Regular verbs are those that usually form the past tense by adding **d** or **ed** to the simple present. The *principal parts* of a verb are the parts from which tense forms are created. Generally, there are three principal parts: the *present tense,* the *past tense,* and the *past participle*—the form used with the verb *have.* The present participle—the **ing** form of the verb—is often also included as a principal part. (See a current dictionary for principal parts of verbs not listed in *Help Yourself.*) The *conjugation* of a verb is the orderly presentation of tense forms of that verb.

Some regular verbs and their principal parts:

Verb	**Principal Parts**
1. help:	help helped helping helped
	help = present tense (I help.)
	helped = past tense (I helped.)
	helping = present participle (I am helping.)
	helped = past participle (I have helped.)
2. love:	love loved loving loved
3. excite:	excite excited exiting excited

Conjugation of the regular verb *help:*

The following terms are commonly used in relation to conjugation of verbs:
First person singular = (refers to) the speaker
Second person singular = the person spoken to
Third person singular = the person or thing spoken about
First person plural = the persons speaking
Second person plural = the persons spoken to
Third person plural = the persons or things spoken about

Simple Present Tense

	Active Voice*	**Passive Voice**
singular	I help (1st person singular)	I am helped
	you help (2nd person singular)	you are helped
	he, she, or it helps (3rd person singular)*	he, she, or it is helped

*For an explanation of voice, see chapter 13.
*Notice that in 3rd person singular an *-s* is added to the verb to form the *simple present tense.* Thus I *help;* you *help;* but he, she, it *helps.*

	Active Voice	**Passive Voice**
plural	we help (1st person plural)	we are helped
	you help (2nd person plural)	you are helped
	they help (3rd person plural)	they are helped

Simple Past Tense

	Active Voice	Passive Voice
singular	I helped	I was helped
	you helped	you were helped
	he, she, it helped	he, she, it was helped
plural	we helped	we were helped
	you helped	you were helped
	they helped	they were helped

Simple Future Tense

	Active Voice	Passive Voice
singular	I shall (or will) help	I shall (or will) be helped
	you will help	you will be helped
	he, she, it will help	he, she, it will be helped
plural	we shall (or will) help	we shall (or will) be helped
	you will help	you will be helped
	they will help	they will be helped

Present Perfect Tense

	Active Voice	Passive Voice
singular	I have helped	I have been helped
	you have helped	you have been helped
	he, she, it has helped	he, she, it has been helped
plural	we have helped	we have been helped
	you have helped	you have been helped
	they have helped	they have been helped

Past Perfect Tense

	Active Voice	Passive Voice
singular	I had helped	I had been helped
	you had helped	you had been helped
	he, she, it had helped	he, she, it had been helped
plural	we had helped	we had been helped
	you had helped	you had been helped
	they had helped	they had been helped

Future Perfect Tense

	Active Voice	Passive Voice
singular	I shall (or will) have helped	I shall (or will) have been helped
	you will have helped	you will have been helped
	he, she, it will have helped	he, she, it will have been helped
plural	we shall (or will) have helped	we shall (or will) have been helped
	you will have helped	you will have been helped
	they will have helped	they will have been helped

Present Progressive Tense

	Active Voice	Passive Voice
singular	I am helping	I am being helped
	you are helping	you are being helped
	he, she, it is helping	he, she, it is being helped
plural	we are helping	we are being helped
	you are helping	you are being helped
	they are helping	they are being helped

Past Progressive Tense

	Active Voice	Passive Voice
singular	I was helping	I was being helped
	you were helping	you were being helped
	he, she, it was helping	he, she, it was being helped
plural	we were helping	we were being helped
	you were helping	you were being helped
	they were helping	they were being helped

Future Progressive Tense

	Active Voice
singular	I shall (or will) be helping
	you will be helping
	he, she, it will be helping
plural	we shall (or will) be helping
	you will be helping
	they will be helping

A NOTE ABOUT SPELLING: Most regular verbs ending in **e** drop the **e** in the ***ing*** form. For example, *move* becomes *moving, shove* becomes *shoving,* and so forth. Thus, *I love, I loved,* but *I am* ***loving.***

A-7 Irregular (strong) verbs, their principal parts and conjugations

Irregular verbs are verbs that do *not* form their past tense by adding *d* or *ed.* They form their **past tense** in some **individual way.**
Compare these *regular* and *irregular* verbs:

Example

Regular verb		Irregular verb	
Present tense	*Past tense*	*Present tense*	*Past tense*
love	loved	arise	arose
want	wanted	am	was
walk	walked	bear	bore
cultivate	cultivated	beat	beat

Principal Parts

Notice that there is considerable variety in the changes those four irregular verbs undergo as they change from present to past tense. Because irregular verbs form their tenses in so many different ways, you will sometimes need to consult a dictionary to determine their various basic tense forms. (These are called the "principal parts" of the verb.) For example, the dictionary will tell you that the *present, past, present participle,* and *past participle* forms for the irregular verb **drive** are **drive, drove, driving,** and **driven** respectively.
Examples of irregular verbs and their principal parts:

Verb	*Present*	*Past*	*Present Participle*	*Past Participle*
be	(I) am	(I) was	(I) am being	(I) have been
have	(I) have	(I) had	(I) am having	(I) have had
go	(I) go	(I) went	(I) am going	(I) have gone
write	(I) write	(I) wrote	(I) am writing	(I) have written
speak	(I) speak	(I) spoke	(I) am speaking	(I) have spoken
think	(I) think	(I) thought	(I) am thinking	(I) have thought

The following chart lists the principal parts for a number of irregular verbs. It is by no means a complete list, however. If you are unsure whether a verb is regular or irregular, consult a dictionary.

Verb	**Past**	**Present Participle** (Used with a form of the verb *be*)	**Past Participle** (Used with a form of the verb *have*)
(I *arise*)	(I *arose*)	(I am *arising*)	(I have *arisen*)
arise	arose	arising	arisen
be	was	being	been
bear	bore	bearing	borne
beat	beat	beating	beaten
become	became	becoming	become
beget	begot	begetting	begotten
begin	began	beginning	begun
bid	bade	bidding	bidden
bend	bent	bending	bent
bind	bound	binding	bound
bite	bit	biting	bitten
bleed	bled	bleeding	bled
blow	blew	blowing	blown
break	broke	breaking	broken
bring	brought	bringing	brought
broadcast	broadcast	broadcasting	broadcast
build	built	building	built
burst	burst	bursting	burst
buy	bought	buying	bought
catch	caught	catching	caught
cast	cast	casting	cast
choose	chose	choosing	chosen

cling	clung	clinging	clung
clothe	clothed or clad	clothing	clothed or clad
come	came	coming	come
cost	cost	costing	cost
cut	cut	cutting	cut
deal	dealt	dealing	dealt
dig	dug	digging	dug
do	did	doing	done
draw	drew	drawing	drawn
drink	drank	drinking	drunk
drive	drove	driving	driven
eat	ate	eating	eaten
fall	fell	falling	fallen
feed	fed	feeding	fed
feel	felt	feeling	felt
fight	fought	fighting	fought
find	found	finding	found
flee	fled	fleeing	fled
fly	flew	flying	flown
forbid	forbade	forbidding	forbidden
foresee	foresaw	foreseeing	foreseen
foretell	foretold	foretelling	foretold
forget	forgot	forgetting	forgotten or forgot
forgive	forgave	forgiving	forgiven
freeze	froze	freezing	frozen
get	got	getting	gotten or got
give	gave	giving	given
go	went	going	gone
grind	ground	grinding	ground
grow	grew	growing	grown
hang (thing)	hung	hanging	hung
hang (a person) (regular)	hanged	hanging	hanged
have	had	having	had
hear	heard	hearing	heard
hide	hid	hiding	hidden or hid
hit	hit	hitting	hit
hold	held	holding	held
hurt	hurt	hurting	hurt
keep	kept	keeping	kept
kneel	knelt	kneeling	knelt
know	knew	knowing	known
lay (an egg)	laid	laying	laid
lead	led	leading	led
leave	left	leaving	left
lend	lent	lending	lent
let	let	letting	let
lie (on the beach)	lay	lying	lain
light	lit	lighting	lit
lose	lost	losing	lost
make	made	making	made

mean	meant	meaning	meant
meet	met	meeting	met
mistake	mistook	mistaking	mistaken
overcome	overcame	overcoming	overcome
pay	paid	paying	paid
put	put	putting	put
read	read	reading	read
rid	rid	ridding	rid
ride	rode	riding	ridden
ring	rang	ringing	rung
rise	rose	rising	risen
run	ran	running	run
say	said	saying	said
see	saw	seeing	seen
sell	sold	selling	sold
send	sent	sending	sent
set	set	setting	set
shake	shook	shaking	shaken
shine (sun)	shone	shining	shone
shine (polish)	shined	shining	shined
shoot	shot	shooting	shot
show	showed	showing	shown or showed
shrink	shrank	shrinking	shrunken or shrunk
shut	shut	shutting	shut
sing	sang	singing	sung
sink	sank	sinking	sunk
sit	sat	sitting	sat
sleep	slept	sleeping	slept
slide	slid	sliding	slid
speak	spoke	speaking	spoken
speed	sped or speeded	speeding	sped or speeded
spend	spent	spending	spent
spread	spread	spreading	spread
stand	stood	standing	stood
steal	stole	stealing	stolen
stick	stuck	sticking	stuck
sting	stung	stinging	stung
strike	struck	striking	struck or stricken
swear	swore	swearing	sworn
swim	swam	swimming	swum
take	took	taking	taken
teach	taught	teaching	taught
tear	tore	tearing	torn
tell	told	telling	told
think	thought	thinking	thought
understand	understood	understanding	understood
wear	wore	wearing	worn
weave	wove	weaving	woven
weep	wept	weeping	wept
win	won	winning	won
wind	wound	winding	wound
wring	wrung	wringing	wrung

Quick Quiz A

In each of the following sentences, write *the* correct verb form *in the blank within the sentence. Indicate whether the verb is* regular or irregular.

Model: I ___went___ to the bookstore yesterday. (to go, past tense)
___irregular___
Jason ___walked___ along the railroad tracks. (to walk, past tense)
___regular___

1. When the knife cut me, I ________. (*to bleed,* past tense) ________
2. The sea ________ calm. (*to become,* past tense) ________
3. He acted as if he ________ me to do it for him. (*to want,* past tense) ________
4. Richardson ________ he had been there. (*to wish,* present tense) ________
5. Principles have not been ________ for the treaty. (*to establish,* past tense) ________
6. The sweaty shirts ________ to the workmen's backs. (*to cling,* past tense) ________
7. The gambler ________ the cards. (*to deal,* past tense) ________
8. Ask the butcher why he ________ the meat so soon. (*to grind,* past tense) ________
9. The sun will have ________ by then. (*to shine,* past tense) ________
10. The boy's foot was ________ between the rocks. (*to stick,* past tense) ________

Answers to Quick Quiz A are on page 74.

Conjugation of the irregular verbs *to be, to have* and *to go*

(See Appendix C for the conjugations of other irregular verbs: *write, speak, lay, lie, set,* and *sit.*)

1. *be:*

Simple Present Tense

singular	I am you are he, she, or it is	plural	we are you are they are

Simple Past Tense

singular	I was	plural	we were
	you were		you were
	he, she, it was		they were

Simple Future Tense

singular	I shall (or will) be	plural	we shall (or will) be
	you will be		you will be
	he, she, it will be		they will be

Present Perfect Tense

singular	I have been	plural	we have been
	you have been		you have been
	he, she, it has been		they have been

Past Perfect Tense

singular	I had been	plural	we had been
	you had been		you had been
	he, she, it had been		they had been

Future Perfect Tense

singular	I shall (or will) have been	plural	we shall (or will) have been
	you will have been		you will have been
	he, she, it will have been		they will have been

Present Progressive Tense

singular	I am being	plural	we are being
	you are being		you are being
	he, she, it is being		they are being

Past Progressive Tense

singular	I was being	plural	we were being
	you were being		you were being
	he, she, it was being		they were being

Future Progressive Tense

singular	I shall (or will) be being	plural	we shall (or will) be being
	you will be being		you will be being
	he, she, it will be being		they will be being

2. *have:*

Simple Present Tense

singular	I have	plural	we have
	you have		you have
	he, she, it has		they have

Simple Past Tense

singular	I had	plural	we had
	you had		you had
	he, she, it had		they had

Simple Future Tense

singular	I shall (or will) have you will have he, she, it will have	plural	we shall (or will) have you will have they will have

Examples of other tenses:
- present perfect: I have had
- past perfect: I had had
- future perfect: I shall (or will) have had
- present progressive: I am having
- past progressive: I was having
- future progressive: I shall (or will) be having

3. ***go:***

Simple Present Tense

singular	I go you go he, she, it goes	plural	we go you go they go

Simple Past Tense

singular	I went you went he, she, it went	plural	we went you went they went

Simple Future Tense

singular	I shall (or will) go you will go he, she, it will go	plural	we shall (or will) go you will go they will go

Examples of other tenses:
- present perfect: I have gone
- past perfect: I had gone
- future perfect: I shall (or will) have gone
- present progressive: I am going
- past progressive: I was going
- future progressive: I shall (or will) be going

A-8 Auxiliary (helping) verbs

Auxiliary verbs are those that join other verbs in the formation of certain tenses. They thus create *verb phrases,* verb forms of more than one word. Some commonly used auxiliary verbs—all irregular—are *be, have, do, can, will, shall, may, must,* and *should.*

Examples I *am* going. I *might have* gone. You *should be* going.

(aux. labels: *am*; *might have*; *should be*)

Conjugations

Verb	Simple Present		Simple Past	
	Singular	*Plural*	*Singular*	*Plural*
be	I am you are he is	we are you are they are	I was you were he was	we were you were they were
have	I have you have she has	we have you have they have	I had you had she had	we had you had they had
do	I do you do it does	we do you do they do	I did you did it did	we did you did they did
may	I may*	we may	I might*	we might
can	I can*	we can	I could*	we could
must	I must*	we must	(no past tense forms)	

*The form of this verb is the same in all persons.

Simple Future: Form the future of some auxiliary verbs by using *will* or *shall* before the verb: I *will* be. You *will* have. They *will* do.

RULE: Verbs in single or adjoining sentences should be in the same tense unless the meaning requires a change, or shift, in tense.

B Tense Change, or Shift, and How to Use It

B-1 *Meaning* is the key to choice of tense.

The meaning of a sentence, a paragraph, or a paper determines whether tense forms should be alike or should be unlike. The key word is **meaning.** A writer should maintain consistency in tense (use the same tense throughout a passage) *except when the meaning requires a change.*

Examples

a. Yesterday, Yorick *celebrated* his birthday.
In this sentence the verb is *celebrated.*
(a) What did Yorick do? He *celebrated.*
(b) **When** did he celebrate? He *celebrated* yesterday.
When? is answered in two ways: (1) through the word *yesterday* and (2) through the **tense form,*** or spelling, of the verb *celebrated* (*celebrate* + ***d***). The last letter—***d***—indicates that the event is over, the action is past.

*tense form: See chart "The Formation of Tenses," page 56.

b. Yorick *celebrated* his birthday.
(a) What did Yorick do? He *celebrated.*
(b) When? **Before now.**
This sentence answers the question *When?* through the tense form of the verb, even though the sentence does not mention a specific time such as *yesterday.* The ***d*** added to *celebrate* tells us that the action occurred at some past time.

The time of action of a verb is expressed through its *tense;* therefore, we can say that the verb *celebrated,* referring to some *past time,* is in the *past tense.*

c. Yesterday, Yorick *celebrated* his birthday and *washed* his car.
(a) What did Yorick do? He *celebrated* . . . and *washed.*
(b) When? Yesterday.
The verbs [*celebrated* and *washed*] both use the past tense form (*verb* + ***d*** or ***ed***) and are correctly in the past tense since both actions happened before now.
Notice that each of the past tense verbs in the examples ends in ***d*** or ***ed,*** as many—but not all—past tense verbs do.

When a sentence contains two or more verbs, as example c does, the verbs are usually in the same tense. We say they *agree*—are alike—*in tense.* When one verb refers to an action that is past, for instance, other verbs in the sentence usually refer to actions that are past.

d. Yesterday, we *celebrated* Yorick's birthday and we *dance* all evening.
(a) What did we do? We *celebrated* and *dance.*
(b) When? Yesterday.
The verb *celebrated* uses the past tense form and is correct, but the verb *dance* does not use the past tense form, even though it refers to a past action. The verb *dance,* therefore, is a **tense shift error.**
The meaning requires the verbs [*celebrated and dance*] *to use the past tense form because both verbs refer to past actions. By adding* ***d*** *to dance,* we have the correct verbs: *celebrated* and *danced.*

B-2 The meaning of a sentence may require all verbs to be in the same tense.

Examples

a. Yesterday I *borrowed* a lawnmower and *mowed* our lawn.
The verbs [*borrowed* and *mowed*] use the same tense form (*verb* + ***ed***) and are correctly in the same tense.

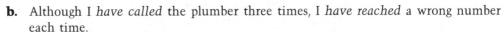

b. Although I *have called* the plumber three times, I *have reached* a wrong number each time.

The verbs	*have called* and *have reached*	use the same tense form (*have* + *verb* + ***ed***) and are

correctly in the same tense.

c. The plane *will land* tonight, and Glinka *will meet* it.

The verbs	*will land* and *will meet*	use the same tense form (*will* + *verb*) and are correctly in

the same tense.

B-3 The meaning of a sentence may require the verbs to be in more than one tense.

Examples **a.** Yesterday I *was* sick, today I *am* well, and tomorrow I *will return* to work.

The verbs	*was* *am* *will return*	correctly use three tense forms to convey their meanings:

was refers to something in the past, *am* refers to something in the present, and *will return* refers to something in the future.

b. Vince *borrowed* a lawnmower yesterday, and he *will return* it tomorrow.

The verbs	*borrowed* and *will return*	use two tense forms (*verb* + ***ed***) and (*will* + *verb*) and are

correctly in different tenses.

c. I *have called* the plumber twice; according to the answering service, he *will call* me tomorrow.

The verbs	*have called* and *will call*	use two tense forms (*have* + *verb* + ***ed***) and (*will* +

verb) and are correctly in different tenses.

B-4 The meaning of two or more adjoining sentences may require their verbs to be in the same tense.

Examples **a.** Recently I *borrowed* a lawnmower from a neighbor. After several reminders from my wife and several phone calls from my neighbor, I finally *mowed* the lawn and *returned* the lawnmower.

The verbs	*borrowed* *mowed* *returned*	use the same tense form (*verb* + ***ed***) and are correctly in

the same tense.

b. I *have called* the plumber twice today. I *have left* a message both times. He still *has* not *returned* my call.

The verbs	(I) (I) (he)	*have called* *have left* *has returned*	use the same tense form	*have* or *has*	+ *past tense* and are

correctly in the same tense.

c. According to the schedule, the plane *will leave* at two o'clock. Deborah and Quillen *will meet* us at the airport for lunch.

The verbs | *will leave* and *will meet* | are correctly in the same tense.

B-5 The meaning of two or more adjoining sentences may require their verbs to be in more than one tense.

Examples

a. Ragtime *is* an original American form that *flourished* before the turn of the century. It still *was flourishing* as late as 1917.

The verbs | *is* *flourished* *was flourishing* | are correctly in three different tenses.

b. Community residents *will attend* the opening of the first group of prefabricated houses. Each house *was designed* by a student in the university's school of architecture.

The verbs | *will attend* and *was designed* | are correctly in two tenses.

c. I know what happened. I was going to keep my appointment with Josie, but I forgot. The earthquake, I guess, upset both me and my memory. I will call tomorrow for another appointment.

As you can see from the underlined verbs, several tenses may be necessary to convey meaning accurately.

Procedure for Recognizing and Correcting Unnecessary Tense Shifts

A marginal notation of *shift* or *tense* or *tense shift* usually refers to an inappropriate change in verb tense.

shift *One of the three majors I am considering was mathematics; one was anthropology; one was physics.*

Step 1: Find the verbs.
The verbs are *am considering, was, was,* and *was.*

Step 2: Decide if the tense forms (tenses) are alike or unlike.
Am considering is in the *present* (progressive) tense, while *was* is in the *past* tense.

Step 3: If the tense forms are *alike,* leave them alike unless the meaning *requires* that they be unlike.

Step 4: If the meaning *requires* the tenses to be *unlike,*
a. look at each verb separately and decide whether it refers to a past, a present, or a future action; then
b. make whatever changes are necessary to have the verbs convey your meaning accurately and to have the tenses go together logically.

Step 5: If the tense forms are *unlike,* but the meaning *requires* them to be *alike* (the most common error!), decide what tense accurately conveys your meaning, then place all verbs in that tense.

In the sample sentence above, the meaning requires the verbs to be alike: all past or all present. The choice depends on the writer's meaning.

present pres.
Corrected, the sentence could read *One of the three majors I am considering is*
pres. pres.
mathematics; one is anthropology; one is physics.

OR

past past past
One of the majors I was considering was mathematics; one was anthropology;
past
one was physics.

REVIEW AND PRACTICE

Each of the sections of this Review and Practice is different. Do some exercises in each section, then decide which sections—if any—you need to continue to work through. Answers are on page 74.

Exercise A *Underline* each of the two verbs in each sentence. If both verbs are alike in tense, *write alike* in the space provided. If the two verbs are unlike in tense, *write unlike.*

Model: I had been waiting for an hour before the bus arrived ___unlike___

1. Henry told me that last summer he went to Alaska with Wally. __________
2. A philosopher is one who doubts. __________
3. The astronauts discovered that the moon is gray. __________
4. The mechanic was overhauling his car when he injured his back. __________
5. Just as the lights dimmed, the curtain rose. __________

Exercise B *Underline* all verbs. Correct any unnecessary tense shift by *crossing out* the incorrect tense form and *writing* the correct tense form above it.

stand
Model: When I want to see the sunset, I ~~stood~~ on the garage roof at sundown.

1. I had an interview for a job, and the personnel manager asks me my middle name.
2. For a number of years, the conference devoted itself to the one subject it considered most important.
3. Creative expression cannot be forced, but it will have been stimulated.
4. The teacher slept while the students work.
5. Carolyn rushed into the plane and sit down.

Exercise C In the space provided, *write* the correct tense form for each verb in parentheses.

Model: Mendel studied the characteristics of peas and thereby (discover) _discovered_ the laws of heredity.

1. While Susie was (grind) ______________ the valves, Blick was (rotate) ______________ the tires.
2. Throughout last winter, the wind (topple) ______________ many trees, and snow (block) ______________ many roads.
3. His name (be) ______________ Archibald, but we (call) ______________ him Arch.
4. Leon often walked past the pet shop and (stop) ______________ to see the cockatoos in the window.
5. The candidate admitted he had never attended a council meeting, but he said, "I (go) ______________ tomorrow."

Exercise D *Cross out* any incorrect tense form and *write* the correct form above it.

Model: He ~~run~~ ran around the track while I waited for him in the shade.

1. The tide come in and washed away the grunion fingerlings.
2. Amy had never ate snails, nor had she tasted frogs' legs.
3. Relda will be visiting you in the summer, and she hopes you are visiting me in the spring.
4. By the time you reached home, we will have decided where to spend the weekend.
5. We do not like to repeat gossip, but we did not know what else to do with it.

Answers to Review and Practice are on page 74.

CHAPTER TEST

Underline all verbs in each sentence. *Write correct* in the space provided when the sample contains no unnecessary tense shift; *write incorrect* when the sample contains an unnecessary tense shift.

Model: I was calling Marge and the phone is ringing. incorrect

1. The boat will dock, and Eva will come ashore. ______
2. Last year the snow was deeper than it had been before. ______
3. I just received your reservations, and you will be leaving tomorrow. ______
4. Myron is doing that now, and it was interesting. ______
5. Julie had a flat tire, and she calls me to help her. ______
6. Delilah, Sue Ellen's dog, goes along with us every evening when we walk through the woods. Without fail, she found some small animal to track. ______
7. Shipments of Australian apples arrive in the United States just before the West-Coast crop is ready to be harvested. American apple producers are concerned at the effect this competition may have on domestic prices. ______
8. Predicting the outcome of the game is impossible. The quarterback for the Dolphins pulled a muscle, and his replacement has not had much experience leading the team. ______

Answers to Chapter Test are on page 75.

ANSWERS: Chapter 3

Answers to Quick Quiz A

1. bled; irregular
2. became; irregular
3. wanted; regular
4. wishes; regular
5. established; regular
6. clung; irregular
7. dealt; irregular
8. ground; irregular
9. shone; irregular
10. stuck; irregular

Answers to Review and Practice

Exercise A

1. told. . . went, alike
2. is . . . doubts, alike
3. discovered . . . is, unlike
4. was overhauling. . . injured, unlike
5. dimmed . . . rose, alike

Exercise B

1. had . . . ~~asks~~ asked
2. devoted . . . considered
3. can be forced. . . ~~will have been~~ can be stimulated
4. slept . . . ~~work~~ worked
5. rushed . . . ~~sit~~ sat

Exercise C

1. grinding, rotating
2. toppled, blocked
3. is, call; or was, called
4. stopped
5. will go

Exercise D

1. ~~come~~ came 2. ~~ate~~ eaten 3. ~~are~~ will be or ~~will be~~ is 4. ~~reached~~ reach 5. ~~do like~~ did like or ~~did know~~ do know

Answers to Chapter Test

1. will dock. . . will come, correct
2. was. . . had been, correct
3. received. . . will be leaving, correct
4. is doing. . . was, incorrect (is)
5. had. . . calls, incorrect (called)
6. goes. . . walk. found, incorrect (finds)
7. arrive. . . is. are . . . may have, correct
8. is. . . pulled . . . has had, correct

CHAPTER 4

Subject-Verb Agreement

- **Items 51–64 in the Pretest are from this chapter.**
- **The procedure for recognizing and correcting errors in subject-verb agreement is on page 86.**

Chapter Contents

RULE: Subject* and verb* must agree (be alike) in number.*

---

*subject: The *subject* of a sentence is what the sentence is about.

subj.
Exams cause ulcers.

subj.
Love is a four-letter word.

subj.
John was driven to the airport.

*verb: The *verb* tells what the subject does, what the subject is, or what action the subject receives.

vb.
Exams *cause* ulcers. (*Cause* tells what the subject does.)

vb.
Love *is* a four-letter word. (*Is* tells what the subject is.)

vb.
John *was driven* to the airport. (*Was driven* tells what action the subject receives.)

*number: *Number* indicates whether one or more than one thing is talked about. Singular (meaning one) and plural (meaning more than one) are the two words that describe number.

sing. subject
The *ticket* costs three dollars.

plural subj.
The *books* are free.

pl. subj.
Cox, Ruckelshaus, and Richardson leave Washington amid furor.

s. subj.
My *physician* and *surgeon* is Dr. Hippocrates.

(Note: When a subject has more than one part, but refers to only one person or thing, it is singular.)

A Making a Subject Agree with Its Verb in Number

A-1 A singular* subject requires a singular verb.

---

*Singular: means **one.**

Examples

a. *Joan lives* alone. (sing. subject; sing. vb.)

b. A football *team needs* practice. (s. subj.; s. vb.)

c. A *member* of my family *takes* vitamins. (s. subj.; s. vb.)

d. *One* out of ten people *likes* beer. (s. subj.; s. vb.)

e. On our vine a *bunch* of grapes *is* ripe. (s. subj.; s. vb.)

NOTE: Nouns and pronouns are the parts of speech that can serve as the subject of the sentence. *Joan, team, member,* and *bunch* are nouns serving as subjects. *One* is a pronoun serving as subject.

A-2 A plural* subject requires a plural verb.

*plural: means ***more* than one.**

Examples

a. Your *holidays* (pl. subj.) *are* (pl. vb.) numbered.

b. The *insects* (pl. subj.) *contribute* (pl. vb.) heavily to crop damage.

c. *Members* (pl. subj.) of the football team *need* (pl. vb.) vitamins.

d. *Both* (pl. subj.) *need* (pl. vb.) dentures.

e. *All* (pl. subj.) *were invited* (pl. vb.) to the opening of the gallery.

f. Actually, *nine* (pl. subj.) out of ten people *do* not *like* (pl. vb.) beer.

g. *Joan* and *Marvin* (comp* subj.) *live* (pl. vb.) in a co-op.

*compound subject: When a subject has more than one part connected by *and* (and refers to more than one person or thing), it is a *compound subject.* A compound subject requires a plural verb.

Peanut butter, bacon, and *tomato* (comp. subj.) make a good sandwich. (*Make* is a plural verb.)

h. Our *house,* our *car,* and our *furniture* (comp. subj.) *are* (pl. vb.) old.

Quick Quiz: A

Underline the subject of each sentence and *circle its number.*

Model: Cigarettes go up in smoke. singular (plural)

1. A stitch in time saves nine. singular plural
2. Members of the soccer team were not chosen yesterday. singular plural
3. I came late. singular plural
4. California and France have excellent wine-producing areas. singular plural
5. Dogs, cats, and hares are hirsute. singular plural

Underline the subject *and* circle the verb that agrees with the subject.

Model: Research findings (suggests, suggest) ways to improve cars.

6. He (run, runs) away from himself.
7. The first question (was, were) this.
8. Words and music (is, are) by Richard Wagner.
9. The members of the caucus (meets, meet) weekly.
10. The crowd (does not number, do not number) a thousand.

Answers to Quick Quiz A are on page 91.

B Recognizing the Subject: Special Cases

Deciding whether the subject is singular or plural is generally easy, though sometimes it is not. The following material should help you recognize the subject of a sentence when that subject might not be easily recognizable.

B-1 Recognizing the subject when it is separated from its verb

Subject and verb must agree in number even when other parts of the sentence separate them.

Examples

a. Just one *error* (s. subj.) in all those numbers *throws* (s. vb.) the total off.
The subject *error* and its verb *throws* are both singular, even though *numbers*—the word just before the verb—is plural.
(. . . one error . . . throws the total off.)

b. The *sprinter* (s. subj.) with the new track shoes *won* (s. vb.) the 100-yard dash.
(The sprinter . . . won the 100-yard dash.)

c. The early *bird* (s. subj.), despite his rewards, *loses* (s. vb.) sleep.
(The early bird . . . loses sleep.)

d. *Towns* (pl. subj.) of only a thousand *are* (pl. vb.) rare in this state.
The subject *towns* and its verb *are* are both plural, even though the word just before the verb—*thousand*—is singular.

pl. subj. pl. vb.
e. These *kinds* of gliders *are* beautiful to fly.
The subject *kinds* is plural and requires a plural verb.

pl. subj. pl. vb.
f. No matter what the weather, *clusters* of onlookers *watch* the excavating.

s. subj. s. vb.
g. The *tragedy*—and the thesis of this book—*is* that the rivalry diminished both artists.
The subject may be separated from its verb by a parenthetical expression enclosed with *dashes, commas,* or *parentheses.*

B-2 Recognizing the subject when it is a collective noun

A collective noun names a *group* that is thought of as a *unit. Class, jury, team, army, herd* are collective nouns.* A singular collective noun generally requires a singular verb, while a plural collective noun, like other plural nouns, requires a plural verb.

*collective noun: See Appendix A for a list of common collective nouns.

A singular collective noun that refers to a single *unit* requires a singular verb.

sing. coll. noun (unit) s. vb.
Examples **a.** Each biological *class* *has* its own characteristics.

sing. coll. n. (unit) s. vb.
b. The *team refuses* to eat at Bar F Ranch.

sing. coll. n. (unit) s. vb.
c. The string *quartet plays* tonight.

A singular collective noun that clearly refers to the members of a group as individuals requires a plural verb. If the plural verb sounds awkward to you, insert "members of" before the collective noun.

s. coll. n. "members of" pl. vb.
Examples **a.** The *family eat* at different hours, except for breakfast.
(The members of the family eat. . . .)

pl. vb.
b. The *faculty have been assigned* to various committees.

When a subject is a plural collective noun, it requires a plural verb.

pl. coll. n. pl. vb.
Examples **a.** The *casts rehearse* daily.

pl. coll. n. pl. vb.
b. The *congregations pray* their traditional prayers.

pl. coll. n. pl. vb.
c. *Committees have studied* this problem for seven years.

Quick Quiz B

Underline the *subject* and *circle* the *correct verb.*

Model: The bundle on his doorstep (surprise, surprises) him.

1. A pile of ashes (marks, mark) the spot.
2. Your articles regarding the airplane (shows, show) irresponsible journalism.
3. The recommendation of the committees for both community councils (agrees, agree) with our findings.
4. The variety of animals inhabiting this island (amaze, amazes) me.
5. The jury (has, have) heard all the arguments.

Answers to Quick Quiz B are on page 91.

B-3 Recognizing the subject when it is a word such as *each*

The words listed below are usually singular. When used as subjects, they require singular verbs.

any	everybody	nothing
anybody	everyone	one
anyone	everything	somebody
each	neither	someone
either	nobody	something

Examples

a. *Each* (s. subj.) of us *creates* (s. vb.) his own hell.

b. *Neither* (s. subj.) of these answers *is* (s. vb.) right.

c. *Everybody* (s. subj.) *is* (s. vb.) eligible to run, but *nobody* (s. subj.) *seems* (s. vb.) ready to sign up.

d. *One* (s. subj.) of the divers repeatedly *loses* (s. vb.) her scuba gear.

e. *Everything* (s. subj.) under the sun, moon, and stars *has* (s. vb.) a reason.

f. *Any* (s. subj.) of these classes *gives* (s. vb.) graduate credit. (Any *one* of these classes. . . .)

NOTE: When *any* means *any one of,* it takes a singular verb.

g. *Are* (pl. vb.) *any* (pl. subj.) of the speakers ready? (Are *some* of the speakers ready?)

NOTE: When *any* means *some,* it takes a plural verb.

h. *Is any* of the speakers ready? (Is *one* of the speakers ready?)

NOTE: When any means *any one,* it takes a singular verb.

B-4 Recognizing the subject when the subject is *all* or *none*

***All* takes a *singular* verb**

***When* all *means* everything *or when* all *is followed by a singular* noun**

Examples **a.** *All is* over. (Everything is over.)

b. *All is* ready. (Everything is ready.)

When* all *is followed by a singular noun or pronoun

Examples **a.** *All* evidence (s. n.) *is* gone.

b. *All* of the paint (s. n.) *is* dry.

c. *All* of it (s. pro.) *is* dry.

***All* takes a *plural* verb**

***When* all *means* all the people *or* places *or* things**

Examples **a.** *All are registering* to vote. (All the people, or students, or parents are registering to vote.)

b. *All were* concerned. (All the people were concerned.)

When* all *is followed by a plural noun or pronoun

Examples **a.** *All* men (pl. n.) *are* created equal.

b. *All* of them (pl. pro.) *dislike* reveille.

None* takes a *singular* verb when *none* means *no one.

Examples **a.** *None was* found. (No one was found.)

b. *None* but the brave *deserves* the fair. (No one . . . deserves the fair.)

***None* takes a *plural* verb when *none* means *not any*.**

Examples **a.** *None are* being published. (Not any are being published.)

b. *None were* located. (Not any were located.)

B-5 Recognizing the subject when a combination such as *either . . . or* joins the parts of the subject

either . . . or *neither . . . nor* *not only . . . but also*	join the parts of a subject

When both parts of the subject are singular, the verb is singular.

Examples **a.** Neither a *borrower* (s. subj.) nor a *lender* (s. subj.) *is* (s. vb.) involved.

b. Either this *book* (s. subj.) or that *one* (s. subj.) *contains* (s. vb.) the information.

c. Not only *strength* (s. subj.) but *agility* (s. subj.) *is* (s. vb.) essential in bicycling.

When both parts of a compound subject are plural, the verb is plural.

Examples **a.** Neither *borrowers* (pl. subj.) nor *lenders* (pl. subj.) *are* (pl. vb.) involved.

b. Either *libraries* or *museums are* open tomorrow.

c. Not only *Republicans* but also *Democrats support* that issue.

When one part of the subject is singular and the other part is plural, the verb agrees with the part* of the subject *nearer the verb.

Examples **a.** Neither the *doctor* (s. subj.) nor the *nurses* (pl. subj.) *were* (pl. vb.) in.

b. Either *I* (s. subj.) or *they* (pl. subj.) *are* (pl. vb.) to drive.

c. Not only *they* but *I am* to drive.

B-6 Recognizing the subject when an expression such as *with* or *along with* follows the subject

An expression such as *with, along with, as well as* does not change the number of a subject.

Examples **a.** *Robin,* (s. subj.) *with* Nora and Della, *is* (s. vb.) *trying* organic farming.

b. The property *tax*, *along with* the flood control assessments, *continues to* rise. (s. subj. / s. vb.)

c. Airborne carcinogens, *as well as* food additives, *threaten* man's future. (pl. subj. / pl. vb.)

B-7 Recognizing the subject when a sentence begins with *There is* or *There are*

In a sentence beginning with *There is* or *There are* the subject follows the verb. When the subject is singular, the verb must be singular. When the subject is plural, the verb must be plural.

Examples

a. There *is* only one *source.* (s. vb. / s. subj.)

b. There *are* several inert *gases.* (pl. vb. / pl. subj.)

c. There *is* one *port* of call on our itinerary. (s. vb. / s. subj.)

Quick Quiz: C

Underline subjects and *circle* correct *verbs.*

Model: Everyone (was, were) applauding.
Neither the oil painting nor the serigraphs (was, were) lost in the fire.

1. Neither of the analysts (was, were) willing to predict the outcome.
2. One of the many fields in which he excels (is, are) herpetology.
3. All these (amount, amounts) to a major transformation in governmental procedure.
4. Everyone on our staff (plan, plans) to take the promotional examination.
5. The engineer, with the mechanics, (intend, intends) to demonstrate his invention tomorrow.
6. Neither the producer nor the newscasters (was, were) informed of the incident.
7. There (is, are) many explanations for unrest.
8. Among the unexpected finds (was, were) a Picasso and two Renoirs.

Answers to Quick Quiz C are on page 91.

Procedure for Recognizing and Correcting Errors in Subject-Verb Agreement

Your instructor's marginal notation generally identifies the error.

subj-v agr. *Each of the candidates are speaking at the town meeting.*

Step 1: Find the subject: Is it *each* or *candidates?*
The subject is *each.*

Step 2: Decide if the subject is singular or plural.
Each is singular.

Step 3: Find the verb.
The verb is *are speaking.*

Step 4: Decide if the verb is singular or plural.
Are makes the verb plural.

Step 5: Make the subject and verb agree in number.
Since the subject *each* is singular, the verb must also be singular.
The corrected sentence reads: **Each** *of the candidates* **is** *speaking.*

REVIEW AND PRACTICE

Each of the sections of this Review and Practice is different. Do some exercises in each section, then check your answers and decide which sections—if any—you need to continue to work through. Answers are on pages 91–94.

Exercise A Circle *the verb that agrees with the singular subject.*

Model: The dam face (is, are) cracked.

1. The quarterback (want, wants) to pass.
2. A stitch in time (save, saves) many a shirt.
3. News nowadays (come, comes) from outer space.
4. (Do, Does) I get ulcers? (Do, Does) I give them?
5. Hobie (carve, carves), while both Hobie and Lee (design, designs) the models.
6. Our group (know, knows) it is more disorganized than your group.
7. (Do, Does) the case of drinks belong to Hans?
8. The judging committee, after hearing one tuba solo, two quartets, three flute solos, and four choral numbers, now (veto, vetoes) any further auditions.
9. Nothing under the sun (happen, happens) by accident.
10. (Is, Are) a battalion of men in Birnam Wood?

Exercise B Circle *the verb that agrees with the plural subject.*

Model: These sportscasters (shout, shouts) when describing the action.

1. Eucalyptus trees (sheds, shed) their bark.
2. Daredevils (dare, dares) and cowards (cower, cowers).
3. (Do, Does) several councilmen in our district agree on the issue?
4. "Radios," Moke said, "(is, are) TV's without picture tubes."
5. What (is, are) her arguments intended to prove?
6. We (feel, feels) free when we can be ourselves.
7. The viruses we are studying (cause, causes) various diseases.
8. People rarely (make, makes) use of all their rights.
9. (Is, Are) we all here?
10. Creditors (have, has) better memories than debtors.

Exercise C Fill in the blank *with the singular form of the verb in parentheses.*

Model: The motor smokes too much. (smoke)

1. He ____________ too much. (expect)
2. A siren ____________ menacing at night. (sound)
3. Any embryologist ____________ why the egg comes before the chicken. (know)
4. Why ____________ a bird in the hand worth two in the bush? (be)
5. The birth of quintuplets ____________ one realize what constitutes an all-out effort. (make)
6. Your band ____________ to a different drummer. (march)
7. One of the bullfighters ____________ a pass. (make)
8. Margaret, like other people, ____________ to know the cause of sin. (want)
9. Of course, everybody ____________ better after the event. (know)
10. The team ____________ coaches who know the game. (need)

Exercise D Fill in the blank *with the plural form of the verb in parentheses.*

Model: The puzzles remain unsolved. (remains)

1. ____________ law and order two different things? (be)
2. Cars and trucks ____________ accidents. (has)
3. Cigarettes ____________ up in smoke. (goes)
4. Children ____________ a greater percentage of dietary protein than do adults. (needs)

5. Dictionaries ____________ wordy. (becomes)
6. Rabbit's-foot charms ____________ good luck to everyone but the rabbit. (brings)
7. Microorganisms from the sea ____________ our greatest untapped natural source of protein. (represents)
8. Some critics ____________ that the novel is a dying art form. (feels)
9. Garbage cans and trash bins ____________ collectors' items. (contains)
10. Because I haven't explained myself clearly, Jane and Phyllis ____________ my motives. (suspects)

Exercise E Correct *any verb that does not agree with its subject.*

Models: What man on earth ~~say~~ says that?

Three of us and six of them still ~~works~~ work with Lee.

1. The real physiological consequence of human weightlessness are still up in the air.
2. Despite all our scientific advances, man remain more important than the machine.
3. Speakers for the extreme right and for the extreme left often sounds remarkably similar.
4. Science and philosophy belongs together.
5. Liberty and justice is for all.
6. The jury of seven men and five women deliberate many hours before rendering a decision.
7. Do the group like the movie?
8. The birds of the flock looks sick.
9. Vipers breeds vermin.
10. Absence sharpen love.

Exercise F *In some of these sentences, subject and verb agree. In others, they do not. Write* **C** *in front of sentences that are correct, and correct those verbs that do not agree with their subjects.*

Models: ________All three of the courses I am taking ~~requires~~ require term papers.

____C____The dust on the tables hides their finishes.

1. ________A word to the wise suffices.
2. ________One car and one truck makes the run daily.
3. ________Every once in a while a carload of eggs overturn on the freeway.
4. ________Neither of the two referees know enough to judge the game.
5. ________Women comprise a numerical majority and a political minority.

6. ________Are the choice of seats in the auditorium limited now?
7. ________Minor temptations, in their small way, proves the character of a man.
8. ________Your freedom becomes license when you step on my toes.
9. ________My freedom remain freedom as long as I take the consequences.
10. ________Is the beginning of all things small?

Exercise G Circle *subjects joined by combinations such as* either . . . or *and* underline *correct verb forms.*

Models: Not only (John) but the (Smiths) (is, <u>are</u>) going.

Neither (violets) nor a (rose) (woo, <u>woos</u>) her.

1. Unfortunately, either your brothers or your sister (has, have) to leave this house.
2. Neither a friend nor a foe (answer, answers) him.
3. Neither sticks nor stones (break, breaks) my bones.
4. Beyond doubt, neither praise nor blame (attach, attaches) to the man.
5. Either Sue or Gwynyth (have, has) his number.
6. Neither of your officers (is, are) safe.
7. Not only eagles but a dove (fly, flies) by.
8. Either of the cars (run, runs) smoothly.
9. Rain, as well as wind, (upset, upsets) our plans every winter.
10. The federal program, with the three local programs, (contribute, contributes) to health care.

Answers to Review and Practice are on pages 91–94.

CHAPTER TEST

Write the subject of each sentence in column *A* and its *correct verb* in column *B.*

		A Subject	B Verb
Model:	Juries whose members sleep (complicate, complicates) justice.	Juries	complicate
1.	Man and boy (walk, walks) shoulder to shoulder.	________	________
2.	The rocks in the road (bruise, bruises) his feet.	________	________
3.	The trace of minerals (excite, excites) the prospector.	________	________
4.	Neither you nor they (give, gives) a plausible excuse.	________	________

5. A board of directors (run, runs) the company. ________ ________
6. Either of them (pick, picks) the winner. ________ ________
7. Fields of corn (stretch, stretches) from one end of the state to the other. ________ ________
8. Fish and white wine (complement, complements) one another. ________ ________
9. Herds (graze, grazes) together. ________ ________
10. Either the soap or the detergents (leave, leaves) a residue. ________ ________
11. The records in the cabinet (is, are) gifts. ________ ________
12. The squads on the varsity (scrimmage, scrimmages) this afternoon. ________ ________
13. Neither Pat nor her friend (eat, eats) with us. ________ ________
14. The surfboard and the ski (is, are) nothing more than extensions of the human foot. ________ ________
15. A hoard of doubloons (lie, lies) at the bottom of the sea. ________ ________
16. Either the clan or its chief (decide, decides) the outlaw's fate. ________ ________
17. The classes (agree, agrees) not to meet this week. ________ ________
18. Neither of the brothers (recognize, recognizes) the other. ________ ________
19. In spite of the warm weather, the flock of geese (head, heads) south. ________ ________
20. Here, on winter days, the wind (blow, blows) from the east. ________ ________

Answers to Chapter Test are on page 94.

ANSWERS: CHAPTER 4

Answers to Quick Quiz A

1. stitch, singular
2. members, plural
3. I, singular
4. California and France, plural
5. dogs, cats, and hares, plural
6. he, runs
7. question, was
8. words and music, are
9. members, meet
10. crowd, does (not) number

Answers to Quick Quiz B

1. pile marks
2. articles show
3. recommendation agrees
4. variety amazes
5. jury has

Answers to Quick Quiz C

1. neither was
2. one is
3. all amount
4. everyone plans
5. engineer intends
6. producer . . . newscasters were
7. explanations are
8. Picasso and Renoirs were

(Notice that in this last sentence the usual word order is altered so that the subject comes last. Usual word order: A Picasso and two Renoirs were among the unexpected finds.)

Answers to Review and Practice

Exercise A

Subject	*Singular Verb*	**Notice that . . .**
1. quarterback	wants	
2. stitch	saves	*stitch,* and not *time,* is the subject.
3. news	comes	*news* is singular

4. I	do	*the word I* takes the verb form do.
5. Hobie Hobie and Lee	carves design	*the second subject, Hobie* and *Lee,* is plural and requires the plural verb *design.*
6. group	knows	*group* is a singular collective noun.
7. case	does	*case* and not *drinks,* is the subject.
8. committee	vetoes	*committee* is a singular collective noun separated from its verb by many words.
9. nothing	happens	*nothing,* and not *sun,* is the subject
10. battalion	is	

Exercise B

Subject	*Verb*	*Subject*	*Verb*
1. trees	shed	6. We	feel
2. Daredevils	dare	7. viruses	cause
cowards	cower	8. People	make
3. councilmen	do	9. we	are
4. Radios	are	10. Creditors	have
5. arguments	are		

Exercise C

Subject	*Verb*	**Notice that...**
1. He	expects	
2. siren	sounds	
3. embryologist	knows	
4. bird	is	word order changes in a question.
5. birth	makes	*birth,* and not *quintuplets,* is the subject.
6. band	marches	*band* is a singular collective noun.
7. One	makes	
8. Margaret	wants	
9. everybody	knows	
10. team	needs	*team* is a singular collective noun.

Exercise D

	Subject	*Verb*	**Notice that . . .**
1.	law (and) order	Are	two or more singular subjects joined by *and* form a compound subject. A compound subject is plural.
2.	Cars (and) trucks	have	*cars* and *trucks* is a compound subject.
3.	Cigarettes	go	
4.	Children	need	
5.	Dictionaries	become	
6.	charms	bring	
7.	Microorganisms	represent	*microorganisms,* and not *sea,* is the plural subject.
8.	critics	feel	
9.	cans (and) . . . bins	contain	the subject is compound.
10.	Jane (and) Phyllis	suspect	

Exercise E

	Original incorrect verb	*Subject*	*Correct verb*
1.	~~are~~	consequence (singular)	is
2.	~~remain~~	man (singular)	remains
3.	~~sounds~~	Speakers (plural)	sound
4.	~~belongs~~	Science and philosophy (plural)	belong
5.	~~is~~	Liberty and justice (plural)	are
6.	~~deliberate~~	jury (singular)	deliberates
7.	~~Do~~	group (singular)	Does
8.	~~looks~~	birds (plural)	look
9.	~~breeds~~	Vipers (plural)	breed
10.	~~sharpen~~	Absence (singular)	sharpens

Exercise F

	Notice that . . .
1. C	
2. ~~makes~~ make	compound subjects require plural verbs. *Make* is plural.
3. ~~overturn~~ overturns	*eggs* is not the subject; *carload* is.
4. ~~know~~ knows	
5. C	
6. ~~Are~~ Is	

7. ~~proves~~ prove	
8. C	*you* always requires a plural verb, whether *you* refers to one or more than one.
9. ~~remain~~ remains	
10. C	

Exercise G	**Notice that . . .**
1. Unfortunately, either your (brothers) or your (sister) has to leave this house.	*sister,* the part of the subject closer to the verb, determines the number of the verb.
2. Neither a (friend) nor a (foe) answers him.	
3. Neither (sticks) nor (stones) break my bones.	
4. Beyond doubt, neither (praise) nor (blame) attaches to the man.	
5. Either (Sue) or (Gwynyth) has his number.	
6. Neither of your officers is safe.	this is not a *neither. . .nor* combination; *Neither* is the singular subject and requires a singular verb.
7. Not only (eagles) but a (dove) flies by.	*dove* is singular and requires a singular verb.
8. Either of the cars runs smoothly.	this is not an *either. . .or* combination. *Either* is the singular subject and requires a singular verb.
9. Rain, as well as wind, upsets our plans every winter.	the singular *rain* remains singular when followed by expressions like *as well as* and requires a singular verb.
10. The federal program, with the three local programs, contributes to health care.	a singular subject (*program* in this sentence) remains singular when followed by expressions like *with...*

Answers to Chapter Test

	Subject	*Verb*		*Subject*	*Verb*
1.	Man. . .boy	walk	11.	records	are
2.	rocks	bruise	12.	squads	scrimmage
3.	trace	excites	13.	Pat. . .friend	eats
4.	you. . .they	give	14.	surfboard. . ski	are
5.	board	runs	15.	hoard	lies
6.	Either	picks	16.	clan. . .chief	decides
7.	fields	stretch	17.	classes	agree
8.	Fish. . .wine	complement	18.	Neither	recognizes
9.	Herds	graze	19.	flock	heads
10.	soap. . .detergents	leave	20.	wind	blows

CHAPTER 5

Pronoun-Antecedent Agreement

- **Items 65–74 in the Pretest are from this chapter.**
- **The procedure for recognizing and correcting errors in pronoun-antecedent agreement is on page 103.**

Chapter Contents

RULE: | A pronoun* and its antecedent* must agree (be alike) in number.*

---

*pronoun: A *pronoun* is a word that stands for a noun and can take the place of that noun in a sentence. (A noun is a word that names something. *Charles, house, freedom* are nouns.) *He, it, I, they* are pronouns. (For a list of pronouns, see Appendix B.)

Example

noun pron.

Eric promised *he* would take the case.

The pronoun *he* stands for the noun *Eric*.

*antecedent: The word that a pronoun stands for is called the *antecedent* of that pronoun. (An antecedent can be one word or a group of words.)

Examples

ant. pron.

Eric promised *he* would take the case.

The noun *Eric* is the antecedent of the pronoun *he*.

ant. pron.

Tom, Dick, and Harry lost *their* shirts.

The antecedent is *Tom, Dick, (and) Harry.*

ant. pron.

Having a second career after one retires has *its* rewards.

The antecedent of *its* is *Having a second career after one retires.*

*number: *Number* tells whether a word is singular (meaning one) or plural (meaning more than one).

Example

sing. pl.

The *attorney* took both *cases.*

Attorney (one) is singular in number, while *cases* (more than one) is plural in number.

A A Singular *Antecedent Requires a Singular Pronoun.

---

*singular: See *number* note above.

A-1 A singular antecedent and its pronoun may be in the same sentence.

Examples

s. ant. s. pron.

a. A careful *driver* always uses *his* seat belt.

s. ant. s. pron.

b. The new *councilwoman* told the reporters *she* would support the mayor's proposal.

s. ant. s. pron.

c. An *army* marches on *its* stomach.

s. ant. s. pron.

d. *Each* of the men bought *his* own ticket.

NOTE: In formal writing, the following words are singular and require singular pronouns: *each, anybody, anyone, everybody, everyone, nobody, no one, somebody, someone, either, neither.*

s. pron.

e. *Everyone* cleared *his* own desk before leaving.

s. ant. s. pron.

f. *Neither* knew *her* mother's birthday.

A-2 A singular antecedent and its pronoun may be in different sentences.

Examples

s. ant. s. pron. s. pron.

a. A safe *driver* is careful. *He* always uses *his* seat belt.

s. ant. s. pron.

b. The *instructor* was merciful. *She* called off the test.

s. ant. s. pron.

c. The *house* was new and spacious. The builder hoped to sell *it* before the first of the year.

s. ant. s. pron.

d. The *news* stunned people everywhere. Mary said that *it* was the first good news in a long time.

Quick Quiz: A

Underline each antecedent and *circle* its pronoun.

Model: The aviator could not afford to keep (his) plane.

1. Zenna flipped her lid when the manuscript arrived.
2. The motorist, finding the repair shop closed, drove his car to a gas station.
3. Each carried insurance on her professional wardrobe.
4. The tree was completely uprooted. It had not survived the storm.
5. Susan watched the little boy wandering around. She began to worry.
6. Susan watched the little boy wandering. He seemed to be lost.

Answers to Quick Quiz A are on page 109.

A-3 A word that comes between an antecedent and its pronoun may be mistaken for an antecedent.

NOTE: You can usually avoid errors in pronoun-antecedent agreement if you answer the question: *What does this pronoun refer to?*

Examples

s. ant. s. pron.

a. *One* of the senators continued *his* argument after the meeting's adjournment. The intervening plural* word *senators* is not the antecedent; the pronoun refers to *one*.

*plural: See note on page 96 under *number*.

s. ant. s. pron.

b. *Each* of the women has *her* reason for being here. The singular antecedent *each* (which means each one) requires the singular pronoun *her*. The intervening plural word *women* is not the antecedent.

s. ant. s. pron.

c. The *list* of architects, draftsmen, and carpenters needed for the project is now double *its* original length.

Its refers to *list*, not to the intervening words *architects, draftsmen, and carpenters*.

NOTE: Items **a.**, **b.**, and **c.** are typical of the kinds of sentences in which errors in pronoun-antecedent agreement frequently occur. Notice that in the three instances the main part of the sentence is as follows:

a. *One* . . . continues *his* argument. . . . (Omit **of** *the senators*.)

b. Each . . . has *her* reason. . . . (Omit **of** *the women*.)

c. The *list* . . . is now double *its* original length. (Omit **of** *architects, draftsmen*, etc.)

Notice that in each of the three instances the omitted phrase ends in a plural word (or words), which makes a plural pronoun *sound* right. But in fact the antecedent (*One, Each, list*) is singular. To check pronoun-antecedent agreement in number, be sure you have identified the antecedent correctly, and that you are not being confused by words in an intervening phrase.

s. ant. s. pron.

d. *Daniels* estimates that during the first year 200 volunteers will take part in *his* program.

s. ant. s. pron.

e. Those trees look like the *kind* that always has *its* roots close to the surface of the soil.

s. ant. s. pron.

f. The *Indian*, along with two friends, represented *her* tribe at the congressional hearings.

s. ant. s. ant s. pron.

g. Neither the *play* nor the *novel* has *its* characters well defined.

NOTE: Two singular antecedents combined in a *neither . . . nor* or *either . . . or* expression require a singular pronoun.

pl. ant s. ant. s. pron.
h. Either the *poems* or the *play* will have *its* place on the program.

NOTE: When two antecedents, one singular and one plural, are combined in a *neither . . . nor* or *either . . . or* expression, the pronoun agrees with the antecedent nearer the pronoun. In this case, the singular *play* is nearer.

Notice the application of this rule in these examples:

ant. 1 sing. ant. 2 nearer sing. pron.
1. Neither the *plays* nor the *novel* has *its* characters well defined.

ant. 1 plural ant. 2 nearer pl. pron.
2. Neither the *play* nor the *novels* have *their* characters well defined.

NOTE: Compare the section you have just studied **(A-3)**, which deals with singular pronouns separated from their singular antecedents, with section **B-3**, which deals with plural pronouns separated from their plural antecedents.

A-4 A singular antecedent may be a collective noun.*

*collective noun: A *collective noun* names a *group* that is thought of as a *unit. Class, team, crowd, family* are collective nouns. (See Appendix A for a list of common collective nouns.)

A collective noun that refers to one group is singular, and pronouns that refer to it are singular.

A collective noun that refers to more than one group is plural, and pronouns that refer to it are plural.

A singular collective noun that implies the *members of* a group—rather than the group as a unit—is plural in meaning, and a pronoun that refers to it is plural.

Examples

s. ant. s. pron.
a. The *audience* expressed *its* enthusiasm by prolonged applause.

s. ant. s. pron.
b. The *platoon* paraded before *its* commanding officer.

s. ant. s. pron.
c. The *flock* of pheasants left *its* nest.

s. ant. s. pron.
d. The ping-pong *team* of six men and six women made *its* highest score of the tournament yesterday.

s. pron. s. ant.
e. At *its* final session, *Congress* failed to pass the constitutional amendment that had been before *it* (s. pron.) for nearly half a century.

Quick Quiz: B

Underline each antecedent and *circle* its pronoun.

Model: The institution celebrated its tenth birthday today.

1. The squad of soldiers left its barracks.
2. The head of the city's rescue units announced her retirement.
3. Deep in the forest, one of the woodsmen lost his way.
4. The herd of cattle suffered from its long drive to new pastures.
5. At the end of her last day of training at the hospital, Dr. Hart donated several books to the medical library.

Answers to Quick Quiz B are on page 109.

B A Plural Antecedent Requires a Plural Pronoun

B-1 A plural antecedent and its pronoun may be in the same sentence.

Examples

pl. ant. pl. pron.
a. Safe *drivers* use *their* seat belts.

pl. ant. pl. pron.
b. Wise *people* keep *their* own counsel.

pl. ant. pl. pron.
c. The older of the *partners* admitted *they* had shared the profits equally.

pl. ant. pl. pron.
d. Successful *businessmen* are turning *their* attention to the solution of social problems.

pl. ant. pl. pron.
e. *Californians* would rather drive than ride, thus maintaining some control over *their* lives.

comp. ant. pl. pron.
f. *Hilda, Drusilda, and I* went *our* separate ways.

NOTE: An antecedent made up of two or more parts joined by *and* is a *compound antecedent*. A *compound antecedent* is usually plural, and, therefore, requires a plural pronoun.

Examples

comp. ant. pl. pron.
g. *Water and oil* seek *their* own levels.

comp. ant. pl. pron.
h. *Time and tide* keep *their* own rhythms.

NOTE: A compound antecedent referring to one person or thing *thought of as a unit* may be treated as singular and then requires a singular pronoun.

Examples

comp. ant. s. pron.
i. The *physician* and *surgeon* opened *his* own clinic.

comp. ant. s. pron.
j. Ivan's *uncle* and *namesake* built *himself* a laboratory.

B-2 A plural antecedent and its pronoun may be in different sentences.

Examples

a. Safe *drivers* (pl. ant.) are careful. *They* (pl. pron.) use seat belts.

b. The *houses* (pl. ant.) were new. *They* (pl. pron.) had not been painted.

c. The *fire fighters* (pl. ant.) were fighting the third fire of the evening. After only three hours of sleep, *they* (pl. pron.) were almost exhausted.

d. *Members* (pl. ant.) of our club are volunteering for a physical fitness project. Although exercising takes time, *they* (pl. pron.) all feel rewarded.

e. *Walter* and *Erica* (comp. ant.) are writing about peace. *They* (pl. pron.) believe peace is humanly attainable.

Quick Quiz: C

Underline each antecedent, *circle* its pronoun, and *indicate* whether the antecedent is singular or plural.

Model: Ronald wrote both congressmen for their voting records. plural

1. Some excellent writers have trouble with their spelling. ____________
2. The success of the project will depend on its efficiency. ____________
3. Hera and Zeus moved to Rome and changed their names. ____________
4. Dianne helped on the project. She ran the district office. ____________
5. Sixteen members of the organization are transferring their memberships to another club. ____________

Answers to Quick Quiz C are on page 109.

B-3 A word that comes between an antecedent and its pronoun may be mistaken for an antecedent.

Examples

a. *Members* (pl. ant.) of the newly created repertory company are wearing *their* (pl. pron.) new costumes.
The singular word *company* is not the antecedent.
Members [of the newly created repertory company] are wearing *their*. . . .
Members . . . are wearing *their*. . . .

b. This tree is one of *those* (pl. ant.) that always have *their* (pl. pron.) roots near the surface of the soil.
The word *tree* is not the antecedent.
This tree is one [of those (trees) that always have their roots. . . .]

pl. ant. — pl. pron.

c. Several statements were challenged as the debating team *members* presented *their* arguments against the war.

pl. ant. — pl. pron.

d. The mass immunization program was planned by the *physicians* through *their* medical society.

comp. ant. — pl. pron.

e. *Synge, Yeats,* and *O'Casey* were distinguished dramatists. *They* were all Irishmen.

s. ant. — pl. ant. — pl. pron.

f. Either the *interview* or the *films* will have *their* place on the program.

NOTE: When two antecedents, one singular and one plural, are combined in a *neither . . . nor* or *either . . . or* expression, the pronoun agrees with the antecedent nearer the pronoun. The plural antecedent *films* is nearer the pronoun and therefore determines the pronoun number.

NOTE: Compare this section (**B-3**) with Section **A-3**.

B-4 A plural collective noun that is an antecedent requires a plural pronoun.

pl. coll. n. ant. — pl. pron.

Examples **a.** The *platoons* marched in *their* first close-order drill.

pl. coll. n. ant. — pl. pron.

b. Several *councils* were negotiating among *themselves.*

pl. coll. n. ant. — pl. pron.

c. Three wolf *packs* had left *their* tracks in the snow.

B-5 A singular collective noun that is an antecedent may require a plural pronoun.

A singular collective noun may refer to a *group as a unit,* or it may refer to the *members* of a group. When it refers to a group as a unit, it is singular and requires a singular pronoun. When it refers to *members* of a group (as individuals), it is plural and requires a plural pronoun.

s. coll. n. ant. — pl. pron.

Examples **a.** The vote of the *clergy* on *their* agenda was divided.

The unexpressed but understood meaning of the subject is *the members of the clergy.* (When the plural sounds awkward, you may provide a plural antecedent by adding the words *members of* in front of the collective noun. The vote of the *members of* the clergy on *their* agenda was divided.)

s. coll. n. ant. — pl. pron.

b. The *team* were weighed before *they* began spring practice.

It is improbable that the team was weighed as a unit.

s. coll. n. ant. / pl. pron.

c. In twos and threes, the *audience* left, quietly but decisively expressing *their* boredom with the play.

Quick Quiz: D

Underline each antecedent and *circle* its *pronoun.*

Model: Both teams rested from practice the night before (their) meet.

1. The governments conceded that the issue touched their countries in different ways.
2. Heather is one of the people always taking their humor seriously.
3. Three groups—each consisting of two lawyers and one doctor—volunteered to present their points of view about euthanasia.
4. Parker, Thurber, and I plan to present the play in the community theater. After a month or two of planning, we should be ready for rehearsals.
5. The crowd yelled their heads off as the team finally pulled ahead of the challengers.

Answers to Quick Quiz D are on page 109.

Procedure for Recognizing and Correcting Errors in Pronoun-Antecedent Agreement

NOTE: The instructor's marginal notations generally identify errors.

pro-ant agr

The list of workers is now double their original length.

Step 1: Find the pronoun.
Their is the pronoun.

Step 2: Find the word you think may be the antecedent.
List may be the antecedent.

Step 3: Read that word *in place of* the pronoun.
(If this does *not* make sense, go through the steps with each possible antecedent, one at a time.)
The *list* is now double the *list's* original length.
List is the antecedent.

Step 4: Decide if the antecedent is singular or plural.
List is singular.

Step 5: Make the pronoun agree with its antecedent in number.
The singular antecedent *list* requires the singular pronoun *its*. Corrected, the sentence is
The list of workers is now double its original length.

NOTE: If you are checking the agreement of more than one pronoun, follow the procedure for one pronoun at a time.

REVIEW AND PRACTICE

Each of the exercises of this Review and Practice is different. Do some exercises in each section, then check your answers and decide which sections—if any—you need to continue to work through. Answers are on pages 109–111.

Exercise A *Underline* each antecedent, *circle* its pronoun, and *write* the number of both, singular or plural, in the space provided.

Model: *singular* The boat sprang a leak in (its) side.

1. ______________ The horse threw its shoe.
2. ______________ The group of geologists lost its way.
3. ______________ My wife and I lived in isolation. We were sixty miles from the nearest town.
4. ______________ People may have to spend a great part of their energy on the education of their children.
5. ______________ The navigators and the cartographer argued about the illustrations for their book.

Exercise B *Underline* the antecedent and *circle* its pronoun.

Model: The flutist ignored (his) conductor.

1. The audience could hardly contain its enthusiasm.
2. The hunter was proud of her marksmanship.
3. One wants his money returned.
4. A citizen should support the government, but she should also be free to criticize that government.
5. The Cheyenne society of porcupine-quill embroiderers was a group in which girls worked their way up from making moccasins to decorating tepees.
6. John slowly and silently got up and brushed the dust from his back.
7. No woman in her right mind believes that TV commercial.
8. The spider and the ad man spin their webs.
9. Hanging from the edge of the roof, the children kicked their feet through the open window.
10. Each of the women has her own reason for being here.

Exercise C *Underline* each antecedent, *circle* its pronoun, and *write* the number of both (singular or plural) in the space provided.

Model: *singular* The child looked for (his) mother.

1. ______________ Although darkness had fallen, the horses found their way through the snowdrift.

2. ______________ At election time, the mayor and the senator pay special attention to their constituents.

3. ______________ A cricket rubs its legs together to produce sound.

4. ______________ After two years, the glue lost its holding power.

5. ______________ In the morning, Donna got up and ate her breakfast in front of the TV.

Exercise D *Underline* each antecedent and *mark* it **S** for singular or **P** for plural, and *circle* the correct pronoun in parentheses.

Model: One (S) of the parachutists forgot (his, their) emergency chute.

1. Half of the human race spends (its, their) time laughing at the other half.
2. Despite the fact that (his, their) speeches were filled with hindsight, the legislators felt like prophets.
3. A sleeping sheep counts people in (its, their) dreams.
4. The acquisition of vast stores of information is at once man's glory and (his, their) undoing.
5. The judges chose Alice B. Toklas to carry (its, their) steins.
6. The murder and the robbery occurred yesterday. The police still don't know who committed (it, them).
7. Sticks and stones can break my bones, but (it, they) can never hurt me.
8. Cobalt blue and burnt umber seem to spread (itself, themselves) across all Vincent's canvasses.
9. The sunlight filtered through the trees. (It, They) glistened on the beer cans in the grass.
10. Each of them stood on (her, their) tiptoes.

Exercise E *Underline* antecedents and *circle* their pronouns.

Model: The witness testifying for the defendants waited until her turn.

1. Any of the counselors will give Doris his advice freely.
2. Not one of the nine men on the team said he was sure the Cougars would show up that day.
3. Nobody, and I do mean nobody, has clearly explained her reasons for wanting to leave quiet Lexington and move to crowded Boston.
4. The house hidden behind the trees should have its walk lighted.
5. When Rick arrives, one of the girls will loan him the car.
6. Either of the wheelbarrows can carry its load.

7. One of the theaters refused to open its doors.
8. One of the significant discoveries about food came when man found that he could plant seeds.
9. What opinions does the author present in her first chapter?
10. In the days before pneumatic hammers, the riveter used a die and a maul. He was dependent on his strength and his skill.

Exercise F *Underline* each collective noun, *label* it **S** for singular or **P** for plural, and *circle* the correct pronoun in parentheses.

Model: The research team (S) took a long time before (it, they) reported the results.

1. Congress sometimes seems to contradict (itself, themselves).
2. The committee is frustrated trying to find out what (its, their) responsibility really is.
3. The team doesn't seem to be very good at recovering (its, their) own fumbles.
4. With surprising speed, the pack of wolves attacked (its, their) prey.
5. The governments reserved to (itself, themselves) the power to declare martial law.
6. The committees told Mr. Sprigg to come directly to (it, them) with the information.
7. Believe it or not, the caucuses elected (its, their) first chairmen.
8. The herd of elephants, some sleeping and some eating, ignored the tourists who were photographing (it, them) one animal at a time.
9. At the far end of the field, the band stood by (itself, themselves).
10. The state assembly of six women and thirty-four men is meeting now to elect (its, their) chairman.

Answers to Review and Practice are on pages 109–111.

CHAPTER TEST

In the spaces provided, write the antecedent in column A and its correct pronoun in column B.

	A Antecedent	B Pronoun
Model: Steve, along with Joan and Brad, spent (his, their) vacation cramming for exams.	Steve	his
1. The man who underwent the world's first larynx transplant died ten months after receiving (his, their) new larynx.	________	________
2. In my group of friends, each of us does (our, his) own thing.	________	________
3. The pitcher and catcher got (her, their) signals crossed.	________	________
4. The facts speak for (itself, themselves).	________	________
5. The body of facts speaks for (itself, themselves).	________	________
6. Every man has (his, their) faults.	________	________
7. The mule and the horse prove (its, their) stamina.	________	________
8. The organization of spelunkers is planning to find a new name for (itself, themselves).	________	________
9. The North Atlantic Treaty Organization presented a list of topics on which (it, they) asked for discussion and negotiation.	________	________
10. The members of the club elected Herbert Q. Potts (its, their) president.	________	________
11. Nobody works as hard for (his, their) money as the person who hoards (it, them).	________	________
12. The jury took a long time before (it, they) reported a deadlock.	________	________
13. Everyone complains of (her, their) own memory, but no one complains of (her, their) own judgment.	________	________
14. After the accident, several of us went to (our, his) own doctors.	________	________
15. Two of Universal Airline's luxury flights are to leave Seattle's airport on December 24 for (its, their) holiday hop to Hawaii.	________	________
16. Everyone in the ranks moves when (he is, they are) told to.	________	________
17. The group sang (its, their) anthem after the results were announced.	________	________

18. The damage caused by drunken drivers in 1930 was considerable, but (it was, they were) insignificant compared with what happened in 1980. ________ ________

19. The movies of the trip were good, but (it was, they were) not as clear as we had hoped. ________ ________

20. Everybody on the boat says (she wants, they want) to learn to handle the tiller. ________ ________

Answers to Chapter Test are on page 112.

ANSWERS: CHAPTER 5

Answers to Quick Quiz A

1. Zenna, her 2. motorist, his 3. each, her 4. tree, It
5. Susan, she 6. boy, He

Answers to Quick Quiz B

1. squad, its 2. head, her 3. one, his 4. herd, its 5. Dr. Hart, her

Answers to Quick Quiz C

1. writers, their, plural 2. project, its, singular 3. Hera . . . Zeus, their, plural 4. Dianne, she, singular
5. members, their, plural

Answers to Quick Quiz D

1. governments, their 2. people, their 3. groups, their 4. Parker, Thurber, I, we 5. (members of the) crowd, their

Answers to Review and Practice

Exercise A

1. singular The horse threw its shoe.
2. singular The group of geologists lost its way.
3. plural My wife and I lived in isolation. We were sixty miles from the nearest town.
4. plural People may have to spend a great part of their energy on the education of their children.
5. plural The navigators and the cartographer argued about the illustrations for their book.

Exercise B

1. The audience could hardly contain its enthusiasm.
2. The hunter was proud of her marksmanship.
3. One wants his money returned.
4. A citizen should support the government, but she should also be free to criticize that government.
5. The Cheyenne society of porcupine-quill embroiderers was a group in which girls worked their way up from making moccasins to decorating tepees.
6. John slowly and silently got up and brushed the dust from his back.
7. No woman in her right mind believes that TV commercial.
8. The spider and the ad man spin their webs.
9. Hanging from the edge of the roof, the children kicked their feet through the open window.
10. Each of the women has her own reason for being here.

Exercise C

1. plural Although darkness had fallen, the horses found their way through the snowdrift.
2. plural At election time, the mayor and the senator pay special attention to their constituents.
3. singular A cricket rubs its legs together to produce sound.
4. singular After two years, the glue lost its holding power.
5. singular In the morning, Donna got up and ate her breakfast in front of the TV.

Exercise D

	antecedent	number	correct pronoun	Notice that . . .
1.	half	S	its	*one-half*, or *half*, is singular. (The same is true of other fractions such as *one-fifth* or *one-third*.)
2.	legislators	P	their	a pronoun sometimes comes before its antecedent.
3.	sheep	S	its	
4.	man's	S	his	
5.	judges	P	their	
6.	murder (and) robbery	P	them	two or more singular antecedents connected by *and* form a compound antecedent that is plural.
7.	sticks (and) stones	P	they	
8.	blue (and) umber	P	themselves	
9.	sunlight	S	It	

10. each	S	her	*each* (like such words as *everyone, everybody*) is singular.

Exercise E

antecedent	*pronoun*	**Notice that . . .**
1. any	his	*any* is sometimes a singular antecedent and sometimes a plural antecedent depending on the meaning of the sentence. In this sentence, *any* is singular, since it means *any one*, and *one* is singular.
2. one	he	*one* remains singular even with *not* in front of it.
3. nobody	her	*nobody*—even when repeated—means *no body* and is singular.
4. house	its	
5. Rick	him	
6. Either	its	*Either* (of the wheelbarrows) means *this one* or *that one*.
7. One	its	
8. man	he	an antecedent and its pronoun may be embedded in a long sentence.
9. author	her	
10. riveter	he his his	an antecedent and its pronoun can be in different sentences, and one word can be the antecedent of more than one pronoun.

Exercise F

coll. noun	*number*	*pronoun*	**Notice that . . .**
1. Congress	S	itself	
2. committee	S	its	
3. team	S	its	
4. pack	S	its	
5. governments	P	themselves	
6. committees	P	them	
7. caucuses	P	their	
8. herd	P	them	*herd* here has the meaning of *members of the herd*.
9. band	S	itself	
10. assembly	S	its	

Answers to Chapter Test

	Antecedent	*Pronoun*		*Antecedent*	*Pronoun*
1.	man	his	11.	nobody money	his it
2.	each	his	12.	jury	it
3.	pitcher (and) catcher	their	13.	everyone no one	her her
4.	facts	themselves	14.	several	our
5.	body	itself	15.	two	their
6.	man	his	16.	everyone	he (is)
7.	mule (and) horse	their	17.	group	its
8.	organization	itself	18.	damage	it (was)
9.	North Atlantic Treaty Organization	it	19.	movies	they (were)
10.	members	their	20.	everybody	she (wants)

CHAPTER 6

Pronoun Reference

- **Items 75–80 in the Pretest are from this chapter.**
- **The procedure for recognizing and correcting errors in pronoun reference is on page 118.**

Chapter Contents

RULE: | A pronoun must refer clearly to its antecedent.

A Clear Pronoun Reference

A *pronoun** is a word that stands for another word or group of words. *I, you, he, she, it, we, they* are pronouns. The word for which a pronoun stands is the *antecedent** of that pronoun. Each of the sentences in A-1 and A-2 contains a pronoun and its antecedent. The reference in each instance is clear because each pronoun has only one possible antecedent. You can substitute the antecedent for its pronoun without changing the meaning of the sentence.

---

*pronouns: See Appendix B for additional pronouns.
*antecedent: See Pronoun-Antecedent Agreement for related material. (Chapter 5).

A-1 When a pronoun antecedent is singular

Examples

ant. pron.
a. *Reymont* worked on the invention for ten years before *he* received a patent.
Reymont is the antecedent of the pronoun *he*. *He* is the pronoun referring to Reymont.

ant. pron.
b. The *editor* met with *her* staff.

ant. pron.
c. *Each* filed *his* own income tax report.

ant. pron. pron.
d. *Everybody* must live with the prospect of *his* or *her* individual death.
The singular pronoun *his* OR the singular pronoun *her* refers to the singular antecedent *everybody*. Notice that *everybody* is singular and that two singular words linked by OR remain singular.

A-2 When a pronoun antecedent is plural

Examples

ant. pron.
a. The *opponents* made *their* reasons clear.
The plural pronoun *their* refers to the plural antecedent *opponents*.

pl. ant. pron.
b. Andrea talked of her *mother* and *father*, and she wondered what *they* were really like.
The plural pronoun *they* refers to the plural antecedents *mother* and *father*. Notice that two singular antecedents joined by *and* form a plural antecedent. (*Her* and *she* are singular pronouns referring to the singular antecedent *Andrea*.)

c. ant. "What *people* mean when pron. *they* say pron. *they* believe in God is extremely various," said Dr. Bellah.
The plural pronouns *they* refer to the plural antecedent *people.* Notice that more than one pronoun in a sentence can refer to the same antecedent.

d. The immunologist found that even when foreign ant. *skin* or foreign ant. *organs* are grown in the laboratory before pron. *they* are grafted or transplanted, pron. *they* are rejected by the recipient.
The plural pronouns *they* refer to the antecedents *skin* and *organs.* Notice that when a singular antecedent *(skin)* and a plural antecedent *(organs)* are joined by OR, both the verb and the pronoun *agree with the antecedent closer to the pronoun.* (The immunologist found that even when foreign organs or foreign *skin* is grown in the laboratory before *it* is grafted or transplanted, *it* is rejected by the recipient.)

e. "You ask about pay ant. *raises*?" cried the manager. pron. "*They* will become effective when you do!"
The plural pronoun *they* refers to the plural antecedent *raises.* Notice that pronoun and antecedent may be in separate sentences.

f. ant. *Peter* and *Susan*—to pron. *their* delight—often spent weekends rummaging through flea markets and exploring garage sales.
Notice that a plural antecedent may have more than one part.

Quick Quiz: A

Circle each pronoun, *underline* its antecedent, and *draw a line* from one to the other.

Model: When Al met the committee, (he) had a black eye.

1. The auditor stirred uncomfortably in his seat.
2. Wilma told Max to stop needling her.
3. At her desk, Millicent worked on her journal.
4. Hubert and Carla raced to the hospital in their car.

Answers to Quick Quiz A are on page 123.

B Unclear, or Ambiguous, Reference

When the connection between a pronoun and an antecedent is unclear, an *error in pronoun reference* exists.

B-1 Correcting an unclear reference when a sentence contains a pronoun that has more than one possible antecedent

Examples

ant.? ant.? pron.

a. *Hugh* and *Edmund* talked together, and then *he* left town.

This sentence contains two possible antecedents, *Hugh* and *Edmund,* but only one pronoun, *he.* Who left town, Hugh or Edmund? Since the pronoun *he* does not give a clear answer, the pronoun reference is unclear, or ambiguous, and is a *pronoun reference error.*

You can ordinarily correct a sentence containing more than one possible antecedent by taking out the pronoun and replacing it with the correct antecedent.

Corrected, the sentence might read: *Hugh and Edmund talked together, and then Hugh left town.*

ant.? ant.? pron.

b. As Fernanda adjusted the *dial* and rotated the *antenna, it* broke.

What broke, the *dial* or the *antenna*? The only pronoun in the sentence, *it,* does not point to a clear answer; therefore, the pronoun reference is unclear.

Corrected, the sentence might read: *As Fernanda adjusted the dial and rotated the antenna, the antenna broke.*

Quick Quiz: B

Circle each pronoun and *underline* its possible antecedents. If the reference is clear, *write clear* above the antecedent. If the reference is unclear, *write unclear* above each possible antecedent.

unclear unclear

Models: Phineas told the dog that (he) had to stay home.

clear

The forgery was verified though (it) was cleverly executed.

1. Myers measured both the liquid and the solid and added them to the beaker.
2. While reporting on lobbyists, the investigator told the committee members they were sometimes rude.
3. Mildred could not talk to Louise until she had a telephone installed.
4. Victor warned Laura that they might get lost in the dense fog.
5. The sailor returned to her ship.

Answers to Quick Quiz B are on page 123.

B-2 Correcting an unclear reference when a sentence contains more than one pronoun

Examples

ant.? ant.? pron. pron. pron.

a. *Iris* asked *Thea* to be *her* traveling companion because *she* understood *her.*

The pronoun-antecedent reference in this sentence is *unclear* because the reader is not told whether

she [Iris] understood *her* [Thea]

OR

she [Thea] understood *her* [Iris]

You can ordinarily correct a sentence containing more than one pronoun by replacing each unclear pronoun with its intended antecedent. Corrected, the sentence might read: Iris asked Thea to be *her* traveling companion because Thea understood Iris.

ant.? ant.? pron. ant.? pron.

b. An ethical *attorney* does not discuss a *client's* case with *his friends* unless *they* agree such a conversation would be wise.

The pronoun-antecedent reference in this sentence is unclear; consequently, the sentence has several possible interpretations:

An ethical attorney does not discuss a client's case with *his* (the attorney's? the client's?) friends, unless *they* (the attorney and the client? the attorney and his friends? the client and his friends? the client's friends?) agree . . . .

You can ordinarily correct such a sentence by replacing each unclear pronoun with its intended antecedent. Corrected, the sentence might read:

An ethical attorney does not discuss a client's case with his own or his client's friends unless the attorney and the client agree such conversation would be wise.

B-3 Correcting an unclear reference when a pronoun has *no antecedent* or when a pronoun has *no logical antecedent*

NOTE: Take particular care to establish clear antecedents for the following pronouns: *it, you, they, this, that, which.*

pron.

Examples **a.** The overweight fighter ate less and exercised more. *This* helped him to lose weight.

What is the antecedent of the pronoun *this*?

ant.?

This [ate less] helped him to lose weight.

ant.?

This [exercised more] helped him to lose weight.

This has no clear antecedent. You can ordinarily correct such a sentence by

1. replacing the pronoun with its intended antecedent

OR

2. providing a clear and logical antecedent for the pronoun.

Corrected, the sentence might read:

The overweight fighter adopted a new plan of eating less and exercising more, a plan that helped him lose weight.

OR

The overweight fighter adopted a new plan of eating less and exercising more,

clear ant.

the plan of his trainer. This approach helped him lose weight.

ant. pron. pron.

b. *Keith* used the desk for *his* typewriter and the table for *his* record player. Jonathan

pron.

did not appreciate *this.*

Pronoun-antecedent reference in the first sentence is clear: the pronoun *his* refers clearly to *Keith.* Pronoun-antecedent reference in the second sentence is *ambiguous* (unclear): no word or group of words can be substituted for the pronoun *this.*

Corrected, the sentence might read:

Keith used the desk for his typewriter and the table for his record player. Jonathan did not appreciate Keith's monopoly of the furniture.

B-4 Correcting an unclear reference when pronoun and antecedent are too far apart to ensure clarity

Example Kate liked the new *project* (ant.?). Obviously, there would be plenty of work to do, but *work* (ant.?) never bothered Kate. Besides, *it* (pron.) might win support for the youth group.

Pronoun-antecedent reference is unclear, since the antecedent of the pronoun *it* is not clear.

You can ordinarily correct such a sentence by replacing the pronoun with its antecedent or by rewriting the sentence so that each pronoun is preceded by only one possible antecedent.

Corrected, the sentence might read:

Kate liked the new project. Obviously, there would be plenty of work to do, but work never bothered Kate. Besides, the new project might win support for the youth group.

Procedure for Recognizing and Correcting Errors in Pronoun Reference

The instructor's marginal notation generally identifies the error.

Examples pro-ref **a.** Place the jar by the window and leave it open.

Step 1: Find the pronoun.
The pronoun is *it.*

Step 2: Find the pronoun's nearest preceding noun.*
The pronoun's nearest preceding noun is *window,* so *window* is a possible antecedent. (If *window* were the only possible antecedent, reference would be clear.)

*A *noun* is a word that names something. *Charles, car, team, idea* are nouns.

Step 3: Find any other possible antecedents.
Jar is another possible antecedent.
Reference in this sentence is unclear, since two possible—and logical—antecedents precede the pronoun *it.*

Step 4: Correct the sentence in either of the following ways:

a. by replacing the pronoun with its antecedent,
Place the jar by the window and leave the jar open.

OR

b. by rewriting the sentence so that only one possible antecedent precedes the pronoun.
Leaving the jar open, place it by the window.

pro-ref **b.** After the trees have shed many leaves, they will have to clean the yard.

Step 1: Find the pronoun.
The pronoun is *they.*

Step 2: Find the pronoun's nearest preceding noun.
The nearest preceding noun is *leaves.*
(Read the sentence with the noun in place of the pronoun: *After the trees have shed many leaves, leaves will have to clean the yard.) Leaves,* obviously, is *not* the correct antecedent.

Step 3: Find any other possible antecedent and substitute it for the pronoun: *After the trees have shed many leaves, the trees will have to clean the yard.*
Neither *trees* nor *leaves* is the correct antecedent of the pronoun *they.* The sentence, then, contains no antecedent for the pronoun *they.*

Step 4: Correct the sentence by substituting a noun or nouns for the pronoun: *After the trees have shed many leaves, Deanna and Drummond will have to clean the yard.*

pro-ref

c. The Novaks traveled to Alaska, which the whole family enjoyed.

Step 1: Find the pronoun.
which

Step 2: Find the pronoun's nearest preceding noun.
Alaska
Read the sentence, substituting the noun for the pronoun. *The Novaks traveled to Alaska Alaska the whole family enjoyed.*
Obviously *Alaska* is not the antecedent.
Which has no logical antecedent in this sentence.

Step 3: Find any other possible antecedent and substitute it for the pronoun: *The Novaks traveled to Alaska Novaks the whole family enjoyed.* Neither *Alaska* nor *Novaks* is a logical antecedent.

Step 4: Correct the sentence by adding a logical antecedent before the pronoun *which.*

ant.
The Novaks traveled to Alaska, a trip which the whole family enjoyed.

REVIEW AND PRACTICE

Each of the sections of this Review and Practice is different. Do some exercises in each section, then check your answers and decide which sections–if any–you need to continue to work through. Answers are on pages 123–125.

Exercise A *Circle* each pronoun, underline its antecedent, and *draw a line* connecting pronoun and antecedent.

Model: When the manager comes back, she will return the call.

1. Edith regretted she had never visited the place.
2. Max took the marlin to the taxidermist and left it to be stuffed.
3. As the governor rode past, he waved to the crowd.
4. Call the reporter to see if he has the information.
5. As they approached the intersection, the car and the bus both swerved.

Exercise B In each sentence, *cross out* the pronoun and *write* its antecedent between the parentheses.

Model: The car had sprung a leak; ~~it~~ (car) needed a new radiator.

1. Sara thought she ( ) had done a good job.
2. As it ( ) neared the loading dock, the truck sideswiped the foreman's car.
3. The authors agree when they ( ) discuss the causes of social unrest.
4. The opera seemed endless as it ( ) dragged on.
5. We attended the rock festival, which ( ) lasted three days.

Exercise C *Circle* each pronoun and *underline* each possible antecedent. If a pronoun has more than one possible antecedent preceding it or no logical antecedent, write *unclear* over that pronoun.

Model: Caleb saw the new car hurrying away from the fire and couldn't help wondering about it. (unclear)

1. Here is the secret. Guard it tenaciously.
2. When fish stop biting, they frustrate anglers.
3. The children started to walk toward town; this seemed like a good idea at first.
4. Rains melted the snows; it caused flooding in the valley below.
5. If the cows are in the barn, tell them to shut the door.

Exercise D Each pronoun below has two possible antecedents and is therefore unclear. *Circle* each pronoun and *underline* its possible antecedents.

Model: The ceiling and the wall were freshly painted, and it looked better than before.

1. Eric and Pierre started out on a vacation after he finished work.
2. The two-ton Stegosaurus had a plum-sized brain. It was frightening.
3. The dogs chased the cats until they dropped.
4. Frieda did not like Rosalie even though she seemed friendly.
5. The bannister was shaky, and the porch floorboards were broken. This should have been repaired.
6. The man drove the injured passenger to his house.
7. Psychology and history left Ivan cold. The instructor could not make its basic concepts clear.
8. Luke would not let Floyd help, even though he was a friend.
9. Isabel told Belinda that she had chills and fever.
10. The plane and the kite dipped and looped. The girl was afraid it would fall.

Exercise E *Find* the pronoun and *write* it in the column marked *pronoun. Find* all possible antecedents and *write* them in the column marked *antecedents.* In the column marked *reference, write clear* for pronoun reference that is clear, and *write unclear* for pronoun reference that is unclear. *Write none* when a sentence contains no antecedent for a pronoun.

	Pronoun	*Antecedent*	*Reference*
Model: By the time the antiserum reached the patient, he was beyond help.	he	patient	clear
1. When Sandy pitched the ball, he knew an outstanding career was over.	________	________	________
2. On her way home, Esther heard the peculiar grinding sound in the engine again.	________	________	________
3. Wendy met with the surveyor and the attorney to discuss the boundaries of the property. They were confused.	________	________	________
4. Scotty argued heatedly with Andrea about the politicians. Finally, it made him storm out of the house.	________	________	________
5. Benjamin met Cornelius when he was twenty-eight.	________	________	________
6. When the sandpipers run along the beach, it looks like a little mechanical toy.	________	________	________
7. When the sandpipers run along the beach, it looks like a freeway for birds.	________	________	________
8. The plays had dozens of characters, and they were all clear in Trudy's mind.	________	________	________
9. On the camping trip, it was beautiful.	________	________	________
10. Bart dreaded the evening. Whenever the parents were together, they caused trouble.	________	________	________

Answers to Review and Practice are on page 123–125.

CHAPTER TEST

In the column marked pronoun, *write the pronoun; in the column marked* antecedent, write *any possible antecedent of that pronoun; in the column marked* reference, write clear *when pronoun reference is clear, and* write unclear *when pronoun reference is unclear.*

	Pronoun	Antecedent	Reference
Model: The motor died and the driver couldn't start it again.	it	motor	clear
1. The highest mountain in the world is Mount Everest. It is five and one-half miles high.			
2. When Adam and Laura got the new apartment, they threw a housewarming party.			
3. When the swan saw Leda, it turned and ran.			
4. On the edge of the river the slime was thick and green, but it flowed sluggishly onward.			
5. A rod tore loose and damaged the engine. It disabled the train.			
6. Ezra told Rupert the rock had nearly hit him.			
7. Conservation seemed like a good topic for an essay because many people liked camping. It was worth writing about.			
8. When the rocket reached Mars, it no longer could be observed.			
9. If the papers are not delivered on time, they will have to take the blame.			
10. Place the jar by the window and leave it open.			

Answers to Chapter Test are on page 125.

ANSWERS: CHAPTER 6

Answers to Quick Quiz A

1. The auditor stirred uncomfortably in (his) seat.
2. Wilma told Max to stop needling (her).
3. At (her) desk, Millicent worked on (her) journal.
   A pronoun may precede (come before) its antecedent, as well as follow it.
4. Hubert and Carla raced to the hospital in (their) car.

Answers to Quick Quiz B

1. liquid . . . solid, (them) — clear
2. lobbyists, members, (they) — unclear, unclear
3. Mildred, Louise, (she) — unclear, unclear
4. Victor . . . Laura, (they) — clear
5. sailor, (her) — clear

Answers to Review and Practice

Exercise A

Notice that . . .

1. Edith (she)
2. marlin (it)
3. governor (he)
4. reporter (he)
5. (they) car (and) bus — *car* + *bus* form the antecedent of the plural pronoun *they*. Here the pronoun precedes its antecedent.

Exercise B

1. ~~she~~ Sara 2. ~~it~~ truck 3. ~~they~~ authors 4. ~~it~~ opera 5. ~~which~~ festival

Exercise C

pron.	*possible ants.*	**Notice that . . .**
1. (it)	secret	you can substitute *secret* for *it:* Guard *it* [the *secret*] tenaciously.

2. they	fish	you can substitute the antecedent *fish* for the pronoun *they.*
3. clear this	to walk toward town	this whole phrase can substitute for *this.*
4. unclear it		the singular *it* cannot refer to the plural *rains* or *snows,* and that *it* cannot replace "Rains melted the snows."
5. unclear them	cows?	*cows* is *not* a logical antecedent for *them: tell them* [the cows] *to shut the door* does not make sense.

Exercise D

possible ants.	*ambiguous pron.*	**Ask yourself . . .**
1. Eric? Pierre?	he	who finished work?
2. Stegosaurus? brain?	it	what was frightening?
3. dogs? cats?	they	which dropped, the dogs or the cats?
4. Frieda? Rosalie?	she	who seemed friendly?
5. bannister? floorboards?	This	which needed repair?
6. man? passenger?	his	whose house?
7. Psychology? history?	its	which is not clear?
8. Luke? Floyd?	he	who was a friend?
9. Isabel? Belinda?	she	who was sick?
10. plane? kite?	it	which did the girl fear would fall?

Exercise E

	pron.	*ants.*	*ref.*	***Notice that. . .***
1.	he	Sandy	clear	you can substitute the antecedent for the pronoun: *He* [*Sandy*] *knew. . .*
2.	her	Esther	clear	
3.	They	Wendy, the attorney, and the surveyor? boundaries?	unclear	

	pron.	*ants.*	*ref.*	***Notice that. . .***
4.	it	none	unclear	
5.	he	Benjamin? Cornelius?	unclear	
6.	it	beach?	unclear	
7.	it	beach	clear	
8.	they	plays? characters?	unclear	
9.	it	trip?	unclear	a clear way of saying the same thing is *The camping trip was beautiful.*
10.	they	parents	clear	

Answers to Chapter Test

	pronoun	*antecedent*	*reference*
1.	it	Mt. Everest	clear
2.	they	Adam (and) Laura	clear
3.	it	swan	clear
4.	it	river? slime?	unclear
5.	it	rod? engine?	unclear
6.	him	Ezra? Rupert?	unclear
7.	It	conservation? camping?	unclear
8.	it	rocket? Mars?	unclear
9.	they	papers?	unclear
10.	it	jar? window?	unclear

CHAPTER 7

Pronoun Case

- **Items 81–104 in the Pretest are from this chapter.**
- **The procedure for recognizing and correcting errors in subjective case is on page 133; in objective case, page 145; in possessive case, page 151.**

Chapter Contents

RULE: The case form of a pronoun must show what part that pronoun plays in a sentence.

A pronoun is a word that *stands for a noun** and that can take the place of that noun in a sentence.

*noun: A *noun* is a word that names something. *Charles, car, team, idea* are nouns.

Example Whenever Charles sings, *he* (pronoun) receives an ovation.
(The pronoun *he* stands for the noun *Charles*. Whenever Charles sings, Charles receives an ovation.)

Case form is the form—or spelling—of a pronoun that expresses the part that pronoun plays in a sentence. This chapter deals with four groups of case forms: subjective (nominative), objective, possessive, and reflexive.

A Subjective (Nominative) Case Forms

The subjective case forms are *I, you, he, she, it, we, they, who, whoever.*

A-1 Use a subjective case form for any pronoun that is the subject* of a verb.*

*subject: The *subject* of a sentence is the person or thing the sentence is about.
The *cow* (subj.) jumped over the moon.

*verb: The *verb* indicates *what the subject does* (John (subj.) *runs* (verb) a fifteen-minute mile.), *what the subject is* (Love (subj.) *is* (vb.) a four-letter word.), or *what action the subject receives* (The murals (subj.) *were painted* (vb.) by Diego Rivera.).

When a pronoun is *all or part of a subject*, use the subjective case form of that pronoun.

NOTE: A subject containing only one noun or pronoun is a *simple subject*. A subject containing two or more nouns and/or pronouns is a *compound subject*.

Examples

a. *He* (simple subj.) left for work.

b. *It* (simple subj.) was broken.

c. *You* and *I* (comp. subj.) fight all the time, but neither *he* nor *she* (comp. subj.) does.

NOTE: Two pronouns joined by *and* or separated by *or* or *nor* are in the same case.

comp. subj.

d. Do *we* and *they* really speak the same language?

simple subj. — simple subj.

e. *Who* performed after *she* finished singing?
Who is the subject of the verb *performed;*
she is the subject of the verb *finished.*

Quick Quiz: A

Circle *all pronouns that are subjects.*

Model: (You) and (he) were sick.

1. They know the address of the theatre.
2. Why do he and they come in so late?
3. We and you cannot leave until she arrives.
4. I left the motor idling.

Circle the correct pronoun in parentheses.

Model: ((I), me) prefer not to work.

5. (Who, Whom) slammed the door?
6. (They, Them) and (I, me) understand the question.
7. Edie resented the intrusion when (she, her) and (he, him) came into the studio.

Substitute the correct pronouns for the words in parentheses.

Model: (David) called last night. [He]

8. (Joe and Sam) ran out of gas halfway home.
9. (Alice) is not coming.
10. (What person) answered when (Carol and Bob) knocked on the door?

Answers to Quick Quiz A are on page 156.

When a pronoun following *than* or *as* is the subject of a verb, use the subjective case form of that pronoun.

pron. subj. — verb

Examples **a.** Eric worked more *than she* worked.

pron.
subj. vb.

b. I am tall.
It is easy to see that the pronoun *I* is the subject of the verb *am* in the sentence *I am tall.*

pron.
subj. vb.

My son is taller *than I* am.
It is still easy to see that *I* is the subject of the verb *am.*

In English, needlessly repetitious words in a sentence are often omitted:

My son is taller *than I.*
In the sentence above, *am* and *tall* have both been omitted. *I* is the subject, however, of the **unexpressed** verb *am*, and is therefore in the subjective case.

Written out completely, the sentence would read:
My son is taller *than I* [am] [tall].

NOTE: When a pronoun is the subject of a verb (either expressed or unexpressed), the pronoun should be in the subjective case.

subj.

c. My friend saw as much *as I.*

I is the subject of the unexpressed verb *saw.*

subj. unexpressed vb.

My friend saw as much as *I* [saw].

Quick Quiz: B

Add *the unexpressed verb to the end of each sentence.*

Model: No one cares but he cares.

1. Gloria can answer that better than I ______________.
2. No one thinks as much as I ______________.
3. He is as eager as who ______________?

Circle *the correct pronouns.*

Model: Leon ate more lentils than (we, us).

4. Can George run farther than (I, me)?
5. Filbert enjoyed the nuts as well as (they, them).
6. No one talks as fast as (he, him).

Answers to Quick Quiz B are on page 156.

When *who* or *whoever* is the subject of a verb

Examples

subj. vb. subj. vb.

a. The judge announced *who* won the contest.
If *who* is correct as the subject of a question (Who won the contest?), *who* is correct in the original sentence.
Example **a** has two subjects and two verbs.

subj. 1 + vb. 1
judge announced

subj. 2 + vb. 2
who won

subj. vb. subj. vb.

b. Pablo gave a picture to *whoever* visited his studio.
Question: *Who*(ever) visited his studio? *Whoever* is correct.

subj. vb. subj. subj. vb. vb.

c. The coach's strategy depends on *who* he thinks will win.
Question: *Who* . . . will win?

subj. 1 + vb. 1
strategy depends

subj. 2 + vb. 2
who will win

subj. 3 + vb. 3
he thinks

Even when the subject *who* is separated from its verb by expressions like *he thinks, I believe, you know, who* remains in the subjective case since it is the subject of a verb.

subj. vb. subj. vb.

d. I build cabinets for whoever needs them.
Notice that *whoever* is the *subject* of the verb *needs.*
The object of the preposition *for* is the group of words "whoever needs them." (A preposition is a word that relates a noun or pronoun to another word in the sentence. *By, to, over* are prepositions. More information on this topic follows in section **B-3**.)

Quick Quiz: C

Circle *the subject of each underlined verb.*

Model: Here (I) am.

1. The man who left the scene of the accident was John.

2. I need to call everyone who will be here tonight.

3. It was he who wrote the controversial article.

In the space provided, write *each subject and its verb.*

Model: The man who called left a message. man left, who called

4. You tell whoever asks that I am out. ____________________

5. The actress who played Juliet is only an amateur.

____

6. The congressman, I think, will speak to anyone who visits him.

____

Circle *the correct pronouns.*

Model: The man with amnesia did not know (who, whom) he was.

7. (Who, Whom) is on the party line now?

8. Children (who, whom) act like adults are sometimes penalized.

9. She (who, whom) knows my story sees its pathos.

10. Offer the invention to (whoever, whomever) will buy it.

Answers to Quick Quiz C are on page 156.

• **When a pronoun following expressions such as *everyone but* ... or *no one except* ... is the subject of a verb, use the subjective case of that pronoun.**

Examples

subj. pron.

a. Everyone but *I* saw the blastoff.

subj. vb. subj. vb.

In other words, *Everyone saw the blastoff, but I* [did not see the blastoff].

subj. pron. pron.

b. Jimmy said no one except *he* and *she* responded.

subj. vb. subj. vb. subj. vb.

In other words, ... *no one responded except he [responded] and she [responded].*

A-2 Use a subjective case form for a pronoun that follows a form of the linking verb * *be.*

Commonly used forms of *be* are *am, are, is, was, were, will be.*

*linking verb (See chapter 1, section A-2 regarding linking verbs.)

Examples

form of vb. *be* pron. form of vb. *be* pron.

a. The writer ***was*** *he. The director* ***was*** *I.*
You can check for correctness by reading each pronoun as a subject:
He was the writer.
I was the director.

NOTE: Although many people use "The writer is him" or "The director was me" in informal conversation, *use the subjective case forms after the verb "to be" in formal writing.*

form of *be*

b. The finalists **were** *they* and *I*.
(*They* were the finalists. *I* was the finalist.)

form of *be*

c. My roommate **will be** *who*?
(*Who* will be my roommate?)

Quick Quiz: D

Underline *the forms of the verb* be *and* circle *the correct pronouns.*
Check *each sentence for correctness by reading each pronoun as a subject.*

Model: The losers are (we, us). (We are the losers).

1. The first to arrive will be (they, them).
2. The members of the steering committee were (she, her) and (I, me).
3. The marchers will be (who, whom)?
4. Those called on the carpet are (we, us) and (he, him).
5. Appearing for the defense were (he, him) and (she, her).

Answers to Quick Quiz D are on page 156.

Procedure for Recognizing and Correcting Errors in the Subjective (Nominative) Case Forms of Pronouns

Case *Despite the rain, him and me went jogging.*

Step 1: Find the pronouns.
The pronouns are *him* and *me*.

Step 2: If any pronoun is the subject of a verb, see that the pronoun is in the subjective case. *Him* and *me* are meant to be subjects of the verb *went*, so they should be in the subjective case. Corrected, the sentence reads *Despite the rain, he and I went jogging.*

Step 3: If any pronoun is the subject of an unexpressed verb following *than* or *as*, see that the pronoun is in the subjective case.
(*Meg is a better jogger than he and I.*)

Step 4: If any pronoun follows a form of the verb *be*, see that the pronoun is in the subjective case.
(*The joggers will be he and I.*)

REVIEW AND PRACTICE: SUBJECTIVE (NOMINATIVE) CASE

Each of the sections of this Review and Practice is different. Do some exercises in each section, then check your answers and decide which sections—if any—you need to continue to work through. Answers are on pages 156–157.

Exercise A Underline *the subject in each sentence.*

Model: We and they got together to play handball.

1. She and he look ridiculous in those costumes.
2. Who could stop the argument?
3. He and I wanted to be included.
4. They camp with Bob and Carol.
5. You and we were the only participants.

Exercise B Underline *the subjects and* circle *the correct pronouns in parentheses.*

Model: (I, me) was left.

1. You and (I, me) have seen that exhibit.
2. (Who, Whom) knows more about baseball than Casey and (he, him)?
3. (We, us) can do anything better than (they, them).
4. No one knows as much as (he, him) about local politics.
5. Wherever you and (I, me) go, (we, us) will always keep in touch.

Exercise C *In the sentences below,* cross out *incorrect pronouns and* write *in correct pronouns.*

Model: George was late for work more often than ~~me~~ __I__.

1. Although Kate was older than her ______, Bianca wanted to get married first.
2. Margaret, whom ______ is as intelligent as him ______, knows less.
3. You and me ______ really know Proust.
4. Whenever her ______ and them ______ get together, trouble starts.
5. After the earthquake, him ______ and me ______ left in a hurry.

Exercise D *In the following sentences, some of the pronouns are correct and some are incorrect.* Write correct *in front of each correct sentence and* incorrect *in front of each incorrect one.* Circle *incorrect pronouns.*

Model: incorrect After (me) left, they continued playing.

1. ______________ After you and they left, we whom remained went swimming.
2. ______________ He and them are waiting on the corner.
3. ______________ Didn't he leave before them and us got there?
4. ______________ I knew what she was thinking.
5. ______________ I can do anything better than her.

Exercise E *In the following sentences,* underline *forms of the verb* be *and* circle *the correct pronouns in parentheses.*

Model: The leading contenders are you and ((she,) her).

1. William insisted the thief was not (he, him).
2. The first grade teachers are George and (I, me).
3. Are the only workmen you and (I, me)?
4. Faster than a speeding bullet was (he, him).
5. The finalists will be Mabel and (I, me).

Answers to Review and Practice are on page 156–157.

B Objective (Accusative) Case Forms*

*objective case forms: An *objective case form* is the form a pronoun takes when that pronoun is the object of a verb, a verbal, or a preposition.

obj. obj.
I saw him near *me.*

The objective case forms are *me, you, him, her, it, us, them, whom, whomever.*

On the next page are the objective case forms and their related subjective case forms. (Subjective case forms are discussed in part A of this chapter.)

Pronouns

Subjective (Nominative) Case Forms	*Objective Case Forms*
I	me
you	you
he	him
she	her
it	it
we	us
you	you
they	them
who	whom
whoever	whomever

B-1 Use an objective case form for any pronoun that is the direct object* of a verb or a verbal*.

---

*direct object: A *direct object* is a word or group of words that *receives the action of a verb.*

vb. dir. obj.
I found a *dime.*

vb. dir. obj.
He broke *a cup and a plate.*

vb. dir. obj.
Claudia met *him.*

NOTE: Some verbs, such as *be* and *seem,* do not take direct objects.

---

*A *verbal* is a word formed from a verb but not used as verb. Two types of verbals are formed by adding ing to a verb: help+ing=*helping,* come+ing=*coming.* Verb+ing is called a *present participle* or *gerund.*

Another type of verbal is formed by putting to in front of a verb: *to help, to come.* To+verb is called an *infinitive.*

verbal
Running the store bored him.

verbal
To stand was impossible for the moment.

For further information on verbals, see chapter 1.

When a pronoun is a *direct object of a verb,* use the objective case form of that pronoun.

Examples

verb / dir. obj. / vb. / dir. obj.
a. Jeffrey *brought* his **sister** to the dance, and Alex *met* **her** there.

vb. / dir. obj.
b. Impulse *led* **him** into the debate.

vb. / dir. obj.
c. The storm *kept* **us** in the house.

vb. dir. obj.

d. Father *remembered* **her** and **him.**

An object having two or more parts is a *compound object.* To choose correct pronoun case, check one part of the object at a time, repeating the subject and the verb like this:

Father remembered *her.*
Father remembered *him.*

dir. obj.

Father remembered | her
| him.

dir. obj.

e. Paul invited *Ralph and you, Timmy and Alice, and Mel and me* to dinner.

In checking pronouns, omit words coming between verb and pronoun.

Paul invited *you.*
Paul invited *me.*

Paul invited | you
| me.

Quick Quiz: E

Underline *verbs and* circle *the direct objects in each sentence.*

Model: The chicken found (him) and (us.)

1. I touched her.
2. We believe him.
3. The memory haunted you and them.
4. The boss found her and me chained to our desks with paper clips.
5. During vacation, we met him and her, and on the way home, we saw you and them again.

Answers to Quick Quiz E are on page 158.

When a pronoun is a *direct object of a verbal,* use the objective case form of that pronoun.

Examples

verbal dir. object

a. Glenda remembered to call *them.*

verbal dir. obj.

b. The film boring *us,* we left.

verbal dir. object verbal dir. obj.

c. Suddenly remembering *him* and *them,* Annette turned to answer *her.*

Quick Quiz: F

Underline *each verbal and* circle *its direct object.*

Model: I wanted to know (him) and (her.)

1. Fatigue overcame Laura and Lenny, making them stop.
2. My mother tried to remember her.
3. Later my brother recalled his childhood friend, remembering her with great pleasure.
4. Entertaining us, he forgot to watch the clock.
5. Any citizen could claim unoccupied wastelands if he were prepared to develop them.

Answers to Quick Quiz F are on page 158.

When a pronoun is a *direct object following than or as,* use the objective case form of that pronoun.

Than or *as* often introduces an incomplete statement (also called an *elliptical* statement) that ends in a pronoun: I like her better *than* him.

In other words, *I like her better than* [I like] *him.*

To determine which pronoun should follow *than* or *as,* use these two steps:

Examples

a. When I compare my two colleagues, I like her better than (he? or him?)

Step 1: Complete the statement following *than* or *as* by adding the **unexpressed words:**
. . . I like her better *than [I like] he.* (incorrect)
. . . I like her better *than [I like] him.*

Step 2: Check the parts of the direct object one at a time by reading aloud subject + verb + pronoun (omitting words between):
. . . I like her. (*Her* is the direct object of the verb *like.*)
. . . I like [he?] (incorrect)
. . . I like [him?]
Your ear will usually help you choose the correct pronoun for a direct object. *Him,* which is an objective case pronoun, is the correct pronoun for a direct object.

The correct sentence is
When I compare my two colleagues, I like her better than I like him.
OR
When I compare my two colleagues, I like her better than him.

b. Lionel photographed *us* (dir. obj.) less often than *them* (dir. obj.).
Compete the statement by adding the unexpressed words:
Lionel photographed us less often than [Lionel photographed] *them.*
Check the parts of the direct object one at a time by reading subject + object + pronoun:
Lionel photographed *us.*
Lionel photographed *them.*
Them is the correct case form for a direct object.

c. The diet helped *Marvin* (dir. obj.) more than *me* (dir. obj.).
Complete the statement: The diet helped Marvin more than [the diet] helped *me*.
Check the parts of the direct object one at a time:
The diet helped *Marvin*.
The diet helped *me*.
Me is the correct case form for a direct object.

d. This hurts *them* (dir. obj.) as much as *us* (dir. obj.).
Complete the statement: This hurts them as much as [this hurts] *us*.
Check the parts of the direct object one at a time:
This hurts *them*.
This hurts *us*.
Us is the correct case form for a direct object.

NOTE: The easiest way to insure claity in sentences including *than* or *as* is to use complete statements instead of elliptical (incomplete) ones.

Quick Quiz: G

Complete *each elliptical statement following* than or as *and* circle *the correct pronoun in parentheses.*

Model: Our employer works you harder than Our employer works (she, her).

1. Biological science excites me more than ____________ (he, him).
2. My friends encourage me as much as ____________ (she, her).
3. The team wanted Milton more than ____________ (we, us).
4. The news conference convinced Michael as much as ____________ (they, them).
5. The earthquake startled the chickens more than ____________ (she, her).

Answers to Quick Quiz G are on page 158.

When a pronoun is a direct object following *but* or *except*, use the objective case of that pronoun.

NOTE: The last examples show that *than* and *as* sometimes introduce elliptical statements (statements in which some of the words are omitted). *But* and *except* also sometimes introduce such incomplete (elliptical) statements.
When *but* or *except* precedes pronouns that are the **objects of unexpressed** verbs, use the objective case of the pronouns.

Examples **a.** The referee knows no one *but me.*
The sentence, complete with unexpressed words, is

unexpressed vb. obj.
The referee knows no one *but* [the referee *knows*] *me.*

b. That reporter questioned everyone *except her.*
The sentence, complete with unexpressed words, is

unexpressed vb. obj.
The reporter questioned everyone *except* [the reporter *did* not *question*] *her.*

c. I mistrust everyone *but you* and *me.*
The sentence, complete with unexpressed words, is

unexpressed vb. obj. unexpressed vb. obj.
I mistrust everyone *but* [I *do* not *mistrust*] *you* and [I *do* not *mistrust*] *me.*

***Whom* and *whomever* are objective case pronouns.**

NOTE: In informal conversation, *who* sometimes replaces *whom* (*Who* does he work for? in place of *Whom* does he work for?). In formal writing, however, *who* is correct only when the subjective case is required. That is, *who* and *whoever* are correct only when they are the *subjects* of verbs.

You can use the "him test" to determine whether to use *who* or *whom* in a sentence.

If you can substitute the word *him, whom* is correct. If you can substitute the word *he, who* is correct:

Examples: **a.** George is one (who? or whom?) I nominated.
I nominated (he? or him?).
I nominated him.
Whom is therefore correct: George is the one *whom* I nominated

b. The roofer (who? or whom?) we hired did an excellent job.
We hired (he? or him?).
We hired him.
Whom is therefore correct: The roofer *whom* we hired did an excellent job.

c. Dirk photographed (whoever? or whomever?) he met.
Dirk photographed (he? or him?).
Dirk photographed him.
Whomever is therefore correct: Dirk photographed *whomever* he met.

Examples **a.,** **b.,** and **c.** require objective case pronouns: *him, whom, whomever.*

d. (Who? or Whom?) doubts the facts?
(He? or Him?) doubts the facts.
He doubts the facts.
Who is therefore correct: *Who* doubts the facts?

e. The answers will be supplied by (whoever? or whomever?) gets them first.
(He? or Him?) gets them first.
He gets them first.
Whoever is therefore correct: The answers will be supplied by *whoever* gets them first.
Examples **d.** and **e.** require subjective case pronouns: *he, who, whoever.*

Quick Quiz: H

In each sentence, circle *the correct pronoun in parentheses.*

Model: The man (who, whom) they nominated won.

1. The man (who, whom) you are calling is away.
2. The worker (who, whom) you are honoring is here.
3. Give (whomever, whoever) you meet my best regards.
4. She was the only person (who, whom) the children trusted.
5. (Who, Whom) is in first place?

Answers to Quick Quiz H are on page 158.

If you are in doubt about any part of this quiz, try the *"him test"* on the sentences: 1. You are calling *him.* 2. You are honoring *him.* 3. Give *him* my best regards. 4. The children trust *him.* 5. *Him* is in first place. (This is *incorrect; He* is in first place is correct, and question 5 should be, *Who* is in first place?)

B-2 Use an objective case form for any pronoun that is the indirect object* of a verb or a verbal.

*indirect object: The *indirect object* of a verb is the person or thing that *receives what the direct object* names. An indirect object expresses the idea of *to someone,* or *to something,* without using the word *to.*

vb. (gave) indirect object (me) dir. obj. (lesson)

Maud gave *me* a lesson in first aid.

Maud gave a lesson (direct object) to me (indirect object).

When a pronoun is an *indirect object of a verb,* use the objective case form of that pronoun. An indirect object expresses the idea of doing something to someone (or something), but without the use of *to.*

Examples

a. Stephanie gave *him* the book. (vb.: gave; indirect object: him; dir. obj.: book)

Stephanie gave the direct object—*book*—to the indirect object—*him.*

Notice that the indirect object is expressed without the *to* and comes before the direct object:

Stephanie gave *him* the book.

b. Nobody told *her* the truth. (vb.: told; indir. obj.: her; dir. obj.: truth)

c. The Constitution gives *you, me,* and *all* of us specific rights and responsibilities. (vb.: gives; indir. obj.: you, me, and all of us; dir. obj.: rights and responsibilities)

Quick Quiz: I

Underline *each verb and* circle *its indirect object.*

Model: The druggist brought (me) the prescription.

1. The pitcher threw me the ball.
2. When the horse became frightened, the jockey gave him a firm tug on the reins.
3. In the middle of the night, a friend called me for help.
4. During their vacation, our neighbors sent us a live lobster.
5. As soon as I received my diploma, I wrote him, her, and them about it.

Answers to Quick Quiz I are on page 158.

When a pronoun is an *indirect object of a verbal,* use the objective case form of that pronoun.

Examples

a. *Giving* (verbal) *him* (indir. obj.) the book was a nuisance.

b. Nobody wanted to *tell* (verbal) *her* (indir. obj.) the truth.

c. The Constitution, *giving* (verbal) *us* (indir. obj.) specific rights, demands responsibility from us.

d. In order to *show* (verbal) *us* (indir. obj.) the experiment, the research team presented the procedure via closed circuit television.

Quick Quiz: J

Underline *each verbal and* circle *the pronoun (in parentheses) that is its indirect object.*

Model: Feeding (he, (him)) the hot soup was difficult.

1. To show (they, them) the machinery, he took them to the mill.
2. Giving (she, her) his watch, he entered the water.
3. Writing my husband and (I, me) a weekly letter became a habit of theirs.
4. He was told to tell (who, whom) the story?
5. Telling (he, him) the secret was a big mistake.

Answers to Quick Quiz J are on page 158.

When a pronoun is an *indirect object* following *than* or *as*, use the objective case form of that pronoun.

Examples **a.** The shop foreman gave him more space than (I? or me?).

To determine the correct case form for a pronoun following *than* or *as*, take the following steps:

Step 1: Complete the statement following *than* or *as* by adding the *unexpressed* words:

indir. obj. ... unexpressed

The shop foreman gave him more space *than* [the shop foreman gave] (I? or me?).

Step 2: Check the parts of the indirect object one at a time by reading aloud subject + verb + pronoun:

The shop foreman gave *him* space.

The shop foreman gave *me* space.

The correct sentence is

indir. obj. ... indir. obj.

The shop foreman gave him more space than me.

Notice that both parts of the comparison—*him* and *me*—are in the same case, the objective case.

indir. obj. ... indir. obj.

b. Lionel gave you more help than *me*.

Complete the statement: Lionel gave you more help *than* [Lionel gave] *me*.

Check the parts one at a time:

Lionel gave you help.

Lionel gave *me* help.

indir. obj. ... unexpressed ... indir. obj.

This sentence means Lionel gave you more help than [Lionel gave] me.

c. The tax assessor's office sent me, *as well as him*, a refund.

The office sent me a refund.

The office sent *him* a refund.

unexpressed

This sentence means the tax assessor's office sent a refund to me as well as [to] *him*.

indir. obj. ... indir. obj.

d. We loaned him *as well as her* our bicycle.

indir. obj. ... indir. obj.

e. My aunt and uncle left us *as well as him* their books.

Quick Quiz: K

Underline *the verb,* circle *the correct pronoun in parentheses, and complete the statement "This sentence means. . ." using an unexpressed* to *and other words you wish.*

Model: The boxing instructor gave Jennings more help than (I, me).

The boxing instructor gave more help [to] Jennings than [to] me.

or

The boxing instructor gave more help to Jennings than the instructor gave to me.

1. The dentist gave Alice more anaesthetic than (I, me).
2. The secretary presented (we, us) the agenda.
3. The architect gave (they, them) a model.
4. The lecturer awarded them as well as (we, us) the citations.
5. The mail carrier brought (he, him) and (I, me) a Christmas card.

Answers to Quick Quiz K are on page 158.

B-3 Use an objective case form for any pronoun that is the object of a preposition*.

*preposition: A *preposition* is a word that *relates* a noun or pronoun *to another word* in a sentence. A preposition with its object is a prepositional phrase, although other words may come between the preposition and its object.

prep. obj. prep. obj. prep. obj. prep. obj.
The train went *over* a hill, *under* a bridge, *into* the town and stopped *at* the newly re-painted station.

Examples

prep. obj.
a. She loaned the album *to* me.
Me is the object of the preposition *to.*

prep. obj.
b. Most of *them* have seen it.
Them is the object of the preposition *of.*

prep. obj.
c. They ran from *him.*
Him is the object of the preposition *from.*

Quick Quiz: L

Underline *prepositions and* circle *pronouns in parentheses that are objects of prepositions.*

Model: The group planned an exhibit for (she, her).

1. Clara played the piano for (they, them).
2. The understudy rode with (he, him) and (I, me).
3. The discussion between (he, him) and (she, her) sparked the party.
4. Make out the check to (whoever, whomever) you wish.
5. Disaster loomed ahead of (they, them) and (we, us).

Answers to Quick Quiz L are on page 159.

Procedure for Recognizing and Correcting Errors in the Objective (Accusative) Case Forms of Pronouns

case

Step 1: Find the pronoun or pronouns.

Step 2: If any pronoun is a direct or an indirect object of a verb, see that the pronoun is in the objective case.
George called *him* last night. (direct object)
George gave *him* the information. (indirect object)

Step 3: If any pronoun is a direct object or an indirect object of a verbal, see that the pronoun is in the objective case.
George wanted to inform *them.* (direct object of verbal)
George likes giving *them* orders. (indirect object of verbal)

Step 4: If any pronoun is the object of a preposition, see that the pronoun is in the objective case.
George sent the phone bill to *him.* (object of a preposition)

REVIEW AND PRACTICE: OBJECTIVE (ACCUSATIVE) CASE

Each of the sections of this Review and Practice is different. Do some exercises in each section, then check your answers and decide which sections—if any—you need to continue to work through. Answers are on pages 159–161.

Exercise A *In the sentences below,* circle *objective case pronouns.*

Model: Hector drove (her) and (me) mad.

1. The interviewer made appointments with Manny, Gloria, and me.
2. Does she remember them?
3. The next order is for Jack and him.
4. Everyone likes them and her.
5. He saw all of his patients except her.
6. Pronouns, she said, drive her and us crazy.
7. They came between Jane and us.
8. Take it from whomever you want to.
9. Write the letter to them and her.
10. The story tells the world about him and us.

Exercise B *In the sentences below,* circle *the correct pronouns in parentheses.*

Model: Tennis interests everyone but Sadie and (I, me).

1. The stories were written by (they, them) for a magazine planned by (we, us).
2. George fought against (he, him) and (they, them).
3. For everyone except (she, her) this car will start.
4. For (who, whom) was this written?
5. Ask the question of (whoever, whomever) you want.
6. The accountant would like to see (they, them) and (we, us) immediately.
7. When you get up, give (she, her) and (we, us) breakfast.
8. These facts should be told to no one but (they, them).
9. The delegation received (we, us) and (he, him).
10. Ask the psychologist about (who, whom)?

Exercise C Cross out *incorrect pronouns and* write *in correct pronouns.*

Model: You will carry ~~who~~ whom across the stream?

1. The lake, unfortunately, lay between they and we.
2. The dean wrote Tom and he a letter of recommendation.
3. Doctor Whippet dogged both she and I.
4. The film gave he and she a new concept of love.
5. Tell the truth to no one but we.
6. The nurse had previously shot Rupert, she, and I full of penicillin.
7. He dedicated the program to the choreographer from who he had learned to dance.
8. Disaster loomed ahead for all but we.
9. The police officer ordered everyone but you and they and us to leave the room.
10. He wants who in his Christmas stocking?

Exercise D *In each sentence* substitute *the correct pronoun for the word or words in parentheses.*

Model: Jim looked everywhere for (~~John~~) him and (~~Mary~~) her.

1. She reviewed the latest book for (Robert and Jack).
2. Rene brought everybody but (the girl) and (the two boys) a gift.
3. The cartoon was a caricature of (what person)?
4. Without (the man) and (the woman), life would be meaningless.

5. The sun will rise regardless of you or (six people).

6. Someone asked everyone but (the girls) and (the boy) for money.

7. When are you giving (Charles) and me the furniture?

8. She knew everyone except (Tommy).

9. Discuss this with (whichever person) you like, but give (Lulu) your answer today.

10. If you are sick, (which person) should I call?

Exercise E *In each sentence below,* cross out *incorrect pronouns and* write in *correct ones. If a sentence contains no errors,* write **correct** *in front of it.*

Models: Correct ______ Give him the ball. me
______ Please give her and I the book.

1. ______ The specialists needed he and I for the experiment.

2. ______ Whom do you love most?

3. ______ Tell he and her why.

4. ______ Who are you willing to call concerning the overdraft?

5. ______ After hearing both stories, who are we to believe?

6. ______ Application blanks were given to everyone but we and they.

7. ______ I gave part of mine to her.

8. ______ Who does the company need?

9. ______ Is she going to marry he?

10. ______ I got the answers from she.

Answers to Review and Practice: Objective Case on pages 159–161.

C Possessive Case Forms

A *possessive case form* is the form a pronoun takes when that pronoun shows ownership or some other form of belonging. On the next page are the possessive case forms and their related subjective and objective case forms.

Case Forms of Personal Pronouns

Subjective Case Forms	*Objective Case Forms*	*Possessive Case Forms*	
(See part A for uses of these pronouns)	*(See part B for uses of these pronouns)*	*used as modifiers**	*used alone*
I	me	my	mine
you	you	your	yours
he	him	his	his
she	her	her	hers
it	it	its	its
we	us	our	ours
you	you	your	yours
they	them	their	theirs
who	whom	whose	whose
whoever	whomever	whosever (rare)	whosever (rare)

Notice that in three instances, both possessive case spellings are alike: *his-his, its-its, whose-whose,* in addition to the rarely used *whosever.*

*modifier: A *modifier,* or a word that *modifies,* adds some specific information about the word to which it applies. *The small, brown* dog *running around the yard* belongs to me. (*Small, brown,* and *running around the yard* modify dog.)

C-1 Use the following possessive case forms alone, without adjoining nouns.

mine, yours, his*, hers, its,* ours, theirs, whose*

*his, its, whose: While it is true that these words are among the pronouns that can be used without adjoining nouns, they also may be used to modify nouns:

His newspaper article revealed *whose* invention had truly demonstrated *its* usefulness.
(See section C-2 below.)

Examples

a. The car with the dead battery is *mine.* (my car) [poss. pron. above *mine*]

b. *Yours* has no brakes. (your car) [poss. pron. above *Yours*]

c. *Whose* has no brakes? (whose car) [poss. pron. above *Whose*]

d. The blue blazer is *his,* and the red raincape is *hers.*

Easily Misused Pronoun Forms

Some possessive case forms of pronouns can easily be confused with similar-sounding expressions. Possessive case forms **never** contain apostrophes (').

Correct Possessive Case Forms	*Incorrect (expressions sometimes mistaken for possessive case forms)*
1. *its* (belonging to it) The club planned *its* tour carefully.	*it's* (it is)
2. *our, ours* (belonging to us) This is *our* home. It is *ours.*	*hour, hours* (time) *are* (verb)
3. *their, theirs* (belonging to them) This is *their* home. It is *theirs.*	*there* (not here) *they're* (they are) *there's* (there is)
4. *your, yours* (belonging to you) This is *your* home. It is *yours.*	*you're* (you are)
5. *whose* (belonging to whom) *Whose* home is this?	*who's* (who is)

Quick Quiz: M

Circle *the correct possessive pronouns in parentheses.*

Model: A family values a home of (his, it's, our, its) own.

1. The cars should be combined; (theirs, there's) will not start and (ours, hours) will not stop.
2. (Whose, Who's) are they?
3. Are these yours? No, they are (our, their, her, theirs).

Answers to Quick Quiz M are on page 161.

C-2 Use the following possessive case forms with nouns and with gerunds*

my, your, his, her, its, our, their, whose

*gerund: A *gerund* is the [ing] *form of a verb* when it *functions as a noun. Skiing, thinking, barking, crying* are gerunds when those words are used as nouns.

gerund
Your *skiing* was excellent.
Thinking is difficult.
The *barking* grew louder.

Examples with Nouns

poss. pron. noun

a. *Our* house is on fire.

b. Crab, *my* dog, chews *his* toys, *my* slippers, and *your* bath towels.

c. Nobody's car goes down hill as well as *my* car.

NOTE: *Nobody,* like such pronouns as *anyone, no one, somebody, everybody,* is an *indefinite* pronoun. *Indefinite* pronouns are not possessive pronouns. *Indefinite* pronouns form their possessives by adding 's: *anyone's, no one's, somebody's, everybody's.*

Examples with Gerunds

gerund gerund

a. *Her* leaving by plane coincided with *my* coming by train.

gerund

b. I object to *her* driving.

gerund

c. We were all exhausted by *our* moving to Keokuk.

Quick Quiz: N

Circle *each possessive pronoun and* underline *its noun or gerund.*

Model: The state of (her) finances led the waitress to look for a second job.

1. The advertisements promised a golden future, but their details were not clear.
2. Our singing sounds better from a distance.
3. Can you tell me whose key this is?
4. Although my smoking has decreased, my eating has increased.
5. Her thinking and their planning could accomplish the task easily.

Circle *the possessive pronouns in parentheses.*

Model: This company offers ((its,) it's) employees low salaries and few fringe benefits.

6. (Their, They're, There) first meeting ended in a brawl.
7. (Whose, Who's) church will (your, you're) brother attend?
8. (Its, It's) initiative in community action won national recognition for (our, are, hour) organization.
9. (Their, Them) talking during the night amused no one.
10. Will (our, us) staying here cause you any inconvenience?
11. (His, Him) joking about (their, they) dancing caused a lot of trouble.

Answers to Quick Quiz N are on page 161.

Procedure for Recognizing and Correcting Errors in the Possessive Case Forms of Pronouns

case Who's life did Christopher try to emulate?

Step 1: Find the pronouns.
The only pronoun is *who's.*

Step 2: If any pronoun expresses possession **and** modifies a noun or a gerund, use one of the following possessive case forms: *my, your, his, her, its, our, their, whose.*

The pronoun *who's* is meant to express possession and to modify the noun *life,* but it is not a possessive case form. Corrected, the sentence reads *Whose life did Christopher try to emulate?*

Step 3: Check to see that you have not used an apostrophe in any possessive pronoun.

REVIEW AND PRACTICE: POSSESSIVE CASE

Each of the sections of this Review and Practice is different. Do some exercises in each section, then check your answers and decide which sections—if any—you need to work through. Answers are on pages 161–162.

Exercise A Circle *possessive pronouns.*

Model: Wise men cherish (their) liberty.

1. The highwayman shouted, "Your money or your life!"
2. It's not mine; it's yours.
3. Their griefs and fears were secret.
4. I like a man whose heart is in his work.
5. You're on your own.

Exercise B Circle *correct possessive pronouns.*

Model: (His, Him) laughing was more frightening than (his, him) shouting.

1. They're on (their, there) way.
2. (It, Hers) was the last number on the program.
3. (Who's, Whose) house are you going to?
4. (You're, Your) pounding on the table annoys us.
5. Can (ours, our) singing be that bad?
6. (Them, Their) arriving has changed (are, our, hour) plans.
7. (Who's, Whose) book did you lose?
8. Does (me, my) humming bother you?
9. The slide rule is (her, hers).
10. Someone must stop (him, his) procrastination.

Exercise C *In each group of sentences,* circle *the letter in front of the correct sentence.*

Model: a. You're account is overdrawn.
b. Your account is overdrawn.

1. a. Illness has prevented me answering your letter.
b. Illness has prevented my answering you're letter.
c. Illness has prevented my answering your letter.

2. a. Their advertisement appears in yesterday's paper.
b. There advertisement appears in yesterday's paper.

3. a. What is it's title?
b. What is its title?

4. a. The horse is mine; the saddle is her's.
b. The horse is mine; the saddle is hers.

5. a. You're first in line.
b. Your first in line.

6. a. Who goes there?
b. Who goes their?

7. a. As a statement of opinion, its true in it's own way.
b. As a statement of opinion, it's true in its own way.

8. a. I wish I knew whose house it is.
b. I wish I knew who's house it is.

9. a. It's an ill wind.
b. Its an ill wind.

10. a. There's no end to it.
b. Theirs no end to it.

Answers to Review and Practice: Possessive Case are on pages 161–162.

D Reflexive Case Forms

The reflexive case pronoun forms, singular and plural, are
myself; ourselves (1st person)
yourself; yourselves (2nd person)
himself, herself, itself; themselves (3rd person)

D-1 Use reflexive case to reflect back to the subject:

Examples
a. The sinking ship righted *itself.*

b. I confused *myself.*

c. They shouted *themselves* hoarse.

D-2 Use reflexive case for emphasis

Examples
a. I *myself* will finish the task.

b. You *yourself* are guilty.

c. We made the mistake *ourselves.*

CHAPTER REVIEW AND PRACTICE

Circle *the correct pronouns in parentheses.*

Model: The rosebush belongs to (I, me).

1. Jane drove faster than (he, him) or (I, me).
2. (Him, His) riding a horse always makes me laugh.
3. The crash killed no one but (she, her) and (they, them).
4. The actor gave his autograph to (whoever, whomever) asked.
5. During the storm (I, me) dove under the bed.
6. That lot is (hours, ours).
7. After Saturday night she did not want (we, us) or (they, them) to visit her again.

8. During the flight (she, her) was the pilot.
9. The man (who, whom) you told me about is coming here.
10. Is it for (we, us)?
11. Please visit (are, our) exhibit.
12. (We, Us) and (they, them) are planning to go.
13. The blueprints were prepared for (he, him) and (I, me).
14. You received advice from (who, whom)?
15. When we arrived, (she, her) and (he, him) greeted us.
16. (Whose, Who's) house is that?
17. The boat is (her, hers) and (hours, ours).
18. It all depends on (who, whom) will do the work.
19. (Whose, Who's) bikini is that lying there?
20. I am as tall as (he, him).
21. Will (me, my) playing and (them, their) singing wake you up?
22. The office space is for (whoever, whomever) can use it.
23. Remember, it is (your, you're) motorbike, not (theirs, there's).
24. The practical joke was planned for no one but (she, her).
25. Take (whoever, whomever) you want to the meeting.
26. Are (he, him) and (she, her) really engaged?
27. Come to (we, us) if you need anything.
28. The attack was mounted against (they, them) and (we, us).
29. It is (who, whom)?
30. Give no one except (she, her) the fortune cookie.
31. The escapees were (he, him) and (they, them).
32. The building slipped from (its, it's) foundation.
33. The clown was (he, him).
34. I am (she, her).
35. The horseman is (who, whom)?

Answers to Chapter Review and Practice are on page 162.

CHAPTER TEST

Circle *the correct pronouns in parentheses.*

Model: (I, me) like you.

1. The awards were given to (they, them) and (she, her).
2. The preview was for the people (who, whom) worked on the picture.
3. The work was his, but the profits were (their, theirs).
4. Before leaving, will (we, us) have time to stop by?
5. I built the boat for (whoever, whomever) I can find to buy it.
6. They are better carpenters than (we, us).
7. The president named (they, them) and (I, me) to the task force.
8. (Who's, Whose) pizza should we sample today?
9. (Our, Are) readers have suffered much from this chapter.
10. In the beginning, (we, us) wanted to attend.
11. I am interested in (whoever, whomever) is interested in me.
12. From (who, whom) did you get the cold?
13. He left the building after John and (she, her) had left.
14. (Them, Their) climbing was watched by many people.
15. For everyone except (they, them) it was an ordeal.

Answers to Chapter Test are on page 163.

ANSWERS: CHAPTER 7

Answers to Quick Quiz A

1. They 2. he and they 3. We and you, she 4. I 5. Who
6. They and I 7. she and he 8. They 9. She 10. Who, they

Answers to Quick Quiz B

1. can 2. think 3. is 4. I [can run] 5. they [enjoyed the nuts]
6. he [talks]

Answers to Quick Quiz C

1. who left 2. who will be 3. who wrote 4. You tell, whoever asks, I am
5. actress is, who played 6. congressman will speak, I think, who visits 7. Who
8. who 9. who 10. whoever

Answers to Quick Quiz D

1. will be they (They will be the first to arrive.)
2. were she and I (She and I were members of the steering committee.)
3. will be who (Who will be the marchers?)
4. are we and he (We and he are those called on the carpet.)
5. were he and she (He and she were appearing for the defense.)

Answers to Review and Practice: Subjective Case

Exercise A

1. She and he
2. Who
3. He and I
4. They
5. You and we

Exercise B

1. You and I
2. Who
   Casey and he
3. We
   they
4. No one
   he
5. you and I
   we

Notice that . . .

2. *Casey and he* is the subject of the unexpressed verb *know:* Casey and he know.

3. *they* is the subject of the unexpressed verb *can:* they can.

4. No one knows as much as he [knows] . . . .

Exercise C

1. ~~her~~ she
2. ~~whom~~ who
   ~~him~~ he
3. ~~me~~ I
4. ~~her~~ she
   ~~them~~ they
5. ~~him~~ he
   ~~me~~ I

Notice that . . .

1. *she* is the subject of the unexpressed verb was: *she was.*

2. . . . who is as intelligent as he [is] . . . .

Exercise D

1. incorrect whom
2. incorrect them
3. incorrect them and us
4. correct
5. incorrect her

Notice that . . .

1. *who* is the subject of the verb *remained:* who remained

2. . . . *they* are waiting on the corner.

3. . . . they [got there] and we got there.

5. than *she* [can do anything].

Exercise E

1. was he
2. are I
3. Are I
4. was he
5. will be I

Answers to Quick Quiz E

1. touched her 2. believe him 3. haunted you and them 4. found her and me 5. met him and her saw you and them

Answers to Quick Quiz F

1. making them 2. to remember her 3. remembering her 4. Entertaining us, to watch the clock 5. to develop them

Answers to Quick Quiz G

1. science excites him 2. my friends encourage her 3. the team wanted us 4. the news conference convinced them 5. the earthquake startled her

Answers to Quick Quiz H

1. whom 2. whom 3. whomever 4. whom 5. Who

Answers to Quick Quiz I

1. threw me 2. became, gave him 3. called me 4. sent us 5. received, wrote him, her, and them

Answers to Quick Quiz J

1. To show them 2. Giving her 3. Writing me 4. to tell whom 5. Telling him

Answers to Quick Quiz K

1. gave me than the dentist gave [to] me 2. presented us, presented the agenda [to] us 3. gave them, gave a model [to] them 4. awarded us, citations [to] us 5. brought him and me, brought cards [to] him and brought cards [to] me

Answers to Quick Quiz L

1. for them 2. with him and me 3. between him and her 4. to whomever 5. of them and us

Answers to Review and Practice: Objective Case

Exercise A

1. The interviewer made appointments with Manny, Gloria, and me.
2. Does she remember them?
3. The next order is for Jack and him.
4. Everyone likes them and her.
5. He saw all of his patients except her.
6. Pronouns, she said, drive her and us crazy.
7. They came between Jane and us.
8. Take it from whomever you want to.
9. Write the letter to them and her.
10. The story tells the world about him and us.

Exercise B

Exercise B	Notice that . . .
1. The stories were written by them for a magazine planned by us.	
2. George fought against him and them.	
3. For everyone except her this car will start.	
4. For whom was this written?	this was written for *"him"*; thus, from the results of the *"him test,"* whom is correct
5. Ask the question of whomever you want.	*"him test"*; you want to ask *"him."*
6. The accountant would like to see them and us immediately.	
7. When you get up, give her and us breakfast.	. . . give her breakfast . . . give us breakfast. Give her and us breakfast.
8. These facts should be told to no one but them.	
9. The delegation received us and him.	the delegation received us; the delegation received him
10. Ask the psychologist about whom?	the "him test" applies: ask the psychologist about *"him."*

Exercise C

1. The lake, unfortunately, lay between ~~they~~ them and ~~we~~ us.
2. The dean wrote Tom and ~~he~~ him a letter of recommendation.
3. Doctor Whippet dogged both ~~she~~ her and ~~I~~ me.
4. The film gave ~~he~~ him and ~~she~~ her a new concept of love.
5. Tell the truth to no one but ~~we~~ us.
6. The nurse had previously shot Rupert, ~~she~~ her, and ~~I~~ me full of penicillin.
7. He dedicated the program to the choreographer from ~~who~~ whom he had learned to dance.
8. Disaster loomed ahead for all but ~~we~~ us.
9. The police officer ordered everyone but you and ~~they~~ them and us to leave the room.
10. He wants ~~who~~ whom in his Christmas stocking?

Exercise D

1. She reviewed the latest book for ~~(Robert and Jack)~~ them.
2. Rene brought everybody but ~~(the girl)~~ her and ~~(the two boys)~~ them a gift.
3. The cartoon was a caricature of ~~(what person)~~ whom?
4. Without ~~(the man)~~ him and ~~(the woman)~~ her, life would be meaningless.
5. The sun will rise regardless of you or ~~(six people)~~ them.
6. Someone asked everyone but ~~(the girls)~~ them and ~~(the boy)~~ him for money.
7. When are you giving ~~(Charles)~~ him and me the furniture?
8. She knew everyone except ~~(Tommy)~~ him.
9. Discuss this with ~~(whichever person)~~ whom or whomever you like, but give ~~(Lulu)~~ her your answer today.
10. If you are sick, ~~(what person)~~ whom should I call?

Exercise E

1. The specialists needed ~~he~~ him and ~~I~~ me for the experiment.
2. correct

Notice that ...

3. Tell ~~he~~ him and her why.

4. ~~Who~~ Whom are you. . . ? — you are willing to call *"him."*

5. ~~who~~ whom are we to believe? — we are to believe *"him."*

6. Application blanks were given to everyone but ~~we~~ us and ~~they.~~ them — . . . but they were not given to us and they were not given to them

7. correct

8. ~~Who~~ Whom does the company need? — the company needs *"him."*

9. Is she going to marry ~~he?~~ him

10. I got the answers from ~~she~~ her.

Answers to Quick Quiz M

1. (theirs), (ours) 2. (Whose) 3. (theirs)

Answers to Quick Quiz N

1. (their) details 2. (Our) singing 3. (whose) key 4. (my) smoking, (my) eating 5. (Her) thinking, (their) planning 6. (Their) 7. (Whose) . . . (your) 8. (Its) . . . (our) 9. (Their) 10. (our) 11. (His) . . (their)

Answers to Review and Practice: Possessive Case

Exercise A	Notice that . . .
1. (Your) . . (your)	
2. (mine) . . (yours)	*It's* is not a possessive pronoun, but a contraction of *it is.*

3. Their
4. whose . . . his
5. your — *You're* is not a possessive pronoun, but a contraction of *you are.*

Exercise B

1. their 2. Hers 3. Whose 4. Your 5. our 6. Their, our
7. Whose 8. my 9. hers 10. his

Exercise C

1. c 2. a 3. b 4. b 5. a 6. a 7. b 8. a 9. a 10. a

Answers to Chapter Review and Practice

If you missed this answer . . .	*see section:*	*If you missed this answer . . .*	*see section:*
1. he or I	A	19. Whose	C
2. His	C	20. he	A
3. her and them	B	21. my their	C
4. whoever	A	22. whoever	A
5. I	A	23. your theirs	C
6. ours	C	24. her	B
7. us or them	B	25. whomever	B
8. she	A	26. he and she	A
9. whom	B	27. us	B
10. us	B	28. them and us	B
11. our	C	29. who	A
12. We and they	A	30. her	B
13. him and me	B	31. he and they	A
14. whom	B	32. its	C
15. she and he	A	33. he	A
16. Whose	C	34. she	A
17. hers and ours	C	35. who	A
18. who	A		

Answers to Chapter Test

1. them and her
2. who
3. theirs
4. we
5. whomever
6. we
7. them and me
8. Whose
9. Our
10. we
11. whoever
12. whom
13. she
14. Their
15. them

CHAPTER 8

Run-on Sentences; the Comma Splice

- **Items 105–110 in the Pretest are from this chapter.**
- **A procedure for recognizing and correcting run-ons is on pages 173–174.**

Chapter Contents

RULE: | Separate sentences correctly or join them correctly.

RO = Run-on sentence
CF = Comma fault
CS = Comma splice
CB = Comma blunder
RT = Run-together sentence

The Problem with Run-on Sentences

Two or more sentences* *may* be joined together to form one longer sentence. They should, however, be connected correctly to avoid confusing the reader. When two sentences are combined in a single sentence form, separate them or join them by one of the following:

1. a semicolon (;)
2. a comma(,) + a *coordinating conjunction**
3. a semicolon + a *conjunctive adverb** + a comma

---

*A *sentence* is a group of words that contains at least one subject + verb unit and that communicates a sense of completeness. A subject + verb unit is a clause. A sentence begins with a capital letter and ends with a period, a question mark, or an exclamation mark.

Examples

subj. vb.
(1) *Dogs bark* at night. (dogs + bark = subject + verb unit)

subj. vb. subj. vb.
(2) *Dogs bark* at night, but *owls hoot.* (dogs + bark = subject + verb unit 1; owls + hoot = subject + verb unit 2.)

*A *coordinating conjunction* is a word that joins sentence elements of equal form or function: for example, two subject + verb units. The coordinating conjunctions are *and, but, for, nor, or, so,* and *yet.*
*A *conjunctive adverb* is a word that joins and shows a relationship between the two elements it connects—usually clauses or sentences. Some common conjunctive adverbs are *accordingly, also, anyhow, besides, consequently, furthermore, however, indeed, moreover, nevertheless, otherwise, still, then, therefore.*

"Run-on" sentences are sentences that are not connected correctly. Sections A, B, and C below indicate three typical kinds of run-on sentences, in which the connections are not correct. Each section shows you how to recognize that type of run-on and how to correct it.

(Other names for incorrectly connected sentences are *comma splice, comma fault, comma blunder, fused sentence,* and *run-together sentence.*)

A The Run-On That Has a Comma but No Connective* Between Sentences: the Comma Splice

---

*A *connective* is a word that joins (connects) words or groups of words. Coordinating conjunctions and conjunctive adverbs are connectives.

A-1 Recognizing a run-on that contains a comma but no connective: the comma splice

sentence 1 — sentence 2

Examples **a.** *Most of the children were playing together, Marcia was alone.*
This is a comma splice because the two sentences have a comma but no connective between them. Each is an *independent clause;** each can stand alone as a sentence.

*A clause that communicates a sense of completeness is an *independent clause:*

dogs bark at night

An independent clause can stand alone as a sentence:

Dogs bark at night.

A sentence may include more than one independent clause:

indep. clause — indep. clause
Dogs bark at night, but owls hoot.

Sentence 1: *Most of the children were playing together.*
Sentence 2: *Marcia was alone.*

sentence 1 / indep. clause — sentence 2 / indep. clause

b. *Marriage is a game for two, it should be played without kibitzers.*
This is a comma splice because the two independent clauses (the two sentences) have a comma but no connective between them. Each clause can stand alone as a sentence.

Sentence 1: *Marriage is a game for two.*
Sentence 2: *It should be played without kibitzers.*

sentence 1: dependent clause, independent clause 1 — sentence 2: independent clause 2

c. *Since I got up this morning, I have had a headache, you are the cause of it.*
This is a comma splice because the two sentences have a comma but no connective between them. (The comma in sentence 1 correctly separates the *dependent clause** from the independent clause.)

Sentence 1: *Since I got up this morning, I have had a headache.*
Sentence 2: *You are the cause of it.*

*A clause that does not communicate a sense of completeness is a *dependent clause:*
although dogs bark at night
A dependent clause cannot stand alone as a sentence. Dependent clauses are commonly introduced by expressions such as the following:
after, although, as, as if, as long as, because, before, even though, if, provided, since, that, though, unless, until, what, whatever, when, whenever, where, whereas, which, who, whoever, whose, why.
A sentence may include one or more dependent clauses together with one or more independent clauses:
Although dogs bark at night, owls hoot.
A comma correctly separates the *dependent clause* from the independent clause.

indep. clause 1 — indep. clause 2

d. *When did he get to town, when will he come over?*
The comma incorrectly splices two sentences together.

Sentence 1: *When did he get to town?*
Sentence 2: *When will he come over?*

NOTE: **An Exception to the Rule:**

While independent clauses usually should not be separated merely by commas, they may be when the independent clauses are *very* short and form a series:

ind. cl. 1 — ind. cl. 2 — ind. cl. 3

Example I ran, I jumped, I fell.

A-2 Three methods of correcting a run-on that contains a comma but no connective

Correct a run-on that contains a comma but no connective *by placing a coordinating conjunction* after the comma.*

*The coordinating conjunctions are *and, but, for, nor, or, so,* and *yet.*

Examples

a. incorrect: *Most of the children were playing together, Marcia was alone.* (run-on)
correct: *Most of the children were playing together*[, but] *Marcia was alone.*

b. incorrect: *When did he get to town, when will he come over?* (run-on)
correct: *When did he get to town*[, and] *when will he come over?*

OR

Correct a run-on that contains a comma but no connective *by changing the comma to a semicolon (;).*

Examples

a. incorrect: *Marriage is a game for two, it should be played without kibitzers.* (run-on)
correct: *Marriage is a game for two*[;] *it should be played without kibitzers.*

b. incorrect: *Since I got up this morning, I have had a headache, you are the cause of it.* (run-on)
correct: *Since I got up this morning, I have had a headache*[;] *you are the cause of it.*

OR

Correct a run-on that contains a comma but no connective *by making each independent clause stand as a separate sentence*.

Examples

a. incorrect: *Most of the children were playing together, Marcia was alone.* (run-on)
correct: *Most of the children were playing together*[.] *Marcia was alone.*

b. incorrect: *When did he get into town, when will he come over?* (run-on)
correct: *When did he get into town*[? W]*hen will he come over?*

Quick Quiz: A

Some of the sentences below are correct; others are run-ons. *Write* **C** in front of each correct sentence, and *write* **run-on** in front of each run-on.

Model: run-on The heat wave broke a record, it lasted ten days.

1. ______________ Since he came to town, he has made a nuisance of himself, I wish he would leave.

2. ______________ Knapsacks were packed, mules were loaded, and hikers started their journey.

3. ______________ The operation went quite well, the surgeon decided not to go back for the lost sponge.

4. ______________ At the bottom of the mine shaft, everything was in darkness, it was difficult to see where the cave-in had occurred.

5. ______________ The knife was dull, so I sharpened it.

6. ______________ The ragweed bloomed, the goldenrod bloomed, and my hay fever bloomed.

Answers to Quick Quiz A are on page 179.

B The Run-On That Has a Connective but No Punctuation Between Sentences

B-1 Recognizing a run-on that contains a connective but no punctuation

Examples

indep. clause 1 — indep. clause 2

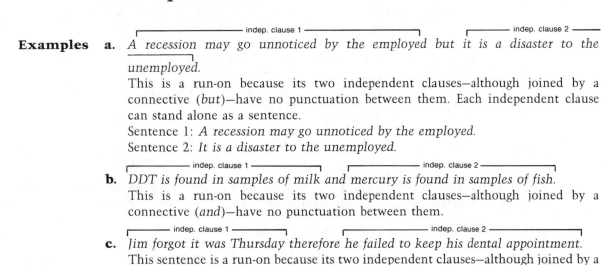

a. *A recession may go unnoticed by the employed but it is a disaster to the unemployed.*
This is a run-on because its two independent clauses—although joined by a connective (*but*)—have no punctuation between them. Each independent clause can stand alone as a sentence.
Sentence 1: *A recession may go unnoticed by the employed.*
Sentence 2: *It is a disaster to the unemployed.*

indep. clause 1 — indep. clause 2

b. *DDT is found in samples of milk and mercury is found in samples of fish.*
This is a run-on because its two independent clauses—although joined by a connective (*and*)—have no punctuation between them.

indep. clause 1 — indep. clause 2

c. *Jim forgot it was Thursday therefore he failed to keep his dental appointment.*
This sentence is a run-on because its two independent clauses—although joined by a connective (therefore)—have no punctuation between them.
Sentence 1: *Jim forgot it was Thursday.*
Sentence 2: *He failed to keep his dental appointment.*

B-2 Three methods of correcting a run-on that contains a connective but no punctuation

Correct a run-on that contains a connective but no punctuation *by separating the run-on into sentences.*

run-on

Examples **a.** incorrect: *A recession may go unnoticed by the employed but it is a disaster to the unemployed.*

correct: *A recession may go unnoticed by the employed . But it is a disaster to the unemployed.*

NOTE: Some authorities consider it incorrect to begin a sentence with *and* or *but.*

run-on

b. incorrect: *DDT is found in samples of milk and mercury is found in samples of fish.*

correct: *DDT is found in samples of milk . Mercury is found in samples of fish.*

run-on

c. incorrect: *Jim forgot it was Thursday therefore he failed to keep his dental appointment.*

correct: *Jim forgot it was Thursday . Therefore, he failed to keep his dental appointment.* (A comma generally follows a conjunctive adverb.)

OR

Correct a run-on that contains a coordinating conjunction but no punctuation *by placing a comma before the connective.*

run-on

Examples **a.** incorrect: *A recession may go unnoticed by the employed but it is a disaster to the unemployed.*

correct: *A recession may go unnoticed by the employed , but it is a disaster to the unemployed.*

run-on

b. incorrect: *DDT is found in samples of milk and mercury is found in samples of fish.*

correct: *DDT is found in samples of milk , and mercury is found in samples of fish.*

OR

Correct a run-on that contains a conjunctive adverb but no punctuation *by placing a semicolon before the connective and a comma after it.*

run-on

Examples **a.** incorrect: *Jim forgot it was Thursday therefore he failed to keep his dental appointment.*

correct: *Jim forgot it was Thursday ; therefore, he failed to keep his dental appointment.*

b. incorrect: *The man's fingerprints were found on the buried murder weapon* (run-on) *moreover the suspect's own dog dug it up.*

correct: *The man's fingerprints were found on the buried murder weapon; moreover, the suspect's own dog dug it up.*

Quick Quiz: B

*Some of the sentences below are correct; others are run-ons. Write **C** in front of each correct sentence, and write **run-on** in front of each run-on.*

Model: run-on An orchestra has string instruments in it but a band does not.

1. ____________ Hal was fired, yet his work was good.
2. ____________ Home cooking is often simple nevertheless it is usually tasty.
3. ____________ Melvin left the beach before the sun came out and the next day he was the only one of the group without a sunburn.
4. ____________ Many of her facts are incorrect however her theory still holds promise.
5. ____________ After the fight, Jeff left Alice, and he has not come back yet.
6. ____________ To err is human; besides, to forgive is sometimes impossible.

Answers to Quick Quiz B are on page 179.

C The Run-On That Has Neither Punctuation nor Connective Between Sentences

C-1 Recognizing a run-on that contains neither punctuation nor connective

Examples **a.** *I cooked the egg for two minutes the white was still nearly raw.* (indep. clause 1: I cooked the egg for two minutes; indep. clause 2: the white was still nearly raw)

This is a run-on because the two independent clauses have neither punctuation nor connective between them.

Sentence 1: *I cooked the egg for two minutes.*
Sentence 2: *The white was still nearly raw.*

indep. clause 1 / indep. clause 2

b. *Yesterday the painters finished decorating our house we moved back today.*

Sentence 1: *Yesterday the painters finished decorating our house.*
Sentence 2: *We moved back today.*

sentence 1 / sentence 2
dep. clause / indep. clause / indep. clause

c. *Because Ron married Cleo, Chuck was unhappy he sulked for two weeks.*
This is a run-on because the two sentences have neither punctuation nor connective between them. (The comma in sentence 1 correctly separates the dependent clause from the independent clause.)

Sentence 1: *Because Ron married Cleo, Chuck was unhappy.*
Sentence 2: *He sulked for two weeks.*

C-2 Four methods of correcting a run-on that contains neither punctuation nor connective

Correct a run-on that contains neither punctuation nor connective *by adding a comma and a coordinating conjunction.*

Examples

a. incorrect: *I cooked the egg for two minutes the white was still nearly raw.* (run-on)
correct: *I cooked the egg for two minutes [, but] the white was still nearly raw.*

b. incorrect: *Yesterday the painters finished decorating our house we moved back today.* (run-on)
correct: *Yesterday the painters finished decorating our house [, and] we moved back today.*

OR

Correct a run-on that contains neither punctuation nor connective *by adding a semicolon.*

Examples

a. incorrect: *I cooked the egg for two minutes the white was still nearly raw.* (run-on)
correct: *I cooked the egg for two minutes [;] the white was still nearly raw.*

b. incorrect: *Because Ron married Cleo, Chuck was unhappy he sulked for two weeks.* (run-on)
correct: Because Ron married Cleo, Chuck was unhappy [;] he sulked for two weeks.

OR

Correct a run-on that contains neither punctuation nor connective *by adding a semicolon, a conjunctive adverb, and a comma.*

Examples

a. incorrect: *Yesterday the painters finished decorating our house we moved back today.* (run-on)
correct: *Yesterday the painters finished decorating our house [; therefore,] we moved back today.*

b. incorrect: *Because Ron married Cleo, Chuck was unhappy* run-on *he sulked for two weeks.*

correct: *Because Ron married Cleo, Chuck was unhappy* [*; consequently,*] *he sulked for two weeks.*

OR

Correct a run-on that contains neither punctuation nor connective *by separating the run-on into sentences.*

Examples **a.** incorrect: *I cooked the egg for two minutes* run-on *the white was still nearly raw.*

correct: *I cooked the egg for two minutes* [*. T*] *he white was still nearly raw.*

b. incorrect: *Yesterday the painters finished decorating our house* run-on *we moved back today.*

correct: *Yesterday the painters finished decorating our house* [*. W*] *e moved back today.*

Quick Quiz: C

Some of the sentences below are correct; others are run-ons. Write **C** *in front of each correct sentence,* and *write* **run-on** *in front of each run-on.*

Model: run-on He came to the window I did not see him.

1. ________ Because Pablo is away, all his friends are cleaning up his studio he is an extremely messy painter.
2. ________ No one actually saw the damage, but it was said to be great.
3. ________ The company will not sell the equipment it will lease it.
4. ________ Since the bookstore has moved, both quality and quantity of books have decreased.
5. ________ He told me the same story he told you I cannot be sure where the truth lies.
6. ________ During the last five days, Mona has been wonderful to me; however, I cannot predict what the next week will bring.

Answers to Quick Quiz C are on page 179.

Procedure for Recognizing and Correcting Run-Ons

run-on The fishing boats rode at anchor they swung their prows toward the incoming tide.

Step 1: Decide the type of run-on you have.

The three common types are

Type I: two sentences *with a comma—but no connective*—between them

Type II: two sentences *with a connective—but no punctuation*—between them

Type III: two sentences *with neither connective nor punctuation* between them.

Step 2: Correct the run-on through one of the following methods:

For Type I

(1) Place a coordinating conjunction after the comma.

OR

(2) Change the comma to a semicolon.

OR

(3) Make two separate sentences.

For Type II

(1) If the connective is a coordinating conjunction, place a comma before it.

OR

(2) If the connective is a conjunctive adverb, place a semicolon before and a comma after it.

OR

(3) Make two separate sentences.

For Type III

(1) Separate the two parts with a comma followed by a coordinating conjunction.

OR

(2) Separate the two parts with a semicolon.

OR

(3) Separate the two parts with a semicolon, a conjunctive adverb, and a comma (in that order).

OR

(4) Separate the two parts into two sentences.

The example is a Type III run-on. Corrected, it might read:

The fishing boats rode at anchor, and they swung their prows. . . .

OR

The fishing boats rode at anchor; they swung their prows. . . .

OR

The fishing boats rode at anchor; consequently, they swung their prows. . . .

OR

The fishing boats rode at anchor. They swung their prows. . . .

REVIEW AND PRACTICE

Each of the sections of this Review and Practice is different. Do some exercises in each section, then check your answers and decide which sections—if any—you need to continue to work through. Answers are on pages 179–182.

Exercise A Some of the sentences below are correct; others are run-ons. *Write* ***C*** in front of each correct sentence, and *write* ***RO*** in front of each run-on.

Model: RO ______ People who wear coats made from the skins of wild animals contribute to the extinction of many species the coats look better on their original owners.

1. ______ Camping is a lot of trouble moreover, it leads to many mosquito bites.
2. ______ Travel gets into a person's blood but it is a legal addiction.
3. ______ When it works, a clothes dryer is wonderful; however, when it breaks down, having wet clothes drying all over the house is not so wonderful.
4. ______ Arnold felt better he was still a very sick man.
5. ______ Their coach was less than a genius, their team never placed higher than sixth.
6. ______ Robert Jones is a native of Portland, Maine; he is a well-known druggist in his community.
7. ______ He had signed a statement saying he would leave the country voluntarily he was not technically deported.
8. ______ The contract specifies that the order must be delivered by June first, and failure to deliver the order could nullify the agreement.
9. ______ Since he told her to work harder, she has practiced six hours a day on the piano, she has improved her playing, and she has lost her roommates.
10. ______ The snow fell for days, drifts covered houses, many people were lost, and normal conditions did not return for almost two weeks.

Exercise B *Correct* each run-on by adding a comma, a coordinating conjunction, or both. Using the model as an example, mark the point of your correction as necessary.

Model: The day was terrible, but the night was worse.

1. I do not hate him I do pity him.
2. Her apple pie may not be perfect but it is better than any other pie I have eaten.
3. The train came to a screeching halt, the man next to me slid off his seat.
4. Dan ordered pizza and garlic bread and I ordered lasagna.
5. You have this job now you might as well try to keep it.
6. The bus runs infrequently in our area of the city, this is the second fare increase in the last eight months.
7. The consequences of political inertia are frightening a nation needs to guard itself from those who would exploit its apathy.
8. It is necessary to know in what directions our social customs are going, it is equally important to know from what roots they derive.

9. He learned the basics of computers on the job and he was able to suggest improvements in production methods.

10. We should go home now or you should warm up the coffee.

Exercise C *Correct* each run-on either by *adding a* ***semicolon*** or by *changing* incorrect punctuation to a semicolon.

Model: If there is any oil, the company will find it ^;^ if there is none, the company will drill elsewhere.

1. Brent did not seem to be lying I continued to doubt him, nevertheless.
2. Anne Boleyn, King Henry's second queen, finally lost her head Mary, Queen of Scots, too, lost hers.
3. Guppies are interesting fish, they give birth to live young.
4. The cup was cracked, the saucer was broken.
5. Some people think the game of curling is fun I don't even know what it is.
6. During the past year I was in Africa now I am home for a two-week vacation.
7. The study of grammar should make one's use of language more effective some people feel grammar exists solely to build character through suffering.
8. If we had followed his directions, we would be there by now, since we did not, it is our own fault that we are lost.
9. It was the usual idyllic picnic we had dry bread sandwiches, warm beer, and ant-covered potato salad.
10. Rock climbing is one sport I can understand intellectually I cannot, however, feel myself in the climber's place.

Exercise D *Correct* each run-on by adding a ***semicolon*** and a ***comma***.

Model: The quartet could have been worse ^;^ indeed ^,^ all the singers could have been sopranos.

1. Zachary was stuck in the window however his head and one arm dangled inside.
2. Jazz is one of the truly American music forms nevertheless few people know that its roots lie deep in Black folk culture.
3. Allergy is a very ticklish subject besides scientists have only scratched its surface.
4. Claustrophobia harms the person who suffers from it however pyromania harms others.
5. Pre-Columbian art is little known nevertheless it is just as rich and varied as European art.

Exercise E *Correct* each run-on by ***adding a conjunctive adverb and necessary punctuation***. *Mark* the point of your addition accurately.

; however,

Model: The Surgeon General says that cigarettes are a health hazard‸ I cannot give them up.

1. He felt at home in Greece, he wondered if he had ever really lived anywhere else.
2. Rome was not built in a day I don't expect you to follow Rome's schedule in finishing this workbench.
3. I missed the last half of the game, I don't know whether to cheer or to cry.
4. The sheep were reported to have died from a toxic weed they had been less than 100 miles from a biological warfare testing ground.
5. I would like to report that this telephone is out of order I am unable to call the phone company.

Exercise F *Correct* each run-on by separating it into two sentences.

⊙ However,

Model: Halibut is a strange-looking fish‸ ~~however, i~~t is delicious to eat.

1. Ike, closely followed by the lion, reached the lake Ike jumped in.
2. The carpenter knew he should brace the wooden beams with metal supports instead, he added only one more nail to each beam.
3. Walter should have come in from the rain he already had a cold.
4. Who called earlier was it Russell or Eva?
5. Frederick the Great was a complex man indeed, he could plan battles and play his flute with equal virtuosity.
6. Much can be said about a culture from its slang English relies on the vegetable kingdom for many of its descriptive slang words.
7. This breakfast food is advertised as making all sorts of noises with the headache I have this morning, I hope mine's quiet.
8. At my house we use the unabridged dictionary my two-year-old son sits on it at the dinner table.
9. Credit card abuse is increasing someday we may have "Credit Card Users Anonymous."
10. In times of social unrest, many people are willing to part with some of their own freedoms rarely, however, are lost freedoms restored.

Answers to Review and Practice are on pages 179–182.

CHAPTER TEST

Some of the following sentences are correct; some are run-ons. *Mark* correct sentences ***C;*** *mark* run-ons ***RO***.

Model: ____C____ Yesterday I rode horseback, and today I am sore all over.

1. ________ It is important that you leave now, I shall pack your bag immediately.
2. ________ The report was made to the chairman, the committee issued a subpoena, and Williams was called to testify.
3. ________ A diamond can be a playing field, or it can be a playing card.
4. ________ Marriage and a family are not the only things people want; most want security, both emotional and economic.
5. ________ He used to go hunting for wild mushrooms now he is recovering from toadstool poisoning.
6. ________ Ask him to come to dinner, he seems to need a square meal.
7. ________ Elsie's nephew stepped in some paint he has left his mark.
8. ________ Hard rock may be good for the soul, but it is hard on the ear drums.
9. ________ Most people celebrate the new year but the time of celebration varies.
10. ________ The local utility company is urging people to use more electrical appliances yet it is also warning about potential power shortages.

Answers to Chapter Test are on page 182.

ANSWERS: CHAPTER 8

Answers to Quick Quiz A

1. run-on 2. C (a series of short independent clauses) 3. run-on 4. run-on 5. C 6. C (a series of short independent clauses)

Answers to Quick Quiz B

1. C 2. run-on 3. run-on 4. run-on 5. C 6. C

Answers to Quick Quiz C

1. run-on 2. C 3. run-on 4. C 5. run-on 6. C

Answers to Chapter Review and Practice

Exercise A	**Notice that . . .**
1. RO	corrected: Camping is a lot of trouble; moreover, it leads to many mosquito bites.
2. RO	corrected: Travel gets into a person's blood, but it is a legal addiction.
3. C	
4. RO	corrected: Arnold felt better. He was still a very sick man. OR Arnold felt better; he was still a very sick man. OR Arnold felt better, but he was still a very sick man. OR Arnold felt better; however, he was still a very sick man.
5. RO	corrected: Example: Their coach was less than a genius; their team never placed higher than sixth.
6. C	
7. RO	corrected: Example: He signed a statement saying he would leave the country voluntarily; therefore, technically, he was not deported.

8. C

9. C — This sentence contains a series: *she has practiced six hours a day on the piano, she has improved her playing, she has lost her roommates.* The following would also be correct: Since he told her to work harder, she has practiced six hours a day on the piano; she has improved her playing; and she has lost her roommates.

10. C — This sentence is a series of four short independent clauses.

Exercise B

In some cases, any one of several coordinating conjunctions might be correct. Some alternate coordinating conjunctions are given in parentheses.

Notice that . . .

1. I do not hate him, but I do pity him. (yet)
2. Her apple pie may not be perfect, but it is. . . .
3. The train came to a screeching halt, and the man. . . .
4. Dan ordered pizza and garlic bread, and I ordered lasagna. — This run-on contains two *ands.* One *and* links two items, pizza and garlic bread. The other *and* links two independent clauses and requires a comma.
5. You have this job, and now . . . . (so)
6. The bus runs infrequently in our area of the city, and this . . . . (but, yet)
   OR
   The bus etc. . . . This is the second . . . ,
7. The consequences of political inertia are frightening, so a nation. . . :
8. It is necessary to know in what directions our social customs are going, but it is. . . . (and, yet)
9. He learned the basics of computers on the job, and. . . .
10. We should go home now, or you should. . . .

Exercise C

1. Brent did not seem to be lying; I. . . .
2. Anne Boleyn, King Henry's second queen, finally lost her head; Mary. . . .
3. Guppies are interesting fish; they. . . .
4. The cup was cracked; the. . . .
5. Some people think the game of curling is fun; I. . . .
6. During the past year I was in Africa; now. . . .
7. The study of grammar should make one's use of language more effective; some. . . .
8. If we had followed his directions, we should be there by now; since we did not, it. . . .
9. It was the usual idyllic picnic; we. . . .
10. Rock climbing is one sport I can understand intellectually; I. . . .

Exercise D

1. Zachary was stuck in the window; however, his. . . .
2. Jazz is one of the truly American music forms; nevertheless, few. . . .
3. Allergy is a very ticklish subject; besides, scientists. . . .
4. Claustrophobia harms the person who suffers from it; however, pyromania. . . .
5. Pre-Columbian art is little known; nevertheless, it. . . .

Exercise E

In most cases, any one of several conjunctive adverbs might be correct. A list of conjunctive adverbs is given on page 166.

1. He felt at home in Greece; indeed, he. . . .
2. Rome was not built in a day; however, I. . . .
3. I missed the last half of the game; consequently, I. . . .
4. The sheep were reported to have died from a toxic weed; however, they. . . .
5. I would like to report that this telephone is out of order; however, I. . . .

Exercise F

1. Ike, closely followed by the lion, reached the lake. Ike jumped in.
2. The carpenter knew he should brace the wooden beams with metal supports. Instead, he. . . .
3. Walter should have come in from the rain. He. . . .

4. Who called earlier? Was it Russell or Eva?

5. Frederick the Great was a complex man. Indeed, he could. . . .

6. Much can be said about a culture from its slang. English. . . .

7. This breakfast food is advertised as making all sorts of noises. With. . . .

8. At my house we use the unabridged dictionary. My. . . .

9. Credit card abuse is increasing. Someday. . . .

10. In times of social unrest, many people are willing to part with some of their own freedoms. Rarely, however, are. . . .

Answers to Chapter Test

1. RO 2. C 3. C 4. C 5. RO 6. RO
7. RO 8. C 9. RO 10. RO

CHAPTER 9

Punctuation

- **Items 111–175 in the Pretest are from this chapter.**

Chapter Contents

A Period ⊡

RULES:	1. Use a period at the end of each declarative and imperative sentence. 2. Use periods with certain abbreviations.

A-1 Ending declarative and imperative sentences

A declarative sentence makes a statement and ends with a period.

Examples **a.** The earth is not quite round.

b. He came to the rehearsal carrying his cello on his back.

c. I asked him if the book was worth reading.

An imperative sentence expresses a *command* or a *request* and ends with a period unless it is said with urgency. (See Exclamation Mark.)

Examples **a.** Get me a hot dog.

b. Take the tools outside.

c. Please scratch my back.

A-2 Ending abbreviations

An abbreviation is a *shortened form* of a word or group of words. Many abbreviations or their parts end with periods. (When in doubt, see the dictionary.)

Examples

a.	B.A.	Bachelor of Arts (She got her *B.A.*)
b.	B.C.	Before Christ (Confucius, in 500 *B.C.*, completed the *Book of Odes.*)
c.	Nev.	Nevada
d.	etc.	et cetera (Notice that some abbreviations contain no capitals.)
e.	rpm	revolutions per minute (Notice that some abbreviations contain no periods.)
f.	PCP	phencyclidine (Notice that some abbreviations do not echo the sound of the word or words they represent.)

B Question Mark [?]

RULE: Use a question mark at the end of a question.

Examples

a. Who invented the electric ice cream freezer?

b. Is the cellist's bow broken?

c. I am quite confident, but are you sure you can do it?

C Exclamation Mark (Exclamation Point) [!]

RULE: Use an exclamation mark at the end of an exclamatory expression.

Exclamatory sentences and exclamatory expressions are meant to convey *strong feeling*.

Examples

a. I hate him!

b. Run for your life!

c. Help!

Review and Practice: Period, Question Mark, Exclamation Mark

End each sentence with the correct punctuation mark and write abbreviations as indicated.

Model: Does Joe drink ?

1. Call the police
2. Henry says that the tractor won't run because it is out of gas

3. Why do you ask me
4. Get out of my way
5. How is Bill going to be able to ask Sue to go to the party if he has already asked Jane to go with him
6. The abbreviation for "et cetera" is ____________
7. Is he here
8. Jim asked if I would go with you
9. Janice said that they came for the ride
10. The abbreviation for "Before Christ" is ____________
11. I don't understand the theory of relativity
12. The speaker asked if anyone had another question

Answers to Review and Practice: Period, Question Mark, Exclamation Mark are on page 233.

D Apostrophe [']

RULES:	1. Use an apostrophe to show omission. 2. Use an apostrophe to show possession.

D-1 Showing omission

Use an apostrophe to show *omission of one or more letters* in a contraction.*

*contraction: A *contraction* is either 1) a single word formed from two or more words from which one or more letters have been omitted or 2) a single word shortened by the omission of letters: *it's* formed from *it is*, *o'clock* formed from *of the clock*, *can't* formed from *can not* are contractions.

NOTE: Even though contractions are common in daily speech and in written dialogue, avoid them in formal writing.

Examples a. Apostrophe replacing the letter ***a*** to form a contraction:
I + am = *I'm*
they + are = *they're*
we + are = *we're*
you + are = *you're*

b. Apostrophe replacing the letter ***i*** to form a contraction:
it + is = *it's*
it + is = *'tis* (archaic*)

*Archaic: Formerly common, but presently seldom used

she + is = *she's*
that + is = *that's*
what + is = *what's*
who + is = *who's*

c. Apostrophe replacing the letter ***o*** to form a contraction:
are + not = *aren't*
could + not = *couldn't*
did + not = *didn't*
do + not = *don't*
has + not = *hasn't*
is + not = *isn't*
should + not = *shouldn't*
were + not = *weren't*
would + not = *wouldn't*

d. Apostrophe replacing ***two or more letters*** to form a contraction:
can + not = *can't*
I + shall = *I'll*
I + will = *I'll*
I + would = *I'd*
I + have = *I've*
it + has = *it's*
of the clock = *o'clock*
will + not = *won't*

e. Apostrophe replacing the letter **v** to form a contraction:
over = *o'er*
even = *e'en*
ever = *e'er*
(See the dictionary for the uses of *o'er, e'en* and *e'er.)*

Quick Quiz: A

Write *the contractions of the words in parentheses.*

Model: He (could not) couldn't come.

1. (I will) ________________ be with you in a minute.
2. (It is) ________________ five (of the clock) ________________.
3. John (would not) ________________ go there if you paid him.

4. (What is) ______________ her name?

5. (I would) ______________ say (they are) ______________ happy.

Answers to Quick Quiz A are on page 233.

D-2 Showing possession

Use an apostrophe + s ['s] to show possession in a noun that does not end in the letter *s*.

*A *noun* is a word that names something. *Charles, book, idea* are nouns.

		nouns (and some pronouns) not ending in s	noun + 's
Examples	**a.** the fender of this	car = this car's fender	
	b. the hobby of the	boy = the boy's hobby	
	c. the stories of the	author = the author's stories	
	d. the coats of the	men = the men's coats	
	e. the voices of the	children = the children's voices	
	f. the activities of the	alumni = the alumni's activities	
	g. the opinion of	anybody = anybody's opinion	
	h. the decision of	someone else = someone else's opinion	

NOTE: For two or more words used as a unit, you generally add an apostrophe to the last word: somebody else's name, but somebody's name.

Use just an apostrophe ['] to show possession in a noun that ends in the letter *s (or ends in an *s* or *z sound*).**

* nouns ending in s: Most *nouns ending in s are plural* (meaning more than one); most nouns *not ending in s are singular* (meaning one).

sing. plural
The *speaker* talked about *gophers*.

		nouns ending in s	nouns + '
Examples	**a.** the fenders of both	cars = both cars' fenders	
	b. the advantages of the	others = the others' advantages	
	c. a leave of three	days = a three days' leave	
	d. the bindings of the	books = the books' bindings	
	e. daisies worth two	dollars = two dollars' worth of daisies	
	f. the work of and the work of the	Charles = Charles' work and the Joneses' work Joneses	
	g. The honesty of	Liz = Liz's honesty (or Liz' honesty)	

NOTE: For a *singular* noun ending in *s (Charles),* you may add an 's or an ' alone.

Quick Quiz: B

Reword *each of the following sentences,* **using an apostrophe** *to show possession.*

Model: I walked along the *edge of the cliff.*

Reworded: *I walked along the cliff's edge.*

1. The end of the day finally arrived.
2. Look at the exhibit of these painters.
3. We were in the eye of the hurricane.
4. Where is the dressing room of the women?
5. The hobbies of the boy include cross-country skiing.
6. They found the tracks of many elephants.

Answers to Quick Quiz B are on page 233.

Form the possessive of a *hyphenated noun* through the part *following the last hyphen.*

Examples

a. the name of my mother-in-law = my *mother-in-law's* name

b. the club of the mothers-in-law = the *mothers-in-law's* club

c. the lid of the jack-in-the box = the *jack-in-the-box's* lid

d. the blossoms of the johnny-jump-up = the *johnny-jump-up's* blossoms

Form the possessive of nouns joined by *and* as follows:
When possession is *individual,* show possession through each noun.
When possession is joint, show possession through the noun following the last *and.*

Examples

a.	individual possession: Each noun shows possession.	The lives of Lewis and Clark were different = *Lewis's* and *Clark's* lives were different.
	joint possession: The noun following the last *and* shows possession.	The expedition of Lewis and Clark started in 1804 = Lewis and *Clark's* expedition started in 1804.
b.	individual possession:	The knapsacks of John, Mary, and Suzie = *John's, Mary's,* and *Suzie's* knapsacks
	joint possession:	the shop of John, Mary, and Suzie = John, Mary, and *Suzie's* shop

Quick Quiz: C

Reword *each of the following sentences using* **an apostrophe** *to show possession.*

Model: The *wool of the sheep* was sheared.

Reworded: The sheep's wool was sheared.

1. What is the name of the president-elect?

____

2. The scales of the fish were luminescent.

____

3. The hats of Tom, Dick, and Harry are made of felt.

____

4. The sentences of the court-martial were unusually severe.

____

5. *H. M. S. Pinafore* is one of the funniest of the operas of Gilbert and Sullivan.

____

Answers to Quick Quiz C are on page 234.

D-3 Using apostrophes for other purposes

To form the plurals of letters

Examples **a.** Cross your *t's.*

b. Learn your *abc's.*

c. Who is going to teach our children the three *R's?*

To form the plurals of dates and other figures

Examples **a.** It happened in the *1930's.*

b. I will need three *4 × 4's* to shore up this wall.

c. Here are two *5's* and two *10's.*

To form the plurals of words named as words

Examples **a.** His promises contain too many *if's, and's,* and *but's.*

b. She didn't like his *thank you's.*

c. They had said their *good-by's.*

To indicate omission in dates

Examples **a.** Most *'49ers* didn't find gold.

b. Do we still have the spirit of *'76?*

c. She will graduate in the class of '87.

NOTE: **The one function of punctuation is to clarify meaning.** Some writers and publishers omit apostrophes in the above cases as long as no possible confusion of meaning results.

Quick Quiz: D

Add *any needed apostrophes.*

Model: The Civil Rights Movement came to prominence in the 1960**'**s.

1. Be sure to dot you is.

2. He said his hellos when he returned.

3. How may 2 × 4s should I get?

Answers to Quick Quiz D are on page 234.

D-4 Correctly omitting apostrophes

Some words—possessive pronouns—have the idea of possession built into them and, therefore, *never use apostrophes.**

*See page 149 for a chart of easily confused pronoun forms.

Examples

a. *yours* — If the house is *yours,* why did you knock at the door?

b. *his* — *His* eyes are brown.

c. *hers* — Honesty is a characteristic of *hers.*

d. *its* — The dog chased *its* tail.
Be careful not to confuse *its* with the *contraction* ***it's.*** Use this test to see if *its* requires an apostrophe: substitute *it is* for *its.* If *it is* ***does not*** make sense in the sentence, use *its* without an apostrophe. (The dog chased *it is* tail. Since this ***does not*** make sense, *its* is correct: The dog chased *its* tail.) Use ***it's*** only where *it is* does make sense.

e. *ours* — We are staying here since the farm is *ours.*

f. *theirs* — He is a friend of *theirs.*

g. *whose* — *Whose* slide rule did he use?
Be careful not to confuse *whose* with the contraction ***who's.*** Use this test to see which is correct: substitute *who is* for *whose* or *who's.* *Who is* slide rule did he use? Since this ***does not*** make sense, the correct word is *whose: Whose* slide rule did he use?

Quick Quiz: E

Circle the correct word in parentheses.

Model: I wonder (who's, whose) house that is.

1. (Whose, Who's) coming?

2. (Its, It's) Sandra.

3. (Whose, Who's) coat is she wearing?
4. (Its, It's) not mine, but I like (its, it's) color.

Answers to Quick Quiz E are on page 234.

REVIEW AND PRACTICE: APOSTROPHE

Exercise A Add ***apostrophes*** *in the sentences below to signify that letters or numbers have been omitted.*

Model: Although *he's* my friend, *I'm* not sure *I'd* trust him.

1. He doesnt need me any more.
2. Youre right, and Im wrong.
3. Its none of my business.
4. Theyre coming for you!
5. Shes the one whos to blame.
6. Arent you ready yet?
7. I shouldnt let you in.
8. The rains of the winter of 39 havent been equalled yet.
9. Ill guess shell be coming around the mountain.
10. Speak when youre angry, and youll make the best speech youll ever regret.

Exercise B Circle *the correct word in parentheses.*

Model: He set aside one (days', day's) profits.

1. Ted doubted the (mans, man's) honesty.
2. Dont tell me (her, hers) age.
3. (Whose, Who's) bright idea was it?
4. (Phyllis', Phyllis's) car chugged slowly over the crest of the hill.
5. He turned the plane toward the (suns', sun's) light.
6. (It's, Its) time for us to think things over.
7. (James', James's) name was on her lips.
8. Even if I sell my property, they will keep (theirs, there's).

Exercise C *One word in each of the following sentences should show possession.* Circle *the word* and add *an* **apostrophe,** *if necessary.*

Model: He found the old raccoon coat in his father's closet.

1. The steeplejack climbed up the steeples north side.
2. When I heard the description, I knew the stolen car was ours.
3. Stanley sent Mr. Sandovals steamroller rumbling down the ravine.
4. I cannot compute this rectangles area.
5. Whose coat is it?
6. Give me Charles overseas address.
7. Both clocks pendulums had stopped swinging.
8. Save me from its grip!
9. When the detective questioned her, she admitted the phone number was hers.
10. The three farmers silos were being cleared of rats.

Answers to Review and Practice: Apostrophe are on page 234.

E Comma ,

RULE: Use a comma (or commas) to separate or to enclose certain elements within a sentence.

The comma insures clear writing and accurate reading. It is a vocal pause.

E-1 Separating certain elements within a sentence

Place a comma before the coordinating conjunction when two independent clauses* are joined by a *coordinating conjunction (and, but, for, nor, or, so, yet).**

*independent clause: An *independent clause* is a group of words that contains a subject + verb unit and that communicates a sense of completeness. (The subject of a clause is the person or thing that the clause is about. The verb tells what the subject *is,* what the subject *does,* or what action the subject *receives.* A clause generally includes more words than just the subject and its verb.)

subj. vb.
John loves Mary

An independent clause can stand alone as a sentence: *John loves Mary.*

*See Chapter 8 for a fuller discussion of this use of the comma.

Examples

indep. clause 1 — indep. clause 2

a. Our one-story house collapsed, *but* this high-rise apartment building stood during the earthquake.

indep. clause 1 — indep. clause 2

b. He returned, *for* his money was gone.
Omitting the comma before the conjunction *for* can result in ambiguity.
He returned for his money . . .

indep. clause 1 — indep. clause 2

c. Leave, *or* I shall leave.

d. According to *Newsweek*, some girls still believe they can get pregnant by swimming in a public pool, *and* some take showers in their underwear.

e. The lightning flashed and the thunder roared.

NOTE: The comma may be omitted when the two clauses are short and closely related, when a pause is not needed, and when ambiguity does not result.

Place a comma after each item in a series* unless all items are joined by coordinating conjunctions.

---

*series: A *series* consists of *three* or more items.
He bought *books, records,* and *etchings.*
He followed her *to the car, to the store,* and *to work.*

Examples

a. We visited Italy, France, *and* England.

b. We climbed over rocks, into ravines, across streams looking for the lost child.

NOTE: A series does not necessarily have a coordinating conjunction separating its last two elements.

c. A delicate, gray, metal mobile won first prize.

d. The dodo is extinct, the brown pelican will be gone, *and* several other species of birds are in grave danger of extinction.

e. I will go by plane or pony or pogo stick.

NOTE: The items in this series are joined by coordinating conjunctions, so no commas are needed.

f. Staging, acting, directing—all were excellent.

Quick Quiz: F

Mark *the correct sentence in each pair.*

Model: (a.) De Mille, Griffith, and Eisenstein were three early motion picture directors.
b. De Mille Griffith and Eisenstein were three early motion picture directors.

1. a. This house is built of brick stone and wood.
   b. This house is built of brick, stone, and wood.

2. a. Walter swam played eighteen holes of golf and went out to dinner.
   b. Walter swam, played eighteen holes of golf, and went out to dinner.

3. a. Get in the car start the engine, and drive away.
   b. Get in the car, start the engine, and drive away.

4. a. The old, battered, rundown warehouse was demolished.
   b. The old battered rundown warehouse was demolished.

Answers to Quick Quiz F are on page 235.

When two or more adjectives* precede a noun, separate those adjectives from one another by commas.

---

*adjective: An *adjective* is a word that describes (modifies) a noun or a noun substitute.

noun
The *tiny, red, semi-precious* garnet sparkled.

Tiny, red, and *semi-precious* are adjectives.

NOTE: Do **not** use a comma between an adjective and a noun that immediately follows that adjective.

Examples **a.** She wore a clean, blue* uniform.

---

*blue: When only two adjectives precede a noun, the comma may be omitted if the sentence is clear without it.

adj. adj. noun
Hardy's long handwritten manuscript is on display.

---

b. She wore a new, clean, blue uniform.

c. The host served a thick, fruit-filled pudding.

d. Although she was a good actress, she had a thin, unpleasant voice.

e. He became a respected, versatile painter.

Quick Quiz: G

Mark *the correct sentence in each pair.*

Model: a. She was wearing a frilly, pink, blouse.

(b.) She was wearing a frilly, pink blouse.

1. a. He put on clean, dry clothes and left the house.
   b. He put on clean dry, clothes and left the house.

2. a. I saw the new, planetarium.
   b. I saw the new planetarium.

3. a. The roof was made of light, durable material.
   b. The roof was made of light, durable, material.

Answers to Quick Quiz G are on page 235.

Place a comma after an introductory expression or explanation.

Introductory expressions

Some common introductory expressions are *after all, by the way, of course, as you know, to be sure, yes, no, well, in the first place, at first.*

Examples

a. *After all,* eclipses are not daily occurrences.

b. *Yes,* that is the right answer.

c. *In the first place,* the lights went out in the theater.

d. *For example,* pharmacy and oceanography are now open to women.

e. *On the contrary,* some still think the earth is flat.

Introductory explanations

intro. exp.

Examples **a.** *Our tax bill having been paid,* we started a budget for the next year.

b. *Brushing aside the warnings of the governor,* they boldly went ahead with their plan.

c. *When children are told one thing and see another,* many things can happen.

d. *For some time after the appearance of his first novel,* he was considered a leading young writer.

e. *In evaluating the movie,* the critic drew upon her experiences in television acting.

Quick Quiz: H

Correctly punctuate *each sentence.*

Model: On the contrary, it cannot wait.

1. Since the power failure sales of flashlights and candles have increased dramatically.
2. In conclusion I wish to explain why I cannot stay.
3. Before considering that let's eat.

Answers to Quick Quiz H are on page 235.

Use a comma to set off contrasting or transposed elements.

Contrasting elements

Examples **a.** He needs money, *not sympathy.*

b. Fiction, *rather than nonfiction,* fit his mood that summer.

c. The more we talked, *the slower we walked.*

Transposed elements (sentence elements placed out of usual word order)

Examples **a.** The witness, *silent and reserved,* answered almost inaudibly.
The usual word order of this sentence would be *The silent and reserved witness answered almost inaudibly.*

b. The wind, *intense, cold, and continuous,* devastated the blossoming orchards.
The usual word order of this sentence would be *The intense, cold, continuous wind devastated the blossoming orchards.*

Quick Quiz: I

Mark *the correct sentence in each pair.*

Model: (a.) He needs a transfusion, not a vacation.
b. He needs a transfusion not a vacation.

1. a. Give him a gallon of milk, not a quart.
   b. Give him a gallon of milk not a quart.

2. a. The building dilapidated and old had not been lived in for nineteen years.
   b. The building, dilapidated and old, had not been lived in for nineteen years.

3. a. They want wisdom not just knowledge.
   b. They want wisdom, not just knowledge.

Answers to Quick Quiz I are on page 235.

Use a comma wherever one is necessary for *clarity* and wherever one is needed to indicate a *pause.*

Examples

a. After the dinner was on, the table was moved to the open window.

b. He hurried to the library, for his books were overdue.

c. The night before, Christmas seemed as if it would never come.

Quick Quiz: J

Mark *the correct sentence in each pair.*

Model: a. In front of the auditorium, demonstrators carried placards and police officers walked through the crowd.
(b.) In front of the auditorium, demonstrators carried placards, and police officers walked through the crowd.

1. a. The agency will send a counselor now and then arrange a permanent schedule later.
   b. The agency will send a counselor now, and then arrange a permanent schedule later.

2. a. If he thinks that he is wrong.
   b. If he thinks that, he is wrong.

3. a. At first, glance to the right.
   b. At first glance to the right.

Answers to Quick Quiz J are on page 235.

E-2 Enclosing certain elements within a sentence

Enclose *appositives* with commas.

An *appositive* is an expression that renames or explains the noun preceding it.

Examples

(appositive: *the painter*)

a. Rembrandt, *the painter,* etched.

(appositive: *a system of underground fortifications*)

b. The Maginot Line, *a system of underground fortifications,* gave France a false sense of security.

(appositive: *a marine mammal that is reported to be able to talk with man*)

c. The dolphin, *a marine mammal that is reported to be able to talk with man,* is the subject of intensive research.

(appositive: *my brother*)

d. Carlos, *my brother,* is a physicist.

Set off words in *direct address* with commas.

Direct address is the *name, title,* or *descriptive term* used in addressing a person or a group.

Examples

a. *Soames,* get off Winifred's foot!

b. Taxes, *ladies and gentlemen,* will continue to go up.

c. The problem, *Senators,* is the Congress.

Quick Quiz: K

Mark *the correct sentence in each pair.*

Model: (a.) Your plane, Doctor Frankenstein, will leave at midnight.
b. Your plane Doctor Frankenstein will leave at midnight.

1. a. Please Martha don't call from there.
   b. Please, Martha, don't call from there.

2. a. Fido, my dog, is unfaithful.
   b. Fido my dog is unfaithful.

3. a. Come to dinner Heidi.
   b. Come to dinner, Heidi.

Answers to Quick Quiz K are on page 235.

Enclose *parenthetical* and *nonrestrictive* elements with commas.

Parenthetical and nonrestrictive elements are elements that are *not essential to the meaning of a sentence;* they are usually enclosed by commas. (Nonrestrictive means nonessential.)

Examples (parenthetical)

parenthetical

a. What, *after all,* threatens them?

parenthetical

b. William, *hurrying,* arrived in time for his appointment.

c. The vernal equinox, *which occurs in March,* is the first day of spring.

NOTE: Parenthetical expressions may also be enclosed by parentheses or dashes.

d. The coat (a hand-me-down that was hand-woven and hand-sewn) was Jim's favorite belonging.

e. The tragedy—and the thesis of the book—is that their rivalry diminished both of them.

Examples (nonrestrictive)

nonrestrictive

f. Ann Smith, *who lives next door,* won the shotput.
The commas show that the only essential part of this sentence is *Ann Smith won the shotput.* (Without the commas, the sentence reads *Ann Smith who lives next door won the shotput.* The lack of commas shows that *who lives next door* is restrictive (essential) since that group of words is needed to identify a particular Ann Smith.)

g. **Nonrestrictive:** (Nonessential information; therefore commas included)
Bring me the box, which is in the corner.
Restrictive: (Essential information; therefore commas left out)
Bring me the box which is in the corner.

h. **Nonrestrictive** (Nonessential)
The character, whom you end up admiring, dies in the last act.
Restrictive (Essential)
The character whom you end up admiring dies in the last act.

Quick Quiz: L

Correctly punctuate *the following sentences.*

Model: My husband, whom you know, just lost his job.

1. John Wilkes Booth who murdered Lincoln was an actor.
2. Gaspe Peninsula which is famous for its scenery is between New Brunswick and the St. Lawrence River.
3. Gargoyles however they are shaped are spouts for carrying off rain water.

Answers to Quick Quiz L are on page 235.

In dialogue, set off expressions like *he said with commas.**

*he said: Expressions like *he said* are sometimes called *dialogue guides.*

Examples

a. "The basic fact of today," *said Nehru,* "is the tremendous pace of change in human life."

b. "Most of the political activity," *he said,* "has been sound."

c. "No," *Marguerita replied irritably,* "I won't go!"

Quick Quiz: M

Correctly punctuate *the following sentences.*

Model: "Earthquakes," he said, "are complex occurrences."

1. She screamed "Get off my toes!"
2. "Mom" Tommy sobbed "never loved me."
3. "A journey of ten thousand miles" the proverb says "begins with a single step."

Answers to Quick Quiz M are on page 236.

Set off *dates* and *addresses* with commas.

Set off days from months and months from years.

Examples **a.** Sunday, December 7, 1941, was called a day that would "live in infamy."

b. Jesse was born January 3, 1970.

Set off street addresses from cities; set off cities from states or countries.

c. He lives at 1234 Lanir Street, Boston, Massachusetts.

d. Elma was raised in Edinburgh, Scotland.

NOTE: When the month and the year are given without the day, the comma may be included or omitted; both are correct: May 1980 or May, 1980.

Quick Quiz: N

Mark *the correct sentence in each pair.*

Model: a. World War I ended November 11 1918.
(b.) World War I ended November 11, 1918.

1. a. The party will be held at 987 Maple Drive, Yonkers, New York.
   b. The party will be held at 987 Maple Drive Yonkers, New York.
2. a. The conferees met on both March 1 1978 and August 10 1979.
   b. The conferees met on both March 1, 1978, and August 10, 1979.
3. a. Which is farther west—Honolulu Hawaii or Nome Alaska?
   b. Which is farther west—Honolulu, Hawaii, or Nome, Alaska?

Answers to Quick Quiz N are on page 236.

E-3 Comma don'ts

Do not use a comma after *the following* or *as follows.*

Examples **a.** correct: The tools included the following: a hammer, a drill, and a saw.
incorrect: The tools included the following, a hammer, a drill, and a saw.

b. correct: The program will be as follows: a violin solo, a poetry reading, and a one-act play.
incorrect: The program will be as follows, a violin solo, a poetry reading, and a one-act play.

Do not use a comma between a *subject and its *verb**.**

---

*subject: The *subject* of a sentence is the *person* or *thing* the sentence is about.

subj.
John loves Mary.

*verb: A *verb* tells *what the subject is, what the subject does,* or *what action the subject receives.*

vb.
John *is* a friend of mine.

Examples **a.** correct: The wind frightened me. (subj.: wind; vb.: frightened)
incorrect: The wind, frightened me.

b. correct: The wind that overturned our porch swing frightened me.
incorrect: The wind that overturned our porch swing, frightened me.

c. correct: Oranges, melons, lettuce, and broccoli are grown in Arizona.
incorrect: Oranges, melons, lettuce, and broccoli, are grown in Arizona.

NOTE: When a subject consists of a *series,* **do not separate the last item in the series from its verb.**

Elements added for explanation (called 'appositives') are, however, correctly set off by a *pair* of commas, one at the beginning and one at the end of the explanatory material:

Dave, *the neighbor's boy,* borrowed the bicycle pump. (subj.: Dave; vb.: borrowed)
The book, *a rare first edition,* had been returned.

The same is true for other short explanatory elements:

Our position, *however,* had not been explained.
I, *on the other hand,* trust that you will keep your word.

Do not use a comma *between* an *adjective* and the *noun* immediately following it.

Examples **a.** correct: Bea wore a blue uniform. (noun: uniform)
incorrect: Bea wore a blue, uniform.

b. correct: Tim became a respected portrait painter.
incorrect: Tim became a respected, portrait painter.
incorrect: Tim became a respected, portrait, painter.

NOTE: Do *not* use a comma between the parts of a compound expression like *portrait painter, football player, steel blue.*

Quick Quiz: O

Circle *incorrect commas.*

Model: Haunch, paunch, and jowl (,) are three of my favorite words.

1. Countries in widely separated parts of the globe, are having similar success.
2. My employer, is hiring three new accountants.
3. The writer, the producer, and the director, disagree on the underlying meaning of the play.
4. The instructions were as follows: weigh the ingredients, store them overnight at room temperature, and combine them the next day.
5. The new, building will be occupied in December.

Answers to Quick Quiz O are on page 236.

REVIEW AND PRACTICE: COMMA

Exercise A *Mark* correctly punctuated sentences ***C;*** *mark* incorrectly punctuated sentences ***Pn.***

Model: Pn Queen Elizabeth I, of England, was the daughter of King Henry VIII.

1. ____We need peace, not war.
2. ____Remember not to walk on the lawn gentlemen.
3. ____Masako read Dickens Austen and Hesse in the novel class.
4. ____We had, of course, to call the doctor.
5. ____Marco Polo, the Italian explorer, introduced spaghetti to Italy.
6. ____The mouse ate the cheese and the crackers and the cat ate the mouse.
7. ____Ruth's car broke down Friday April 11, 1971.
8. ____The report that was published last Tuesday was not accurate.
9. ____Yes George will be there, even if I have to carry him.
10. ____In that case you will find a screwdriver in the glove compartment.

11. ____Watching the sun set James wished he had brought his sunglasses.

12. ____The doctor who saw me yesterday is your aunt.

13. ____Republicans, Democrats, and Libertarians, registered at the same desk.

14. ____The customs officer refused to meet me.

15. ____Ulcers I don't have to remind you are easily acquired.

Exercise B *Circle* incorrect commas, and *add* ***commas*** where needed.

Model: In the first place**,** make up(,) your mind.

1. July 14 1789 was the first, Bastille Day.
2. When they found him, he had, a bad sunburn, a broken arm, and a tall tale to tell.
3. It is unfortunate that Renata Tebaldi the soprano did not make more recordings with Jussi Björling the tenor.
4. Her invitations, are rarely accepted.
5. Send the coupons to 12345 Seventh Street New York New York 10000.
6. No I won't come.
7. As he has told you he likes garlic not sage.
8. Albert collected plant fossils and Milt collected old but usable machine parts.
9. The treaty, dated May 7 1808 and signed by the three countries, was never honored.
10. Al, came out of the service and, entered college.

Answers to Review and Practice: Comma are on pages 236–237.

F Semicolon ;

RULE:	Use a semicolon to separate certain independent clauses* and to separate certain units in a series.

*See Chapter 8 for a fuller discussion of this use of the semicolon.

F-1 Separating independent clauses not joined by coordinating conjunctions

Use a semicolon to separate two closely related independent clauses that are *not* joined by one of the *coordinating conjunctions: and, but, for, nor, or, so, yet.*

Examples

a. correct: Phyl was the only nurse; the surgeon needed her. [indep. clause] [indep. clause]
incorrect: Phyl was the only nurse, the surgeon needed her.

b. correct: The dam broke; the area was flooded. [indep. clause] [indep. clause]
incorrect: The dam broke, the area was flooded.

c. correct: The sun had set; lights came on in all the houses. [indep. clause] [indep. clause]
incorrect: As the sun had set;* lights came on in all the houses.

**As the sun had set* is a dependent clause. A dependent clause contains a subject and verb unit but cannot stand alone as a sentence because it lacks a sense of completeness. Some other expressions that introduce dependent clauses are *after, although, as if, as long as, because, before, even, if, provided, since, that, though, unless, until, what, whatever, when, whenever, where, which, while, who, whoever, whose, why.*

Quick Quiz: P

Combine each pair of sentences to form a single sentence containing a **semicolon.**

Model: Two sentences: General Lee gave the command. The battle started.
Single sentence: General Lee gave the command; the battle started.

1. The contract gave him certain rights. He had insisted they be included.
2. The arrow sped through the dark. It struck him between the shoulders.
3. The photograph must have been taken from a helicopter. The angle seemed impossible otherwise.

Answers to Quick Quiz P are on page 237.

F-2 Separating independent clauses joined by coordinating conjunctions

Use a semicolon to separate two independent clauses that are joined by a coordinating conjunction *when at least one of the clauses is long or contains commas.*

Examples

a. He overhauled the engine, repaired the dent, and replaced the tires; and, when he had finished, he sold the car.

b. Lina was, to be sure, the only person to have seen him that day; and so we must, the inspector told us, ask Lina.

c. The internal temperature of the compound as determined by Reid, Stainback, and Turgot differs significantly from our measurements; and the problem is to determine why.

Quick Quiz: Q

Mark *correctly punctuated sentences* ***C;*** mark *incorrectly punctuated sentences* ***Pn.***

Model: __C__ The candle sputtered; the wick was damp.

1. ____Nero fiddled; while Rome burned.
2. ____Victor found his keys; they had fallen under the table.
3. ____Lend me your car; until mine is repaired.
4. ____The jury returned; the members had reached a verdict.
5. ____Whenever men assemble; these heroes will be remembered.

Answers to Quick Quiz Q are on page 237.

F-3 Separating independent clauses joined by words such as *therefore*

Use a semicolon to separate two independent clauses that are joined by a word such as *therefore* or *however. Generally, a comma follows such a word.**

*however: ***Therefore*** and ***however*** are conjunctive adverbs. See page 166 for a list of some common conjunctive adverbs. See Chapter 8 for a fuller discussion of this use of the semicolon.

Examples

a. This book contains two tables of contents; *however,* only one is alphabetically arranged.

b. Children are basically honest; *therefore,* it is unfortunate when adults teach them, by example, to lie.

c. Styles in music change; *consequently,* today's top ten harmonies will be tomorrow's lost chords.

NOTE: Do **not** put a semi-colon before *therefore, however,* or other similar expressions when such words are used *within* one clause:
He will, *therefore,* succeed. (not ; therefore)
Freud did, *however,* influence Jung. (not ; however)
I will, *moreover,* make this public. (not ; moreover)

Quick Quiz: R

Mark *correctly punctuated sentences* **C;** mark *incorrectly punctuated sentences* **Pn.**

Model: Pn He arrived late, therefore; his dinner was cold.

1. ____Violence begets violence; nevertheless, films are rated with no regard for this fact.
2. ____Water behaves as few other solvents do; because, it expands just before freezing.
3. ____We are beginning to be concerned about dumping beer cans on earth; however, no one seems to mind dumping hardware into space.

Answers to Quick Quiz R are on page 237.

F-4 Separating units in a series

Use semicolons to separate units of a *series* when the units themselves contain commas.

Examples

a. Maud, the violinist; Herbert, the flutist; and Grace, the noted harpist, were waiting for their instruments to arrive. **Notice** that a *comma,* not a *semicolon,* follows the last item in the series.

b. Witches and medicine men knew the curative powers of the foxglove plant derivative, digitalis; the cinchona tree derivative, quinine; and the deadly nightshade plant derivative, atropine, long before physicians did.

c. As I reported to you last night, I filled out the forms carefully; my secretary, to whom you spoke, mailed them promptly to your office; and I still have not received the refund due me.

Quick Quiz: S

Change commas *to* **semicolons** *where necessary for clarity.*

Model: Parsley, an herb, begonia, a flower, and ivy, a vine, grow in the windowbox.

Corrected: Parsley, an herb; begonia, a flower; and ivy, a vine, grow in the windowbox

1. Chicago, Illinois, Atlantic City, New Jersey, and Miami Beach, Florida, all have beaches.
2. Using a telescope, he showed them Sirius, the star, Venus, the planet, and Halley's comet.
3. This experimental diet drink supplies vitamin A, provided by fishliver oil, vitamin C, provided by lemon juice, and vitamin K, provided by hempseed.

Answers to Quick Quiz S are on page 238.

REVIEW AND PRACTICE: SEMICOLON

Exercise A *Mark* each of the following sentences ***C*** if the semicolon is used correctly, or ***Pn*** if the semicolon is used incorrectly.

Model: Pn I didn't know Freddy was listening; while we talked the whole thing over.

1. _____Leroy walked along the road; he wondered where it might lead.

2. _____I'll remember you; no matter how long we are parted.

3. _____I asked him to wait for me; until I completed the long-distance call.

4. _____The bell rang; it roused the Sunday sleepers.

5. _____Under both bridges and across the lake we skimmed; the boat moved without a sound.

6. _____I need your support; therefore, I come to speak to you.

7. _____Virginia will have heard all about it; when she phones this evening.

8. _____He will help you move; although it is my job to arrange for storage of the furniture.

9. _____When at last Françoise's telegram arrived; Monique knew their plans had succeeded.

10. _____At last Françoise's telegram arrived; Monique knew their plans had succeeded.

Exercise B *Place* appropriate punctuation—**comma** or **semicolon**—in each blank.

Model: Thomas Edison__,__as a reward for saving a child's life__,__received telegraphy lessons__;__he went on to patent several telegraphic devices__;__and he later gained fame for inventing the microphone__,__the phonograph__,__and the incandescent electric lamp.

1. I will follow you uncomplainingly___I will even listen to you attentively___however___I will not necessarily obey you.

2. The heat generated during the reaction___although considerable___is adequately controlled by water circulating through this coil.

3. Owen will meet Maggie___the carpenter___Leonard___the plumber___and Oscar___the policeman___and the four will ride to work together.

4. There he stands___cleaning his whiskers and flicking his tail.

5. The rain was so heavy that she missed the street___it was also possible that the sign had been knocked down.

6. During the summer, I read Ralph Ellison's *Invisible Man*___a novel___Jean Genet's *The Blacks*___a play___and Barbara Tuchman's *The Guns of August*___a history of the first few weeks of World War I.

7. The trip took them through Paris___France___Rome___Italy___and Heidelberg___Germany.

8. Eleanor will show you the rooms where we prepare our clay___store our supplies___and set our pots___and you can show her where you want your drawing board set up.

Answers to Review and Practice: Semicolon are on page 238.

G Dash [–]

RULE: Use dashes to set off parenthetical expressions and abrupt changes in thought when other marks of punctuation are inadequate.

Examples

a. Snyder spoke to Jones—*a hard man to please*—about the assignment in Boston.

b. The weather report—*wrong for the sixth day in succession*—necessitated a change in my plans.

c. The candidate—*I should have introduced you to her*—was very impressive.

d. Her offstage antics—*and rumors about them*—were dramatic.

Do *not* use dashes as substitutes for more appropriate punctuation marks.

Examples **a.** with unnecessary dashes: The Lily of the Valley—*my favorite flower*—is out of season.

revised: The Lily of the Valley, my favorite flower, is out of season.

b. with unnecessary dashes: The speaker—*looking like a Neanderthal man*—discussed the perils of speculation in an unstable stock market.

revised: The speaker, looking like a Neanderthal man, discussed the perils of speculation in an unstable stock market.

REVIEW AND PRACTICE: DASH

Exercise A *Set off* parenthetical expressions and abrupt changes in thought with ***dashes***.

Model: The onion soup mine had Gruyere cheese in it was the best I had ever tasted.

Revised: The onion soup—*mine had Gruyere cheese in it*—was the best I had ever tasted.

1. He was tall six feet seven and carried himself well.
2. His handwriting it resembled my mother's was almost indecipherable.
3. The sample of my blood I volunteered to give it will be used for enzyme studies.
4. Sid's auto accident I forgot to tell you about it resulted in his license being revoked.
5. The Four Horsemen of the Apocalypse conquest, slaughter, famine, death are pictured as riding horses of various colors.

Exercise B *Replace* any unnecessary dashes with **preferred punctuation**.

Model: On November 22nd—*a clear and sunny day*—the assassination took place in Dallas.

Revised: On November 22nd, a clear and sunny day, the assassination took place in Dallas.

1. This solution—which Jack never considered—proved to be a good one.
2. The machinery—although stored in the barn for a year—may be reparable.
3. Edward—Fourth Earl of Glockenspiel—was drummed out of court.

4. Cud-chewing, hollow-horned animals—oxen, sheep, antelope—belong to the Family *Bovidae*.

5. The lake water—brackish and stinking—is no longer fit for human use.

Answers to Review and Practice: Dash are on pages 238–239.

H Colon :

RULE: Use a colon in introducing quotations, lists, and explanations and in relating one clause to another.

The colon is a mark of introduction: it may introduce a quotation; it may introduce a list of items; it may introduce an explanation; it may introduce a clause that reflects something that is in the clause preceding the colon.

H-1 Introducing a quotation

Use a colon to introduce a short quotation that immediately follows an independent clause.

Example Epictetus encouraged individuality in one of his writings: "As bad performers cannot sing alone, but in a chorus, so some persons cannot walk alone." He urged men to remain independent and to learn to know themselves.

Use a colon to introduce a long quotation that is set off from the body of the paper. *Notice* that such quotations are often indented and that quotation marks are not used when a quotation is set apart in this manner.

Example Epictetus devoted his fourteenth chapter to a discussion of individualism. This is his opening paragraph:

> As bad performers cannot sing alone, but in a chorus, so some persons cannot walk alone. If you are anything, walk alone, talk by yourself, and do not skulk in the chorus. Laugh a little at yourself; look about you; stir yourself, that you may know what you are.

NOTE: The colon is *not used* when the introductory words are necessary to form the sentence.

Examples **a.** Epictetus encouraged individuality when he said, "As bad performers cannot sing alone. . . ."

b. We will find the promised "city overrun with vipers."

H-2 Introducing a list

Use a colon to introduce a list, when an independent clause precedes the colon:

indep. clause

Examples **a.** *The recipe calls for a variety of fish:* sardines, anchovies, halibut, and herring.

indep. clause

b. *The recipe calls for the following:* sardines, anchovies, halibut, and herring.

Colon don'ts

Do not place a colon between a verb and the rest of the sentence:

The recipe includes(:)sardines, anchovies, halibut, and herring. (incorrect)

Do not place a colon after *such as:*

The recipe includes various fish, such as(:)sardines, anchovies, halibut, and herring. (incorrect)

Do not place a colon between a preposition* and its object*:

The recipe calls for(:)sardines, anchovies, halibut, and herring. (incorrect)

---

*preposition: A *preposition* is a word that explains *position* or *relationship*.

prep. prep.

The man is sitting *on* a chair *beside* a table.

*object: The *object of a preposition* is the noun (or anything that stands for a noun) that follows that preposition. (A noun names something. *Charles, ball, team, idea,* are nouns.)

obj. of prep. obj. of prep.

The man is sitting on a *chair* beside a *table*.

Quick Quiz: T

Circle *the letter before the correct sentence in each pair.*

Model: (a.) You will need the following: a bell, a book, and a candle.
b. You will need: a bell, a book, and a candle.

1. a. They knew she was: a writer, an actor, and a director.
   b. They knew she was several things: a writer, an actor, and a director.

2. a. The collector mailed us: an old globe, a snuffbox, and three brooches.
   b. The collector mailed us an old globe, a snuffbox, and three brooches.

3. a. The string section consists of: violins, violas, cellos, and bass viols.
   b. The string section consists of the following: violins, violas, cellos, and bass viols.

Answers to Quick Quiz T are on page 239.

H-3 Introducing an explanation

Use a colon to introduce an explanation (sometimes expressed as a series of steps or events).

Examples

a. The accident occurred as follows: Car 1 struck the signal light, which fell on Car 2. Car 2 then bounced into the fire hydrant, breaking it. Car 3, illegally parked by the hydrant, was flooded.

b. You will need to bring two essentials for the trip: a sleeping bag that is adequate for desert nights and a flashlight with extra batteries.

H-4 Introducing a clause that reflects something in the clause preceding the colon

Use a colon between two *independent* clauses when the second clause reflects all or part of the first clause through illustration, rewording, or explanation.

Examples

first indep. clause — second indep. clause

a. Accommodations in San Miguel are remarkably inexpensive: two of us shared a room with full board for three dollars a day.
(The second independent clause illustrates or gives an example of the idea expressed in the first clause.)

first indep. clause — second indep. clause

b. Like others, I fear for the quality of our lives: many of us feel the quality is deteriorating.
(The second clause rewords the idea expressed in the first clause.)

first indep. clause — second indep. clause

c. We like both playwrights: Moliere arouses our admiration and O'Neill, our sympathy.
(The second clause explains the idea expressed in the first clause.)

Quick Quiz: U

Mark *any sentence* **correct** *in which the second clause reflects all or part of the first. Otherwise,* mark *it* **incorrect**.

Model: *correct* It had always been like this: She would ask him to stop to visit Mr. Michaels, and the fight would begin.

1. ______ Follow these directions: Take one pill before meals and two at bedtime.
2. ______ Follow these directions: then come back to see me on Monday.
3. ______ Here is the house she described: It has yellow shutters and a blue roof.
4. ______ Here is the house she described: Let's see if anyone is home.

Answers to Quick Quiz U are on page 239.

REVIEW AND PRACTICE: COLON

Exercise A Mark *the following sentences either* **correct** *or* **incorrect**.

Model: *incorrect* There is one thing to remember: and tomorrow I will remember it.

1. ______ There is only one thing to remember: Check to see which way the wind is blowing.

2. ______ Try running some water over the stone's surface: The characters may thus become visible.

3. ______ Try running some water over the stone's surface: then let it dry.

4. ______ Brand X is better than other brands: besides, it is available in this store.

5. ______ Brand X is better than other brands: It costs less and lasts longer.

Exercise B Mark *the following sentences either* **correct** *or* **incorrect**.

Model: *incorrect* The regiment packed up: its belongings, kissed its girls goodbye, and boarded the ship for home.

1. ______ They dissected the following, a starfish, an earthworm, and a clam.

2. ______ Let me point out to you that: Paul is honest, industrious, and prompt.

3. ______ We can be sure of the following: a quick trip, a good meal, and a pleasant host.

4. ______________ To catch abalone, you will need the following: a gunny sack, a tire iron, and patience.

5. ______________ Let me have them all: your guns, your knives, and your slingshots.

Answers to Review and Practice: Colon are on page 239.

I Hyphen [-]

RULE: Use a hyphen to divide a word at the end of a line of writing or typing and to connect words or word elements in forming compound words.

I-1 Dividing words

At the end of a line of writing or typing, divide a word between syllables.*

*syllable: Most American dictionaries indicate syllable division with centered periods as in this example: dic·tion·ar·y. Consult a dictionary for correct division of words into their syllables.

Example *Uncomfortable* is a four-syllable word: un·com·fort·able (1 2 3 4). *Uncomfortable* can be divided in several places:

He felt *un-*
comfortable.

He felt *uncom-*
fortable.

He felt *uncomfort-*
able.

Divide already hyphenated words at their original hyphens.

Examples

a. *brother-in-law*
He is my *brother-*
in-law.

b. *forty-five*
We spent *forty-*
five minutes waiting for our tickets.

Divide a word having a double consonant*between the consonants, unless the dictionary divides the word in another way.

*consonant: *Consonants* are all of the letters in the alphabet except *a, e, i, o, u,* and sometimes *y* (which are vowels).

Examples **a. different**

It is a *dif-*
ferent ball game now.

b. connecting

He fixed the *con-*
necting rod.

Do not separate one letter from the rest of the word, even when that letter is a syllable as in *drear·* y.

Examples **a. adoption**

correct: On that date, *the adop-*
tion proceedings began.

incorrect: On that date, the *a-*
doption proceedings began.

b. ready

correct: The statue was *ready* for the unveiling.

incorrect: The statue was *read-*
y for the unveiling.

Do not divide a word of one syllable, no matter how many letters it contains.

Example **strength**

correct: You have the *strength*
to go on.

incorrect: You have the *stre-*
ngth to go on.

Do not divide the last word on a page.

Example

page 1

correct: . . . the eggs of those birds. No amount of *argument*

page 2

could persuade the manufacturers to change. . . .

page 1

incorrect: . . . the eggs of those birds. No amount of *argu-*

page 2

ment could persuade the manufacturers to. . . .

I-2 Forming compound words

Hyphens often join two or more words to form new words. A *hyphenated word* is a *compound word* that acts as a single unit.

Examples

a. Send the *sergeant-at-arms* here.

b. The *ten-year-old* chair was not considered antique.

c. The *dual-purpose* vehicle was tested *twenty-three* times.

Use a current dictionary as a guide to hyphenation.

I-3 Separating word elements from the rest of a word

A hyphen sometimes separates *re-*, or other word elements, from the rest of a word when omission of the hyphen would result in confusion of meaning.

Examples

a. He is going to *re-cover* those chairs.
He is going to recover his losses.

b. They have to *re-lay* the tile floor.
They have to relay the message.

c. I went to the *co-op*.
I went to the chicken coop.

REVIEW AND PRACTICE: HYPHEN

Mark the correct sentence in each pair.

Model: (a.) Please write the commen-
tary.
b. Please write the commentar-
y.

1. a. The principle of the invention was not stated.
   b. The principle of the invention was not stated.

2. a. The paper said the a-
   ttack failed.
   b. The paper said the attack failed.

3. a. Alfred resigned as a trustee of the universit-
   y.
   b. Alfred resigned as a trustee of the university.

Answers to Review and Practice: Hyphen are on page 239.

J Quotation marks “ ” ‘ ’

RULE: Use quotation marks to mark the beginning and the end of a direct quotation; to enclose titles of literary, musical, and other artistic works; to distinguish special terms from the rest of the sentence; to set off dialogue.

Quotation marks are of two types: *double* (“ ”) and *single* (‘ ’). Single quotation marks consist of a single mark at the beginning of a quotation and a single mark at the end. Unless the word *single* is expressed, *quotation marks* refer to double marks.

J-1 Marking the beginning and end of a direct quotation

A *direct quotation* is a word-for-word presentation of something the writer has heard or read. A written direct quotation must be an *exact* reproduction of wording, spelling, and punctuation. (See *sic* in the Glossary.)

Generally, when a quotation is no more than three or four lines in length,* make it continuous with the material preceding it and/or following it, and enclose it in quotation marks.

*length: This *length* limitation for a prose quotation is not rigid. Although many authorities recommend a four- or five-line limitation, some suggest a limit of 100 words, often of ten typed lines. Your instructor may choose to set his own limit on length.

Examples **a.** Mark Twain, describing the excitement of two steamboats racing down the Mississippi, said, "A horserace is pretty tame and colorless in comparison."

b. Thoreau said, "Thought breeds thought. It grows under your hands."

When a prose quotation is more than four or five lines long, set it off from the body of the paper, single-spaced and indented. Use quotation marks only if they are part of the quoted material. *Prose* is writing *other than poetry.*

Example Mark Twain preferred the excitement of a steamboat race to a horserace:

> Two red-hot steamboats ranging along, neck-and-neck straining every nerve—that is to say, every rivet in the boilers—quaking and shaking and shaking and groaning from stem to stem, spouting white steam from the pipes, pouring black smoke from the chimneys, raining down sparks, parting the river into long breaks of hissing foam—this is sport that makes a body's very liver curl with enjoyment. A horserace is pretty tame and colorless in comparison.

When a quotation consists of one or two lines of poetry, enclose it in quotation marks and make it continuous with the text. Use a slash (/) to separate lines of poetry usually printed beneath one another.

Example Coleridge started his poem, "In Xanadu did Kubla Khan/A stately pleasure dome decree." He was never clear about the meaning of *Xanadu*.

When a poetry quotation contains three or more lines, set it off from the body of the paper, with the longest quoted line centered on the page. Quotation marks are generally not needed.

Example

In Xanadu did Kubla Khan
A stately pleasure-dome decree:
Where Alph, the sacred river, ran
Through caverns measureless to man
Down to a sunless sea.

Enclose a quotation that contains another quotation in the usual double quotation marks, but enclose the *quotation within* in *single quotation marks*.

quotation within a quotation

Example John said, "This is my father's latest letter. He writes, *'Plan to spend a weekend in Minnesota with me.'* What shall I write in reply?"

J-2 Enclosing titles of certain literary, musical, and other artistic works

Chapter titles (but not book titles)*

*Titles of books and magazines are underlined in writing or typing and *italicized* when printed.

Example The first chapter of *The Mother Tongue* is entitled "Our Hybrid Heritage."

Article titles (but not magazine or journal titles)

Example The most interesting article in that issue of *Transaction* is "Sociology of Christmas Cards."

Poem, story, or essay titles (but not anthology titles)

Example "The dead are not gone forever," says Birago Diop in his poem "Forefathers" in *An African Treasure.*

Short musical compositions (but not symphonies and operas)

Example Everyone was surprised when the soprano sang the tenor aria "The Flower Song" in last Saturday's performance of *Carmen.*

Works of art

Example At the art museum, we bought a slide of "Red Pyramid," an Alexander Calder mobile.

Titles within direct quotations

Example The reviewer of this book says, "Mr. Jerry Mander's collection of political essays opens with a provocative proposal entitled 'You Draw Your Line; I'll Draw Mine.' "

NOTE: Single quotation marks enclose the title, since double quotation marks are required to enclose the entire quotation.

Quick Quiz: V

Mark *the correct sentence in each pair.*

Model: a. The book opened with a poem, "Frost at Midnight," and closed with a short story, Gift of the Magi.
(b.) The book opened with a poem, "Frost at Midnight," and closed with a short story, "Gift of the Magi."

1. a. See if you can still recite The Night Before Christmas.
   b. See if you can still recite "The Night Before Christmas."

2. a. The Star Spangled Banner and God Save the Queen are national anthems. Both appear in a collection entitled "Anthems of the Ages."
   b. "The Star Spangled Banner" and "God Save the Queen" are national anthems. Both appear in a collection entitled *Anthems of the Ages.*

3. a. My favorite magazine, *The Saturday Review,* includes a weekly column called "Manner of Speaking" by John Ciardi.
   b. My favorite magazine, "The Saturday Review," includes a weekly column called Manner of Speaking by John Ciardi.

Answers to Quick Quiz V are on page 240.

J-3 Distinguishing special terms from the rest of a sentence

Special terms may be *nicknames, slang, newly coined words, words meant to convey irony or other double meaning.* In general, special terms are words or expressions that are somehow different from the language of the writing in which they appear.

Examples

a. Her friends called her "Verny," but her mother called her Vernita. (nickname)

b. They both felt "up tight" on the day of the interview. (slang)

NOTE: Avoid slang in your formal papers, however. While putting slang words within quotation marks at least shows that you know slang when you see it, the use of slang usually is inappropriate in formal writing. Instead, consult a thesaurus or dictionary to find effective words.

c. I suggest we call young people "pre-ads" for pre-adults, instead of calling them teenagers. (newly coined word)

d. With a "best friend" like him, who needs enemies? (irony)

e. The word "satisfaction" has several meanings. (a word called by name, or a word "used as a word")

Quick Quiz: W

Mark *the correct sentence in each pair.*

Model: (a.) It was a real "mind blower."
b. It was a real mind blower.

1. a. The word "ontogony" refers to the history of the individual.
b. The word ontogony refers to the history of the individual.

2. a. I was the groom, but I was still the best man at the wedding.
b. I was the groom, but I was still the "best man" at the wedding.

3. a. Unfortunately, his mind was really spaced out.
b. Unfortunately, his mind was really "spaced out."

Answers to Quick Quiz W are on page 240.

J-4 Enclosing words spoken in conversation or dialogue

Paragraph 1. "Where is the light switch?" John asked.
Paragraph 2. "On your left," Rich replied.
Paragraph 3. "Found it," John said, "but it doesn't seem to work."
Paragraph 4. Rich was silent a moment, then moaned, "That's right! I forgot to pay the electric bill!"
Paragraph 5. John said to himself, "That's Rich for you"; however, being a guest in Rich's house, he smiled and said, "We'll survive!"
Paragraph 6. Rich thought, "Why did he have to ask, 'Where's the light switch?' as soon as he walked in?"
Paragraph 7. Why did Rich always say "I forgot"?
Paragraph 8. John said that the light switch didn't seem to work.
Paragraph 9. Rich told John that the light bill hadn't been paid.

Rules: The nine paragraphs above illustrate the following rules for punctuating conversation or dialogue.

a. Enclose all spoken words in quotation marks. (Paragraphs 1, 2, 3, 4, 5, 6, 7)
b. Start a new paragraph for *every* change in speaker, and enclose each uninterrupted speech in quotation marks. (Paragraphs 1, 2, 3, 4, 5, 6, 7)
c. Do not enclose comments like *John said* or *Rich replied* in quotation marks. (Paragraphs 1, 2, 3, 4, 5, 6)
d. Place commas and periods inside quotation marks. (Paragraphs 2, 3)
e. When a question mark or exclamation mark applies to the quoted words, place it inside the quotation marks. (Paragraphs 1, 4, 5, 6)
f. When a question mark or exclamation mark does not apply to the quoted words, *but applies to the whole sentence,* place it outside the quotation marks. (Paragraph 7)

g. In general, place a colon or a semicolon outside the quotation marks unless it belongs inseparably to the passage it follows. (Paragraph 5)
h. Do *not* enclose *indirect* quotations in quotation marks. An indirect quotation is a rewording of someone else's idea, rather than a word-for-word direct quotation. (Paragraphs 8, 9)

REVIEW AND PRACTICE: QUOTATION MARKS

Exercise A Mark *the correct sentence in the following pairs.*

Model: (a.) "How do we get back to the highway?" she asked.
b. "How do we get back to the highway" she asked?

1. a. Turn to the article entitled "A New Look."
b. Turn to the article entitled 'A New Look.'

2. a. "Don't you care about your health?" the physician asked.
b. "Don't you care about your health," the physician asked?

3. a. Jabberwocky is a poem containing many nonsense words.
b. "Jabberwocky" is a poem containing many nonsense words.

4. a. The lifeguard told the boys "to stay out of the deep water."
b. The lifeguard told the boys to stay out of the deep water.

5. a. When he said the film was heavy, his father misunderstood him.
b. When he said the film was "heavy," his father misunderstood him.

6. a. The commentator said clearly, We have succeeded.
b. The commentator said clearly, "We have succeeded."

7. a. How do you define "antidisestablishmentarianism"?
b. How do you define "antidisestablishmentarianism?"

8. a. "Look, Jean said, this is our chance."
b. "Look," Jean said, "this is our chance."

9. a. She said, "At last this stupid paper is done!"
b. She said, "At last this stupid paper is done"!

10. a. Patrick Henry said, 'Give me liberty or give me death!"
b. Patrick Henry said, "Give me liberty or give me death!"

Exercise B Mark *the following sentences* ***correct or incorrect.***

Model: correct "Is this the house?" Jim asked.

1. ____________ The economist asserted that inflation would result.

2. ______________Every year Sam recites The Wreck of the Hesperus for us.

3. ______________If someone told me to review the article "Blue Chip Stocks," I wouldn't know what to say.

4. ______________"That," my roommate said, "is a matter of opinion."

5. ______________"What do you want for lunch?" he asked.

6. ______________I heard you say that you are tired.

7. ______________The woman asked, "Is that your opinion"?

8. ______________"Lifeguard" is a good short story, Jim said.

9. ______________In surfing jargon, what does hang ten mean?

10. ______________Did he say "that he was interested, too?"

Exercise C Punctuate *the following sentences.*

Model: "Hurry," John whispered, "and write out the second verse of 'Home on the Range'!"

1. Find a copy of Thurber's The Unicorn in the Garden
2. In England, the word grotty means messy
3. John said Throw me the essay book if you're finished with it. I still have to read The Case Against Teaching Grammar
4. Peter said Phooey
5. Can you define archipelago
6. Let me kow when you can come again Sue said.
7. What dramatist said Let no man count himself fortunate until he is dead
8. When he leaves, I'll whistle Alton said.
9. Write your description of Michelangelo's Pieta
10. Here Hilary said take this

Answers to Review and Practice: Quotation Marks are on page 240.

K Parentheses ( )

RULE: Use parentheses to enclose useful, related, supplementary material.

Examples **a.** Bake the cake in a moderate oven *(350°)* for 30 minutes.

b. At the time the treaty was signed *(Rapallo, 1920)*, few people understood its implications.

NOTE: Although punctuation marks may follow closing parentheses, marks of punctuation are *not* used before opening parentheses.

c. The rust remover cleans in eight seconds. *(At least that is what the ad claims.)*

When parentheses enclose a complete sentence, the end punctuation (in example C, a period) is within the parentheses.

Use parentheses thoughtfully. See that material enclosed within them adds to, rather than distracts from, the ongoing text.

L Brackets [ ]

RULE: Use brackets to enclose explanations or corrections inserted by you into quoted material.

In *quoted* material, brackets usually enclose words written by someone other than the author of the quotation. In published material, brackets generally indicate additions made by an *editor*. In your material, use brackets to enclose words you have added to something you are quoting.

Examples

a. "The significance of this discovery [*made in 1892*] was that it opened the entire area for further exploration."

b. "Neanderthal man had been on the planet for 50,000 years when his existence became threatened. [*This estimate no longer seems correct.*] Climatic changes hastened his extinction."

c. "When storing an unused freezer or refrigerator, lock its door [*or remove it altogether*] so children cannot get locked into the cabinet."

REVIEW AND PRACTICE: PARENTHESES, BRACKETS

Place **parentheses** or **brackets** around the underlined material.

Model: At that time (<u>1503</u>) writing was the pastime of an elite few.

1. "The last two Verdi operas Otello and *Falstaff* were based on plays by Shakespeare."

2. Few people felt that the war World War I would last until spring.

3. Air pollution particularly with oxides of nitrogen and sulphur is worldwide.

4. My soufflé was a letdown even though I followed the directions carefully. I later discovered that the recipe was incorrect.

5. "The city's founders Allen and Green never gave any consideration to its orderly expansion."

Answers to Review and Practice: Parentheses and Brackets are on page 241.

M Ellipsis ... .

RULE: Use an ellipsis to show where words have been omitted from a passage you are quoting.

Examples **a.** quotation: "The director of the company, John Jones, has resigned."
quotation with omission: "The director of the company . . . has resigned."
quotation with omission: ". . . John Jones has resigned."

NOTE: You may wish to omit unnecessary words from a useful quotation, in which case ellipsis marks are helpful. Be sure, however, that in replacing words with ellipses you do not alter the basic meaning of the quote.

b. quotation: The salinity of several bodies of water, including Lake Erie, the Caspian Sea, and Lake Garda, has increased in recent years."
quotation with omission: "The salinity of several bodies of water . . . has increased in recent years."
quotation with omission: "The salinity of several bodies of water. . .has increased. . . ."
Notice that this sentence ends with four dots. When an omission includes the end of a sentence, the end punctuation of the sentence follows the ellipsis, resulting in four dots.

c. quotation: "Are there any great men alive today like Caesar or Churchill?"
quotation with omission: "Are there any great men alive today. . . ?"
Notice that this sentence ends with an ellipsis and a question mark.

REVIEW AND PRACTICE: ELLIPSIS

Use an **ellipsis** to indicate the omission of the underlined material.

Model: "Sky divers have given various reasons for participating in sky diving including achieving a sense of freedom, overcoming anxiety about height, and compensating for feelings of inferiority."
"Sky divers have given various reasons for participating in sky diving. . . ."

1. "Is there anyone here with a gray hat and a white tie?"

2. "The tragedy of the death of a child is not the dying, but the loss of unfulfilled promise."

3. "The countries that border the Mediterranean—Italy, Greece, Israel, and Egypt—are among the oldest with recorded histories."

Answers to Review and Practice: Ellipsis are on page 241.

CHAPTER REVIEW AND PRACTICE: PUNCTUATION

Circle *the correct punctuation, or circle* **none** *if no additional punctuation is needed.*

Model: The boy stood [, ; **none**] on the burning deck [, .]

1. While cleaning [, ; **none**] Ed stumbled over his pail [: .]
2. He needs a doctor [, **none**] not a wife [: .]
3. She asked for a [" **none**] snood [, **none**] [" **none**] but I didn't know what she meant [. ?]
4. I want to test drive the new models of that car [, ; **none**] I'm not sure which to buy.

5. John Lennon [, none] the singer [, none] achieved his initial fame in England.

6. The large [, none] slow [, none] gray [, none] and white [, none] rabbit panicked at our headlights.

7. Drop dead [. ! none]

8. In the third place [, : none] I don't know your name.

9. Try this sample [: , none] then let me know how it compares with the earlier one [. ?]

10. "Where are you going [, ? none] " the passenger demanded [. ?]

11. [" none] This is the end of the line [, none] [" none] the conductor announced. [" none]

12. [" none] Why should I give you the answer [? .] [" none] Sue asked. [" none] You never helped me. [" none]

13. She is the [mans' man's] daughter.

14. What happened to the members of the class of [' " none] 33 [. ?]

15. "This reaction is known to occur with several elements [. . ." . . . ."]

16. The soloist [— : none] I knew him in grammar school [— : none] finally came onto the stage.

17. [Whose Who's] etching is that [. ?]

18. He told me that [" none] he would do it. [" none]

19. Eight of my [cat's cats' cats] nine lives have been used up.

20. He bought the following things [: ; none] meat [, ;] bread [, ;] lettuce [, ;] and cigarettes.

21. The house was empty [, ; none] but a cigar still burned in an ashtray.

22. Gourami [, ;] the fish [, ;] Chelonia [, ;] the turtle [, ;] and Rattler [, ;] the reptile [, none] were evicted from the science lab.

23. The large, green [, none] slug is eating the roses.

24. John Stuart Mill, the philosopher [; none ,] wrote with wisdom and compassion.

25. He said [" none ,] that this was the end [" .]

Answers to Review and Practice are on pages 241–242.

CHAPTER TEST

Mark *the correctly punctuated sentences* **C.** Mark *the incorrectly punctuated sentences* **Pn.**

Model: Pn We will begin ladies, and gentlemen where we left off last week.

1. ____She should write you at 22 West Pine Street, Santa Fe New Mexico.
2. ____No, don't tell me that again; I have heard the story before, and it does not bear repeating.
3. ____His day began strangely: "He awoke in a room that he had never seen before."
4. ____Pass your hand over this tables' surface, and see how much dust has collected in the last ten minutes.
5. ____She visited the house on the hill—which, has been known to be haunted since 1919.
6. ____That, he said, made him wonder what it's composition was."
7. ____John asked, "If I said, 'Give me a *Silphium perfoliatum,*' would you know which flower I wanted?"
8. ____This is what you might call a "gas"!
9. ____"Quadraphonic" refers to sound that comes from four separate sources, just as "stereophonic" refers to sound that comes from two separate sources.
10. ____Bake the bread (after the dough has risen to twice it's original bulk) for 45 to 50 minutes.

Answers to Chapter Test are on page 242.

ANSWERS: CHAPTER 9

Answers to Review and Practice: Period, Question Mark, Exclamation Mark

1. ! or .
2. .
3. ?
4. ! or .
5. ?
6. etc. (not *ect.*)
7. ?
8. .
9. .
10. B.C.
11. .
12. .

Notice that . . .
Some declarative sentences can be confused with questions:
a. Jim asked if I would go with you. (sentence 8)
b. The speaker asked if anyone had questions. (sentence 12)
Both of these sentences correctly end with a period—rather than a question mark—since each sentence makes a statement, the first about what Jim *did* (he asked something), the second about what the speaker *did.*

Answers to Quick Quiz A

1. *I'll* be with you in a minute.
2. *It's* five *o'clock.*
3. John *wouldn't* go there if you paid him.
4. *What's* her name?
5. *I'd* say *they're* happy.

Answers to Quick Quiz B

1. The *day's* end finally arrived.
2. Look at these *painters'* exhibit.
3. We were in the *hurricane's* eye.
4. Where is the *women's* dressing room?
5. The *boy's* hobbies include cross-country skiing.
6. They found many *elephants'* tracks.

Answers to Quick Quiz C

1. What is the *president-elect's* name?
2. The *fish's* scales were luminescent.
3. *Tom's, Dick's and Harry's* hats are made of felt.
4. The *court-martial's* sentences were unusually severe.
5. *H.M.S. Pinafore* is one of the funniest of Gilbert and *Sullivan's* operas.

Answers to Quick Quiz D

1. i's 2. hello's 3. 2 × 4's

Answers to Quick Quiz E

1. Who's (who is) 2. It's (it is) 3. Whose (belonging to whom) 4. It's (it is), its (belonging to it)

Answers to Review and Practice: Apostrophe

Exercise A

1. doesn't
2. You're . . . I'm
3. It's
4. They're
5. She's . . . who's
6. Aren't
7. shouldn't
8. '39 haven't
9. I'll . . . she'll
10. you're . . . you'll . . . you'll

Exercise B

1. man's 2. her 3. Whose 4. Phyllis' or Phyllis's
5. sun's 6. It's 7. James' or James's 8. theirs

Exercise C

1. steeple's 2. ours 3. Mr. Sandoval's 4. rectangle's 5. Whose
6. Charles' or Charles's 7. clocks' 8. its 9. hers 10. farmers'

Answers to Quick Quiz F

1. (b) 2. (b) 3. (b) 4. (a)

Answers to Quick Quiz G

1. (a) 2. (b) 3. (a)

Answers to Quick Quiz H

1. Since the power failure, sales of flashlights and candles have increased dramatically.
2. In conclusion, I wish to explain why I cannot stay.
3. Before considering that, let's eat.

Answers to Quick Quiz I

1. (a) 2. (b) 3. (b)

Answers to Quick Quiz J

1. (b) 2. (b) 3. (a)

Answers to Quick Quiz K

1. (b) 2. (a) 3. (b)

Answers to Quick Quiz L

1. John Wilkes Booth, who murdered Lincoln, was an actor.
2. Gaspe Peninsula, which is famous for its scenery, is between New Brunswick and the St. Lawrence River.
3. Gargoyles, however they are shaped, are spouts for carrying off rain water.

Answers to Quick Quiz M

1. She screamed, "Get off my toes!"
2. "Mom," Tommy sobbed, "never loved me."
3. "A journey of ten thousand miles," the proverb says, "begins with a single step."

Answers to Quick Quiz N

1. (a.) 2. (b) 3. (b)

Answers to Quick Quiz O

1. Countries in widely separated parts of the globe are having similar success.
2. My empoyer is hiring three new accountants.
3. The writer, the producer, and the director disagree on the underlying meaning of the play.
4. Correct
5. The new building will be occupied in December.

Answers to Review and Practice: Comma

Exercise A

1. C
2. Pn Remember not to walk on the lawn, gentlemen.
3. Pn Masako read Dickens, Austen, and Hesse . . .
4. C
5. C
6. Pn The mouse ate the cheese and the crackers, and the cat ate the mouse.
7. Pn Ruth's car broke down Friday, April 11, 1971.
8. C
9. Pn Yes, George will be there, even if . . .
10. Pn In that case, you will . . .
11. Pn Watching the sun set, James . . .
12. C
13. Pn Republicans, Democrats, and Libertarians registered at the same desk.

14. C

15. Pn Ulcers, I don't have to remind you, are easily acquired.

Exercise B

1. July 14, 1789, was the first Bastille Day.
2. When they found him, he had a bad sunburn, a broken arm, and a tall tale to tell.
3. It is unfortunate that Renata Tebaldi, the soprano, did not make more recordings with Jussi Björling, the tenor.
4. Her invitations are rarely accepted.
5. Send the coupons to 12345 Seventh Street, New York, New York 10000.
6. No, I won't come.
7. As he told you, he likes garlic, not sage.
8. Albert collected plant fossils, and Milt collected old, but usable, machine parts.
9. The treaty, dated May 7, 1808, and signed by three countries, was never honored.
10. Al came out of the service and entered college.

Answers to Quick Quiz P

1. The contract gave him certain rights; he had insisted they be included.
2. The arrow sped through the dark; it struck him between the shoulders.
3. The photograph must have been taken from a helicopter; the angle seemed impossible otherwise.

Answers to Quick Quiz Q

1. Pn 2. C 3. Pn 4. C 5. Pn Notice that in sentences 1, 3, and 5 the semicolon is incorrectly used since it does not separate two independent clauses.

Answers to Quick Quiz R

1. C 2. Pn 3. C

Answers to Quick Quiz S

1. Chicago, Illinois; Atlantic City, New Jersey; and Miami Beach, Florida, all have beaches.
2. Using a telescope, he showed them Sirius, the star; Venus, the planet; and Halley's comet.
3. This experimental diet drink supplies vitamin A, provided by fishliver oil; vitamin C, provided by lemon juice; and vitamin K, provided by hempseed.

Answers to Review and Practice: Semicolon

Exercise A

1. C	2. Pn	3. Pn	4. C	5. C
6. C	7. Pn	8. Pn	9. Pn	10. C

Exercise B

1. I will follow you uncomplainingly; I will even listen to you attentively; however, I will not necessarily obey you.
2. The heat generated during the reaction, although considerable, is adequately controlled by water circulating through this coil.
3. Owen will meet Maggie, the carpenter; Leonard, the plumber; and Oscar, the policeman; and the four will ride to work together.
4. There he stands, cleaning his whiskers and flicking his tail.
5. The rain was so heavy that she missed the street; it was also possible that the sign had been knocked down.
6. During the summer I read Ralph Ellison's *Invisible Man*, a novel; Jean Genet's *The Blacks*, a play; and Barbara Tuchman's *The Guns of August*, a history of the first few weeks of World War I.
7. The trip took them through Paris, France; Rome, Italy; and Heidelberg, Germany.
8. Eleanor will show you the rooms where we prepare our clay, store our supplies, and set our pots; and you can show her where you want your drawing board set up.

Answers to Review and Practice: Dash

Exercise A

1. He was tall—six feet seven—and carried himself well.
2. His handwriting—it resembled my mother's—was almost indecipherable.
3. The sample of my blood—I volunteered to give it—will be used for enzyme studies.
4. Sid's auto accident—I forgot to tell you about it—resulted in his license being revoked.

5. The Four Horsemen of the Apocalypse—conquest, slaughter, famine, death—are pictured as riding horses of various colors.

Exercise B

1. This solution, which Jack never considered, proved to be a good one.
2. The machinery, although stored in the barn for a year, may be reparable.
3. Edward, Fourth Earl of Glockenspiel, was drummed out of court.
4. Cud-chewing, hollow-horned animals (oxen, sheep, antelope) belong to the Family *Bovidae*.
5. The lake water, brackish and stinking, is no longer fit for human use.

Answers to Quick Quiz T

1. (b) 2. (b) 3. (b)

Answers to Quick Quiz U

1. correct 2. incorrect 3. correct 4. incorrect

Answers to Review and Practice: Colon

Exercise A

1. correct 2. correct 3. incorrect 4. incorrect 5. correct

Exercise B

1. incorrect 2. incorrect 3. correct 4. correct 5. correct

Answers to Review and Practice: Hyphen

1. (a) 2. (b) 3. (b)

Answers to Quick Quiz V

1. (b) 2. (b) 3. (a)

Answers to Quick Quiz W

1. (a) 2. (b) 3. (b)

Answers to Review and Practice: Quotation marks

Exercise A

1. (a)	2. (a)	3. (b)	4. (b)	5. (b)
6. (b)	7. (a)	8. (b)	9. (a)	10. (b)

Exercise B

1. Correct	2. Incorrect	3. Correct	4. Correct	5. Correct
6. Correct	7. Incorrect	8. Incorrect	9. Incorrect	10. Incorrect

Exercise C

1. Find a copy of Thurber's "The Unicorn in the Garden."
2. In England, the word "grotty" means "messy."
3. John said, "Throw me the essay book if you're finished with it. I still have to read 'The Case Against Teaching Grammar.' "
4. Peter said, "Phooey." OR Peter said, "Phooey!"
5. Can you define "archipelago"?
6. "Let me know when you can come again," Sue said.
7. What dramatist said, "Let no man count himself fortunate until he is dead"?
8. "When he leaves, I'll whistle," Alton said.
9. Write your description of Michelangelo's "Pieta."
10. "Here," Hilary said, "take this."

Answers to Review and Practice: Parentheses, Brackets

1. "The last two Verdi operas [*Otello* and *Falstaff*] were based on plays by Shakespeare."
2. Few people felt that the war (World War I) would last until spring.
3. Air pollution (particularly with oxides of nitrogen and sulphur) is worldwide.
4. My soufflé was a letdown even though I followed the directions carefully. (I later discovered that the recipe was incorrect.)
5. "The city's founders [Allen and Green] never gave any consideration to its orderly expansion."

Answers to Review and Practice: Ellipsis

1. "Is there anyone here with a gray hat . . . ?"
2. "The tragedy of the death of a child is . . . the loss of unfulfilled promise."
3. "The countries that border the Mediterranean . . . are among the oldest with recorded histories."

Answers to Chapter Review and Practice: Punctuation

1. While cleaning, Ed stumbled over his pail.
2. He needs a doctor, not a wife.
3. She asked for a "snood," but I didn't know what she meant.
4. I want to test drive the new models of that car; I'm not sure which to buy.
5. John Lennon the singer achieved his initial fame in England.
6. The large, slow, gray and white rabbit panicked at our headlights.
7. Drop dead!
8. In the third place, I don't know your name.
9. Try this sample, then let me know how it compares with the earlier one.
10. "Where are you going?" the passenger demanded.
11. "This is the end of the line," the conductor announced.
12. "Why should I give you the answer?" Sue asked. "You never helped me."
13. She is the man's daughter.
14. What happened to the members of the class of '33?
15. "This reaction is known to occur with several elements . . . ."
16. The soloist—I knew him in grammar school—finally came onto the stage.

17. Whose etching is that?
18. He told me that he would do it.
19. Eight of my cat's nine lives have been used up. OR
    Eight of my cats' nine lives have been used up.

    Notice that ...

    One cat lost eight of its proverbial nine lives. However, if you thought there were eight cats, the sentence would read

    Eight of my cats' nine lives . . . .
20. He bought the following things: meat, bread, lettuce, and cigarettes.
21. The house was empty, but a cigar still burned in an ashtray.
22. Gourami, the fish; Chelonia, the turtle; and Rattler, the reptile, were evicted from the science lab.
23. The large, green slug is eating the roses.
24. John Stuart Mill, the philosopher, wrote with wisdom and compassion.
25. He said that this was the end.

Answers to Chapter Test

1. Pn	2. C	3. Pn	4. Pn	5. Pn
6. Pn	7. C	8. C	9. C	10. Pn

CHAPTER 10

Dangling, Squinting, and Other Misplaced Modifiers

- **Items 176–190 in the Pretest are from this chapter.**
- **The procedure for correcting dangling modifiers is on page 247.**
- **The procedure for correcting squinting modifiers is on page 253.**
- **The procedure for correcting common forms of misplaced modifiers other than dangling and squinting modifers is on page 257.**

Chapter Contents

RULE:	Apply each modifier clearly and accurately to the specific word (or words) you want it to modify.

mod = modifier
dang = dangling modifier
dp = dangling participle
mm = misplaced modifier
sq = squinting modifier

A *modifier* is a word or a group of words that adds something specific to the meaning of the word it modifies (the word it applies to).

Examples

a. *The zoology deparment* pets are *a white* mouse, a *green-backed* turtle, and a bird *with a broken wing.*
(modifiers of pets: *The zoology deparment*; mod. of mouse: *a white*; mod. of turtle: *green-backed*; mod. of bird: *with a broken wing*)

b. *Being capable of daydreaming,* Ivan was able to escape *boring* lectures.
(mod. of Ivan: *Being capable of daydreaming*; mod. of lectures: *boring*)

A modifier that does not apply clearly and accurately to the specific word or words you want it to modify is a *misplaced modifier*. A misplaced modifier often attaches itself to the wrong word and thereby makes the meaning of the sentence ambiguous.*

---

*A sentence or part of a sentence is *ambiguous* when it presents more than one possible meaning to the reader.
Example
I wrote them *when summer came* to join us at the beach.
Does the writer mean I wrote *when summer came* . . . or to join us *when summer came*? The sentence is ambiguous since it presents more than one possible meaning.
When summer came, I wrote them to join us at the beach is unambiguous.

Misplaced modifiers may be

1. *Dangling modifiers* (dang. mod.), also called dangling participles (dp)

   Example: *Going to the door,* the bell rang.
   (Did the bell go to the door?)

2. *Squinting modifiers* (sq. mod.)

   Example: The travel agent told us *eventually* the new schedules would be ready.
   (Eventually the agent told us? or schedules would be ready eventually?)

3. *Other misplaced modifiers* (mm)

   Example: I nearly fell fifty feet.
   (Did I nearly fall? or did I fall nearly fifty feet?)

A Dangling Modifiers

A modifier "dangles" when a sentence contains no word—or at least no logical word—for the "dangler" to modify.

A-1 Recognizing dangling modifiers

Examples

a. dang. mod.: *Running to the bus*, Steven's glasses broke.
(Were Steven's glasses running to the bus?)

b. dang. mod.: *Coming over the hill*, a field of California cotton lay spread before us.
(Was a field of cotton coming over the hill?)

c. dang. mod.: *Having made my bed and straightened my room*, Susan phoned to invite me for a swim.
(Did Susan make my bed and straighten my room?)

d. dang. mod.: *After painting the garage*, a fly got stuck in the paint.
(Did a fly paint the garage?)

e. dang. mod.: *Finishing dinner*, the pickles and ice cream had my stomach growling for hours.
(Did the pickles and ice cream finish dinner?)

A-2 Testing for meaning in dangling modifiers

Example Running to the bus, Steven's glasses broke.

1. Fill in the following:
glasses / running to the bus
subject* modifier

*subject: The *subject* of a sentence is the person, place, or thing the sentence is about.
subj.
We are here.

Now circle logical or (illogical)

2. Fill in the following:
Steven / running to the bus
logical subject for modifer modifier

Now circle (logical) or illogical.

3. Rewrite the sentence correctly in the following order:
Steven / running to the bus
logical subject modifier
broke / his glasses
verb the rest of the sentence

Correct: Steven, running to the bus, broke his glasses.

Exercises **a.** Coming over a hill, a field of California cotton lay spread before us.

1. Fill in the following:

____

subject modifier

Now *circle logical* or *illogical.*

NOTE: There is no logical subject **in the sentence itself.** ***We***, however, is a logical subject.

2. Fill in the following:

_______________ / _______________

logical subject for modifier — modifier

Now *circle logical* or *illogical.*

3. Rewrite the sentence correctly, in the following order:

_______________ / _______________

logical subject — modifier

_______________ / _______________

verb — (what?)

Correct: Coming over a hill, we saw a field of California cotton.

b. After painting the garage, a fly got stuck in the paint.

1. Fill in the following:

_______________ / _______________

subject — modifier

Now *circle logical* or *illogical.*

NOTE: There is no logical subject in the sentence itself. *Mary*, however, is a logical subject.

2. Fill in the following:

_______________ / _______________

logical subject for modifier — modifier

Now *circle logical* or *illogical.*

3. Rewrite the sentence correctly, in the following order:

______________ / ______________

logical subject modifier

______________ / ______________

verb (what?)

Correct: After painting the garage, Mary found that a fly got stuck in the paint.

Quick Quiz: A

Circle *the subject and* underline *the modifier of the subject.*

Model: Abandoned on the beach, Ariadne was troubled by obnoxious thoughts.

1. Hearing the siren, Orpheus pulled over to the curb.
2. Jerome and Terry, expecting a long ticket line, arrived early.
3. Parched, wrinkled, and obviously old, Peregrine still danced the Virginia reel.

Identify *each correct sentence with a* ***C,*** *and* underline *each dangling modifier.*

Model: _____ Batting left-handed, the ball went over the fence.

_____4. Having held the victim captive for two days, the kidnappers sent a ransom note.

_____5. Going to the door, the bell rang.

_____6. Stephanie, already awake, turned off the alarm.

_____7. Shuffling the cards, an ace slipped to the floor.

_____8. Ceasing fire, the negotiations began.

Answers to Quick Quiz A are on page 261.

Procedure for Correcting Dangling Modifiers

dang. Going to the door, the bell rang.

Step 1: Find the subject of the sentence.
Bell is the subject of the sentence.

Step 2: Find any word—or group of words—that seems to modify the subject.
The clearly modifies *bell* and therefore does not dangle.
Going to the door seems to modify *bell.*

Step 3: Read subject + modifier (or seeming modifier), in that order.
The bell / going to the door

NOTE: Take this step separately for each modifier that you suspect is dangling. If what you read *makes sense,* the sentence probably has no dangling modifier.
If what you read *does not make sense,* the sentence probably has a dangling modifier.

Going to the door is a dangling modifier, since it attaches itself to the wrong word—*bell.*

Step 4: Correct a dangling modifier in one of two ways:
a. If the word that was meant to be modified by the dangling modifier is not in the sentence, add it next to, or close to, its modifier:
Going to the door, I heard the bell ring.
OR
b. Rewrite the sentence, seeing that each modifier applies clearly and accurately to the specific word, or words, you mean it to modify:
As I was going to the door, the bell rang.

REVIEW AND PRACTICE: DANGLING MODIFIERS

Each of the sections of this Review and Practice is different. Do some exercises in each section, then check your answers and decide which sections—if any—you need to continue to work through. Answers are on pages 261–262.

Exercise A Circle *the subject of each sentence.*

Model: While cleaning our car, my (wife) and (I) were both stung by bees.
(Notice that a subject may have more than one part.)

1. Hunger was the theme of the conference.
2. Where do the rules of grammar come from?
3. Brushing his teeth was his only exercise.
4. The sun having set, the air was heavy with heat.
5. Sticks and stones may break my bones, but names will never hurt me.
6. In politics, too, television presents problems.
7. One of the chief reasons for Thackeray's visit to America was his great desire to eat some Massachusetts oysters.
8. Nothing is new under the sun.
9. Reacting to the bell, Stephanie and Alex dashed to the phone simultaneously.
10. Gathering wildflowers and analyzing flower structure occupied the entire week.

Exercise B Circle *the subject and* underline *anything that modifies the subject.*

Models: Having a hole in its shell, the big turtle could be held on a leash.

1. Threatened by famine, the villagers demanded help.
2. The fire alarm made Rosemary jump.
3. Living with the natives, the anthropologist came of age in Samoa.
4. Slamming on the brakes, the bus driver avoided a collision.
5. A popular, lasting theme for comedy seems to be mistaken identity.

Exercise C *In each pair of sentences below, one is correct, while one contains a dangling modifier.* Mark *each correct sentence with a* ***C****, and* underline *each dangling modifier.*

Model: a. __C__ While cleaning my car, I was stung.

b. ____ While cleaning my car, a bee stung me.

1. a. ____Having deposited a quarter in the fare box, Gordon pushed his way through the turnstile.

   b. ____Having deposited a quarter in the fare box, the turnstile stuck.

2. a. ____While doing dishes, an ambulance raced down our street.

   b. ____While doing dishes, I heard an ambulance race by.

3. a. ____The fraternity, in completing its community project first, earned both praise and satisfaction.

   b. ____In completing its community project first, the prize was awarded to our club.

4. a. ____Marching to the beat of a different drummer, Helen dropped her baton.

   b. ____Marching to the beat of a different drummer, the baton slipped from her hands.

5. a. ____Marian, have completed all but one course, decided to stay in school.

   b. ____Having completed all but one course, the department allowed Marian to apply for her credential.

Exercise D *Each sentence contains a dangling modifier.* Rewrite *each sentence.* Start each sentence with the dangling modifier, *then make the word that* **belongs with** *the dangling modifier the subject of the new sentence.* Underline *the modifier and the new subject.*

Model: With dangling modifier:
Entering college, new experiences are confronted by all students.

Corrected:
Entering college, all students confront new experiences.

1. Running freely, the yelping of dogs was heard across the valley.

2. In order to be sure to get up on time, the alarm clock was set for 6 A.M.

3. To obtain a driver's license, your car must be in good condition.

4. Upon entering the theater, the curtain rose, and we took our seats.

5. To be able to type for long periods of time without tiring, your seat should be comfortable.

6. Tired and troubled, the swim soothed him.

7. Acting under the new pest-control law, the bollworm has been controlled by the growers.

8. Like the robin, painters have often depicted the swan.

9. Damaging the nervous system, impaired vision was caused by the chemical.

10. To continue his journey, the train went on through Ohio.

Answers to Review and Practice are on pages 261–262.

B Squinting Modifiers

A squinting modifier is an *either-or modifier*: it stands in the middle of a sentence and can apply either to something that precedes it in the sentence or to something that follows it. A squinting modifier makes the meaning ambiguous and is, therefore, an error. Every sentence containing a squinting modifier has three parts:

1. the part preceding the squinting modifier
2. the squinting modifier
3. the part following the squinting modifier.

B-1 Recognizing squinting modifiers

Examples

a. The ticket agent told us *eventually* (sq. mod.) new schedules would be available.
(told us eventually? or eventually available?)

b. After the mayor made the request *with the approval of the city council* (sq. mod.) the item was added to the budget.
(made the request with the approval of the city council? or was added to the budget with the approval of the city council?)

c. Arriving in Boston *before the day was over* (sq. mod.) we found a motel.
(Arriving before the day was over? or finding a motel before the day was over?)

d. They agreed *after both sides ceased firing* (sq. mod.) to renew negotiations.
(agreed after both sides ceased firing? or renewed after both sides ceased firing?)

e. Ichabod decided *the next day* (sq. mod.) to start studying.
(decided the next day? or start studying the next day?)

B-2 Testing for meaning in squinting modifiers

1. The ticket agent told us *eventually* new schedules would be available.

(a) Fill in the following:

The ticket agent told us
1. The part preceding the squinting modifier

eventually
2. the squinting modifier

new schedules would be available
3. the part following the squinting modifier

(b) Fill in the following:

The ticket agent told us eventually
part before squinting modifier + squinting modifier

new schedules would be available eventually
part after squinting modifier + squinting modifier

(c) Decide which of the two examples conveys your intended meaning.
Correct: *The ticket agent told us that eventually new schedules would be available.*

2. After the mayor made the request *with the approval of the city council* the item was added to the budget.

(a) Fill in the following:

____
1. the part preceding the squinting modifier

____
2. the squinting modifier

____
3. the part following the squinting modifier

(b) Fill in the following:

____

____
the part before squinting modifier + squinting modifier

____

____
the part after squinting modifier + squinting modifier

(c) Decide which of the two above conveys your intended meaning.
Correct: *After the mayor made the request with the approval of the city council, the item was added to the budget.*

3. Arriving in Boston *before the day was over* we found a motel.

(a) Fill in the following:

____
1. the part preceding the squinting modifier

____
2. the squinting modifier

____
3. the part following the squinting modifier

(b) Fill in the following:

____
the part before squinting modifier + squinting modifier

____
the part after squinting modifier + squinting modifier

(c) Decide which of the two above statements conveys your intended meaning.
Correct sample: *Arriving in Boston, we found a motel before the day was over.*

Quick Quiz: B

Identify *each correct sentence below with* **C** *and each sentence containing a squinting modifier with* squint. **Box** *each squinting modifier.*

Model: *squint* The organizer said [Friday] the conference was adjourning.

1. ____________When the conductor approached the center stage abruptly the audience became silent.
2. ____________Each state was already involved in the census.
3. ____________As the ship sank suddenly the life boats were lowered.

Answers to Quick Quiz B are on page 262.

Procedure for Correcting Squinting Modifiers

sq. *Ichabod decided the next day to start studying.*

Step 1: Identify the three parts of the sentence:

1. the part preceding the squinting modifier
   Ichabod decided
2. the squinting modifier (boxing it may be helpful)
   [*the next day*]
3. the part following the squinting modifier
   to start studying

Step 2: Read the sentence in two ways:
first, the part preceding the squinting modifier [+] the squinting modifier
Ichabod decided [*the next day*]
second, the part following the squinting modifier [+] the squinting modifier
to start studying [*the next day*]
Decide which of the two ways conveys your intended meaning.

Step 3: Correct the squinting modifier through one of the following:

- punctuation
  Ichabod decided, the next day, to start studying.
- change in word order (particularly change in the position of the squinting modifier).
  The next day, Ichabod decided to start studying.
- rewriting
  Ichabod decided that he would start studying the next day.
- any combination of these
  On the following day, Ichabod decided to start studying.

Step 4: Check to see that each modifier applies clearly and accurately to the specific word or words you want it to modify and that the correct sentence is not ambiguous.
Correct sample: *Ichabod decided that the next day he would start studying.*

REVIEW AND PRACTICE: SQUINTING MODIFIERS

Each of the sections of this Review and Practice is different. Do some exercises in each section, then check your answers and decide which sections—if any—you need to continue to work through. Answers are on page 263.

Exercise A *In each pair of sentences, one sentence contains a squinting modifier and the other does not.* Mark *each correct sentence* **C** *and each sentence containing a squinting modifier* squint.

Model: a. squint Seeing the fans leave the bleachers quietly we started for the exit gate.
b. C Seeing the fans leave the bleachers quietly, we started for the exit gate.

1. a. ____The Senate decided after discussion to reconsider the bill.
b. ____After discussion, the Senate decided to reconsider the bill.

2. a. ____He said at first they were inclined to be nervous and trigger-happy.
b. ____At first they were inclined to be nervous and trigger-happy, he said.

3. a. ____The man she met in the Orient last week said he was going to marry her.
b. ____The man she met in the Orient said, last week, he was going to marry her.

4. a. ____Since we will have rented a car by then we will be able to meet you anywhere.
b. ____Since we will have rented a car by then, we will be able to meet you anywhere.

5. a. ____The employer agreed to raise salaries after negotiations.
b. ____The employer agreed after negotiations to raise salaries.

6. a. ____A council motion to end all urban oil drilling will be made immediately.
b. ____A council motion to end all urban oil drilling immediately will be made.

7. a. ____Regularly, Fidelio vowed to wax his car.
b. ____Fidelio vowed regularly to wax his car.

8. a. ____She said during the intermission they could go backstage.
b. ____During the intermission she said they could go backstage.

9. a. ____The five scripts we considered this week were scheduled for tryouts.

b. ____The five scripts, which we considered this week, are scheduled for tryouts today.

10. a. ____A South Pacific travel program is being launched by three airlines this spring.

b. ____A South Pacific travel program this spring is being launched by three airlines.

Exercise B Add commas *to eliminate squinting modifiers in the sentences below.* Box *each added comma.*

Model: While we studied marine animals for a month[,] the rest of the staff was on vacation.

1. Artemus walked around the apartment absentmindedly brushing his teeth.
2. Alton hesitated nervously debating his decision.
3. When the cage was opened for a moment the leopard looked up in surprise.
4. The inspector who had entered quickly opened his attache case.
5. Any up-and-coming young person susceptible to seasickness repeatedly will have a difficult time in the navy.
6. The prisoner took his place reluctantly answering the attorney's questions.
7. Knowing their act had to go on at sundown they ended their rehearsal.
8. The trampoline artist practiced in a flippant manner joking with her partner.

Answers to Review and Practice: Squinting Modifiers are on page 263.

C Other Misplaced Modifiers

C-1 Recognizing other misplaced modifiers

In English, the meaning of a sentence depends—to a great extent—on word order, or the position of words in that sentence. In the example below, notice how the change in position of the modifier ***only*** can change the meaning of the sentence.

Example **Only** a passenger plane stopped at our town on weekends.
A passenger plane **only** stopped at our town on weekends.
A passenger plane stopped **only** at our town on weekends.
A passenger plane stopped at **only** our town on weekends.
A passenger plane stopped at our town **only** on weekends.
A passenger plane stopped at our town on weekends **only**.

You must decide what your intended meaning is: *only* a passenger plane, *only* stopped, *only* at our town, or *only* what? Then you must place the modifier *only* so that it unmistakably applies to the word or words you want to modify. ***Only** would be a misplaced modifier in any position that did not convey your exact meaning.*

NOTE: Any modifier is misplaced if it is separated awkwardly from the word it belongs with. However, some modifiers are more ***easily misplaced*** than others. These include:

almost	hardly	most
either . . . or	just	nearly
even	merely	only
ever	more	rather
		very

C-2 Testing for meaning

Examples **a.** Even Morgan harvested apples between semesters.
Where should the writer place the modifer **even**?
Intended Meaning: For this example, assume that the sentence should emphasize the fact that Morgan used vacation time to harvest apples.
Read or write the sentence in several ways, each time changing the position of the modifier **even**.

(a) *Even* Morgan harvested apples between semesters.
(b) Morgan *even* harvested apples between semesters.
(c) Morgan harvested *even* apples between semesters.
(d) Morgan harvested apples *even* between semesters.
(e) Morgan harvested apples between *even* semesters.
(f) Morgan harvested apples between semesters *even.*

Which position of the modifier best conveys the intended meaning?
Corrected: Morgan harvested apples **even** between semesters.

b. Lincoln wrote *The Gettysburg Address* while traveling from Washington to Gettysburg on the back of an envelope.
The modifiers are the phrases* *while traveling from Washington to Gettysburg* and *on the back of an envelope.*

**phrase*: A phrase is a group of words that functions as a unit. A phrase generally lacks all or part of a subject + verb unit and lacks a sense of completeness.

Intended meaning: The speech was written on a particular piece of paper. This action occurred at a particular time.
In the sample sentence, *on the back of an envelope* incorrectly modifies *while traveling from Washington*, rather than modifying *The Gettysburg Address.*

Corrected: Lincoln wrote *The Gettysburg Address on the back of an envelope* while traveling from Washington to Gettysburg.

NOTE: In each example above, one using a single word as a modifier, another using a phrase, the modifier was "misplaced" when the writer separated it too far from the word it modified. You will avoid many misplaced modifiers, and write clearer sentences, if you keep modifiers as close as possible to the words they modify.

Procedure for Correcting Common Forms of Misplaced Modifiers Other Than Dangling and Squinting Modifiers

mm *Legislators heard proposals to amend these laws one at a time.*

Step 1: Identify any modifier whose change in position can change the meaning of the sentence.
One at at time is a modifer whose position can change the meaning of a sentence. Is the intended meaning that the laws were to be amended one at a time or that the proposals were heard one at a time? Or were legislators contacted one at a time?

Step 2: Decide what your intended meaning is.
Intended meaning: Legislators were contacted one person at a time. Each of them listened to proposals to change certain laws.

Step 3: Ask yourself if by moving the modifier you can make your meaning clearer.
One at a time is located far from the word it should modify, *legislators*. It is next to a word it is not intended to modify, *laws*.

Step 4: Consider various ways of writing the sentence so that the modifier clearly applies to the word it modifies.

Step 5: Correct the error through one or more of the following:
- punctutation
- change in word order (the modifier should be next to, or close to, the word it modifies)
- rewriting

NOTE: Any correction may require a change in wording or punctuation.
Corrected: One at a time, legislators heard proposals to amend these laws.

OR

Legislators, who were contacted one at a time, heard proposals to amend these laws.

Step 6: Check to see that each modifier applies clearly and accurately to the specific word or words you want it to modify and that the corrected sentence is neither ambiguous nor awkward.

REVIEW AND PRACITCE: OTHER MISPLACED MODIFIERS

In each pair of sentences below, *mark* the correct sentence **C**, and *mark* the sentence containing a misplaced modifier ***MM.***

Model: a. mm I washed the car along with two friends last night.
b. C Last night, along with two friends, I washed the car.

1. a. ____It is difficult for a writer to use exactly the words he wants to.

b. ____It is difficult for a writer to use the exact words he wants to use.

2. a. ____You only can be effective if you are properly trained, I was told.

b. ____You can be effective only if you are properly trained, I was told.

3. a. ____The barber shaved the man with the motorbike.

b. ____The barber shaved the man who had the motorbike.

4. a. ____He knew almost everyone in town.

b. ____He almost knew everyone in town.

5. a. ____We watched workmen extracting grape juice from the barn roof.

b. ____From the barn roof, we watched workmen extracting grape juice.

6. a. ____Statistics show that thousands of young people in the Dalsi Islands are not going to college.

b. ____Statistics show that thousands of young people are not going to college in the Dalsi Islands.

7. a. ____We saw the two-car accident going to work.

b. ____Going to work, we saw the two-car accident.

8. a. ____Entering the museum, we saw the stegosaurus and the mastodon.

b. ____We saw the stegosaurus and the mastodon entering the museum.

9. a. ____On his way to Atlanta, my father saw *Hamlet*.

b. ____My father saw *Hamlet* on his way to Atlanta.

10. a. ____I want you especially to review the plans for the trip.

b. ____I especially want you to review the plans for the trip.

CHAPTER REVIEW AND PRACTICE

In each pair of sentences below, mark the correct sentence **C** *and the incorrect sentence* ***MM.*** Underline *all misplaced modifiers.*

Model: a. _mm_ At the age of two, his father started his own repair shop.
b. _C_ When Olaf was two, his father started his own repair shop.

1. a. _____They decided around five o'clock to meet.

b. _____They decided to meet around five o'clock.

2. a. _____I have heard over and over again some parents injure their own children.

b. _____I have heard some parents injure their own children over and over again.

3. a. _____I do not want anyone, no matter how well-intentioned, passing his beliefs on to my children.

b. _____I do not want anyone passing his beliefs on to my children, no matter how well-intentioned.

4. a. _____After hearing the panel, she decided immediately to change her major.

b. _____After hearing the panel, she decided to change her major immediately.

5. a. _____Before his lecture, he revised his notes a little.

b. _____He revised his lecture notes a little before each lecture.

6. a. _____To be well done, you should simmer the meat for a long time.

b. _____For the meat to be well done, you should simmer it for a long time.

7. a. _____Even though large, we are not members of the group.

b. _____Even though it is a large group, we are not members of it.

8. a. _____The movie is grossing millions of dollars, whose director is wealthy.

b. _____The movie, whose director is wealthy, is grossing millions of dollars.

9. a. _____After being dressed, we found the chicken weighed four pounds.

b. _____After being dressed, the chicken weighed four pounds.

10. a. _____Through a one-way vision window, we photographed the infants who were learning to walk.

b. _____We photographed the infants who were learning to walk through a one-way vision window.

Answers to Chapter Review and Practice are on page 264.

CHAPTER TEST

Mark *each correct sentence* ***C*** *and each incorrect sentence* ***MM*** *(for any kind of misplaced modifier).* Underline *misplaced modifiers.*

Model: mm Pulling the trigger, the gun went off.

1. ____On first walking into the doctor's office, the skeleton stared me in the face.
2. ____The longshoremen voted after concluding their debate to return to their jobs.
3. ____The hikers stopped feeling the earthquake plodding up the hill.
4. ____While studying the Civil War period, Carl Sandburg learned much about Walt Whitman.
5. ____Owners of multi-family housing spent $840 million annually for maintenance, repairs, and improvements.
6. ____My husband told me during church service he was going for a swim.
7. ____The couple sat watching the sun set in sandy bathing suits.
8. ____By appropriating tax money for the support of public broadcasting, Congress hopes to give citizens a diversity of views.
9. ____The encounter group I belong to this year meets Thursday evenings.
10. ____The book that he is writing will be revised before Christmas.
11. ____On Ellis Island a self-help organization for immigrants was established.
12. ____Wakening in the oppressive heat, the porch swing cooled me off.
13. ____Business analysts suggested today it might be worthwhile to buy corporate bonds.
14. ____The phone rang while tuning his guitar.
15. ____Every morning Barney ran around the block after a shower.

Answers to Chapter Test are on page 264.

Answers: Chapter 10

Answers to Quick Quiz A

1. Hearing the siren, Orpheus
2. Jerome and Terry expecting a long ticket line
3. Parched, wrinkled, and obviously old, Peregrine
4. C
5. Going to the door
6. C
7. Shuffling the cards
8. Ceasing fire

Answers to Review and Practice: Dangling Modifier

Exercise A

1. Hunger
2. rules
3. Brushing or brushing his teeth
4. air
5. sticks . . . stones; names

   Notice that this is a "compound sentence," one made up of two shorter sentences: Sticks and stones may break my bones (Sentence one: subject = sticks and stones), but names will never hurt me (Sentence two: subject = names). See page 40 regarding compound sentences.
6. television
7. One
8. Nothing
9. Stephanie . . . Alex
10. Gathering . . . analyzing

Exercise B

1. Threatened by famine, the villagers
2. The fire alarm
3. Living with the natives, the anthropologist

4. Slamming on the brakes, the bus driver

5. A popular, lasting theme for comedy

Exercise C

1. a. C

   b. Having deposited a quarter in the fare box

2. a. While doing dishes

   b. C

3. a. C

   b. In completing its community project first

4. a. C

   b. Marching to the beat of a different drummer

5. a. C

   b. Having completed all but one course

Exercise D

Several possible answers may be correct for each item. However, corrections must include the underlined material.

1. Running freely, the dogs yelped across the valley.
2. In order to be sure to get up on time, he set the alarm clock for 6 A.M.
3. To obtain a driver's license, you must have your car in good condition.
4. Upon entering the theater, we took our seats as the curtain rose.
5. To be able to type for long periods of time without tiring, you should select a comfortable seat.
6. Tired and troubled, he felt soothed by the swim.
7. Acting under the new pest control law, growers have been able to control the bollworm.
8. Like the robin, the swan is often depicted by painters.
9. Damaging the nervous system, the chemical caused the impairment of vision.
10. To continue his journey, he took a train that went through Ohio.

Answers to Quick Quiz B

1. squint abruptly   2. C   3. squint suddenly

Answers to Review and Practice: Squinting Modifiers

Exercise A

1. a. squint
   b. C
2. a. squint
   b. C
3. a. squint
   b. C
4. a. squint
   b. C
5. a. C
   b. squint
6. a. C
   b. squint
7. a. C
   b. squint
8. a. squint
   b. C
9. a. squint
   b. C
10. a. C
    b. squint

Exercise B

Notice that . . .
two possible corrections are given for each sentence. Others may be possible.

1. Artemus walked around the apartment[,] absentmindedly brushing his teeth.
   Artemus walked around the apartment absentmindedly[,] brushing his teeth.
2. Alton hesitated[,] nervously debating his decision.
   Alton hesitated nervously[,] debating . . . .
3. When the cage was opened[,] for a moment the leopard looked up in surprise.
   When the cage was opened for a moment[,] the . . . .
4. The inspector[,] who had entered[,] quickly opened his attache case.
   The inspector[,] who had entered quickly[,] opened . . .
5. Any up-and-coming young person[,] susceptible to seasickness[,] repeatedly will have a difficult time in the navy.
   Any up-and-coming young person susceptible to seasickness repeatedly[,] will . . . .
6. The prisoner took his place[,] reluctantly answering the attorney's questions.
   The prisoner took his place reluctantly[,] answering . . . .
7. Knowing their act had to go on[,] at sundown they ended their rehearsal.
   Knowing their act had to go on at sundown[,] they . . . .
8. The trampoline artist practiced in a flippant manner[,] joking with her partner.
   The trampoline artist practiced[,] in a flippant manner joking with her partner.

Answers to Review and Practice: Other Misplaced Modifiers

1. a. MM (exactly) b. C
2. a. MM (only) b. C
3. a. MM (with the motorbike) b. C

4. a. C b. MM (almost)
5. a. MM (from the barn roof) b. C
6. a. C b. MM (in the Dalsi Islands)
7. a. MM (going to work) b. C
8. a. C b. MM (entering the museum)
9. a. C b. MM (on his way to Atlanta)
10. a. MM (especially) b. C

Answers to Chapter Review and Practice

1. a. MM (squinting) around five o'clock b. C
2. a. MM (squinting) over and over again b. C
3. a. C b. MM (other) no matter how well-intentioned
4. a. MM (squinting) immediately b. C
5. a. C b. MM (squinting) a little
6. a. MM (dangling) To be well done b. C
7. a. MM (dangling) Even though large b. C
8. a. MM (other) whose director is wealthy b. C
9. a. MM (dangling) After being dressed b. C
10. a. C b. MM (other) through a one-way vision window

Answers to Chapter Test

1. MM On first walking into the doctor's office
2. MM after concluding their debate
3. MM feeling the earthquake
4. C
5. C
6. MM during church service
7. MM in sandy bathing suits
8. C
9. MM this year
10. C
11. C
12. MM Wakening in the oppressive heat
13. MM today
14. MM while tuning his guitar
15. MM after a shower

CHAPTER 11

Parallel Construction

- **Items 191–196 in the Pretest are from this chapter.**
- **The procedure for recognizing and correcting errors in parallel construction is on page 273.**

Chapter Contents

RULE: | Use parallel construction *to express parallel ideas.*

/ /, para, paral = lack of parallelism

Explanations

If you were to build three tables using one plan, the tables would be constructed of similar parts, similarly put together. You could say that the tables had parallel construction. The tables would form a series, since a series is a group of things: *a series of lectures, a series of baseball games, a series of tables.*

In the diagram below notice that the elements in series A are alike: In A1 each is a triangle. Because the elements are alike, we say series A1 has parallel construction. In series B1, however, two elements are triangles and one element is a square; therefore, the series lacks parallel construction. Each of the series in the diagram can be analyzed in the same way: Each of the groups on the ***left*** is a series that **has** parallel construction. Each of the groups on the ***right*** is a series that **lacks** parallel construction.

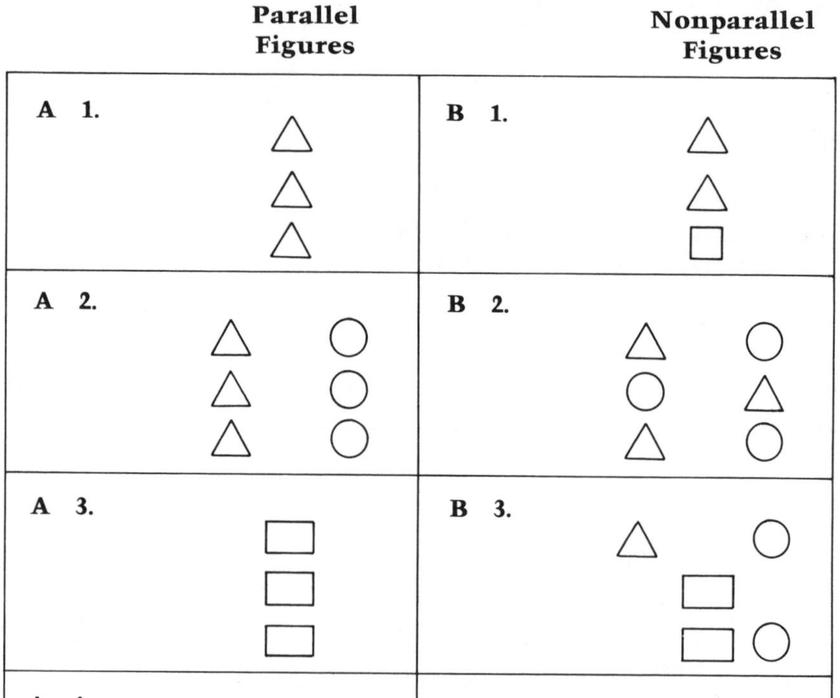

When expressing parallel ideas in a sentence, use parallel construction. That is, use similar kinds of words or groups of words to express the ideas.

You do not have to know technical terms to be able to recognize or to use parallel construction. If, however, you are interested in technical terms, see the notes in this chapter and see chapter 1, *Parts of Speech,* for the names and functions of words.

Below are words and groups of words in series. Notice that the expressions that make up each series are parallel to one another in structure.

Examples

a. a football, a baseball, a basketball

b. a motorboat, a sailboat, a rowboat

c. screwdrivers, wrenches, hammers, saws

d. comes, stays, leaves

e. came, stayed, left

f. throws the ball, bats the ball, catches the ball

g. running, jumping, diving

h. to sing, to talk, to read, to listen

i. in the mountains, by the seashore, on the desert

j. graduated from college, joined the Peace Corps, went to law school, graduated from law school

Quick Quiz: A

In each item, circle *the element that does not belong in the series.*

Model: sings, laughs, rowboat, dances

1. houses, apartments, cabins, running
2. bear, lion, hunting, sheep
3. ate lunch, dinner, ate breakfast
4. a chair, table, a sofa, a lamp
5. going to work, coming home, to eat dinner
6. in the country, fishing, at the river

Answers to Quick Quiz A are on page 277.

Words or phrases or clauses that express parallel ideas should be parallel in construction.

Below are two sets of sentences. The sentences on the **left** express parallel ideas through parallel construction. The sentences on the **right** express the same ideas through nonparallel construction.

Words in a series should be parallel.

Examples

Parallel	Nonparallel
a. They both used to like *people,** *football,* and *chess.*	They both used to like *people, football,* and to play chess.

**People, football,* and *chess* are nouns. A *noun is a word that names something.*

people	△	*people*	△
football	△	*football*	△
chess	△	**to play chess**	□

Parallel	Nonparallel
b. Be sure to pick up *the* passport, the tickets,* and *the visa* before you get on the plane.	Be sure to pick up *the passport, the tickets,* and visa before you get on the plane.

**The, a,* and *an* are *articles.*

the passport	○	*the passport*	○
the tickets	○	*the tickets*	○
the visa	○	**visa**	△

Parallel	Nonparallel
c. He spent most of his time *talking,** *shouting,* and *apologizing.*	He spent most of his time *talking,* to shout, and *apologizing.*

**Talking, shouting,* and *apologizing* are *gerunds.* A *gerund* is a word formed by adding *ing to a verb. Gerunds* are used as nouns.

talking	*talking*
shouting	**to shout**
apologizing	*apologizing*

Parallel	Nonparallel
d. Venus's flytrap *resembles** the orchid, *smells* unpleasant, and *bites* the hand that feeds it.	Venus's flytrap *resembles* the orchid, smelling unpleasant, and *bites* the hand that feeds it.

**resembles, smells, bites* are *verbs,* "action words" that tell what the subject of the sentence does, what the subject is, or what action the subject receives.

resembles	*resembles*
smells	**smelling**
bites	*bites*

Phrases* in a series should be parallel.

*A *phrase* is *a group of words used as a unit: to deaden thought, to dull feelings, in the storm, walking the dog.*

Examples (continued)

e.	At sixty she learned *to bicycle,** *to skate* and *to dance.*	At sixty she learned bicycling, *to skate,* and *to dance.*

*to bicycle: *To bicycle, to skate,* and *to dance* are infinitives. An ***infinitive*** consists of *to* and a verb. *Infinitives* are frequently used as *nouns* or as *modifiers of nouns or of verbs.*
He likes *to fish* and *to hunt.* (infinitives used as nouns)
His plan *to go* failed. (infinitive used to modify the noun *plan*)
We rushed *to finish.* (infinitive used to modify the verb *rushed.*)

	to bicycle *to skate* *to dance*	**bicycling** to skate *to dance*
f.	Television is able *to close minds,** *to deaden thought,* and *to dull feelings.*	Television is able *to close minds,* cause thought to be deadened, and *to dull feelings.*

*to close minds: *To close minds* is a phrase. Generally, a phrase is named after its first element. *To close minds* is an *infinitive phrase* because it begins with the infinitive *to close.*

	to close minds *to deaden thought* *to dull feelings*	*to close minds* **cause thought to be deadened** *to dull feelings*
g.	He chose **neither** *to referee* **nor** *to play.*	He close **neither** to referee **nor** playing.
	to referee *to play*	*to referee* **playing**

NOTE: Both of the following are correct: neither *to referee* nor *to play*

AND

neither *refereeing* nor *playing*

In an *either . . . or*
neither . . . nor
not only . . . but also

expression, the constructions that follow each part should be parallel.

Quick Quiz: B

Circle *the nonparallel element in each sentence.*

Model: Please bring home a record, magazine, and an envelope.

1. He did not have enough time to work, to sleep, to study, and for socializing.
2. Hopping, skipping, and with a jump, Ralph set a new world record.
3. The assemblyman liked debates, caucuses, and to make speeches.
4. She caught a trout, perch, and an eel.
5. I regret that it occurred to me neither to duck nor running away.

Answers to Quick Quiz B are on page 277.

Examples (continued)

h.	*In the woods,** *under a tree, beside a babbling stream,* I left the insect repellent.	*In the woods, under a tree,* a stream babbling nearby, I left the insect repellent.

*in the woods: *In the woods, beside a babbling stream,* and *under a tree* are *prepositional phrases* because each group of words begins with a *preposition: in, beside, under.* A *preposition* is a word that *explains position or relationship.* (See also chapter 1, ***Parts of Speech.***)

	in the woods *under a tree* *beside a babbling stream*	*in the woods* *under a tree* **a stream babbling nearby**
i.	Constitutional amendments can be ratified *by the legislatures of three-fourths of the states, or by conventions in three-fourths of the states.*	Constitutional amendments can be ratified *by the legislatures of three-fourths of the states,* or when the states meet in convention and three-fourths of them vote in favor of an amendment.
	by the legislatures of three-fourths of the states *by conventions in three-fourths of the states*	*by the legislatures of three-fourths of the states* **when the states meet in convention and three-fourths of them vote in favor of an amendment**
j.	The boy, *frightened beyond measure** and *shaken by the ordeal,* collapsed after the rescue.	The boy, in great fear and *shaken by the ordeal,* collapsed after the rescue.

*frightened beyond measure: *Frightened beyond measure* and *shaken by the ordeal* are *participial phrases* because each begins with a *participle: frightened, shaken.* Participles are verb forms and are often used to modify nouns. (See also chapter 1.)

	frightened beyond measure *shaken by the ordeal*	**in great fear** *shaken by the ordeal*
k.	*Studying for the graduate examination* and *taking it* made them jittery.	To study for the graduate examination and *taking* it made them jittery.
	studying for the graduate examination *taking it*	**to study for the graduate examination** *taking it*

Quick Quiz: C

Cross out *the nonparallel element in each sentence and* rewrite *the element above in parallel form.*

Model: The restaurant is famous for its elaborate menu, for its haughty waiters, and ~~overcooked food~~. *for its overcooked food.*

1. We must begin to clean our rivers, to replant our forests, and the restoration of our cities.
2. Eating my breakfast, to read my newspaper, and planning my day occupy each morning of my life.
3. The fire engine raced down the road with its siren screaming, its bell clanging, and roaring its motor.
4. Flying high, avoiding hunters, and by infrequently resting, the birds finally arrived at their nesting grounds.
5. Either various vitamins or eating foods rich in certain elements will help her recover.

Answers to Quick Quiz C are on page 277.

Clauses* in a series should be parallel.

*clause: A *clause* is *a group of words containing a subject + verb unit.* The *subject* indicates the *person* or *thing being talked about.* The *verb tells what the subject does, what the subject is,* or *what action the subject receives.*

Examples (continued)

l. During last year's rains, *the river rose, roads washed out,* and *crops rotted in the fields.*	During last year's rains, *the river rose, roads washed out,* and crops rotting in the fields.
the river rose *roads washed out* *crops rotted in the fields*	*the river rose* *roads washed out* **crops rotting in the fields**
m. This is the story *that you wrote, that I liked,* and *that John reviewed.*	This is the story *that you wrote, that I liked,* and was reviewed by John.
that you wrote *that I liked* *that John reviewed*	*that you wrote* *that I liked* **was reviewed by John**
n. *The sun set, the moon rose,* and *the cold,* sharp wind blew.*	*The sun set,* the moon rising, and *the cold, sharp wind blew.*

*cold: *Cold* and *sharp* are adjectives. An *adjective* is a word that *describes or modifies* (changes, alters) *the meaning of a noun.* (See also chapter 1.)

adj. adj. noun
Cold, sharp, winds are starting.

the sun set *the moon rose* *the cold, sharp wind blew*	*the sun set* **the moon rising** *the cold, sharp wind blew*

o. Although they were rushed, *the food was prepared, the house was cleaned,* and *the party was planned.*	Although they were rushed, *the food was prepared,* they cleaned the house, and *the party was planned.*
the food was prepared *the house was cleaned* *the party was planned*	*the food was prepared* **they cleaned the house** *the party was planned*

*Clauses can be written in the active voice (subject doer of the action) or in the passive voice (subject receiver of the action). In the nonparallel sample above, the voice incorrectly shifts from active to passive. See chapter 13.

p. After removing the egg membranes, the biologist *divided the eggs into groups* and *placed them in saline.*	After removing the egg membranes, the biologist divided the eggs into groups and places them in saline.
divided the eggs into groups *placed them in saline*	the biologist divided* the eggs into groups **places* them in saline**

*The verb carries a sense of time: past, present, or future. Verbs in a series are parallel if they are all in the past, all in the present, or all in the future. See chapter 3.

Examples of clauses

subj. vb.
as she went home (verb in the past) *she* + *went* = *subject* + *verb unit*

subj. vb.
he drives to work (verb in the present) *he* + *drives* = subject + verb unit

subj. vb.
money will be found (verb in the future) *money* + *will be found* = subject + verb unit

Quick Quiz: D

Cross out *the nonparallel element in each sentence and* rewrite *it in parallel form.*

Model: The barber to whom you go, from whom I bought this hair restorer, and ~~I go fishing with~~ changes his mind too often.

with whom I go fishing

1. After his last trip, Tarzan took his films to be developed, his car he had tuned up, and renewed his friendship with Jane.
2. Before Tuesday, the books had to be returned, the experiment had to be set up, and the job interview being held.
3. The clock on the mantel struck midnight, in the basement the cat howled, and the program on TV ended.
4. On the road he talked to everyone he met, in the city he saw seven plays in six days, and at home amusing his friends with his adventures.

Answers to Quick Quiz D are on page 277.

Procedure for Recognizing and Correcting Errors in Parallel Construction

// They liked to fly, to hike, and surfing.

Step 1: Look at the sentence.
Does the sentence contain a series of similar ideas?
Yes, it contains *to fly, to hike,* and *surfing.*

Step 2: If the answer is *yes,* look at each element in the series.
Is each element in the series built like every other element?
No, *surfing* is unlike *to fly* and *to hike.*

a. If the answer is *yes,* the sentence probably is parallel in construction.

b. If the answer is *no,* construct the series so that all elements are built alike—are in parallel construction. Corrected the sentence would read *They liked to fly, to hike, and to surf.*

REVIEW AND PRACTICE

Each of the sections of this Review and Practice is different. Do some exercises in each section, then check your answers and decide which sections—if any—you need to continue to work through. Answers are on pages 278–279.

Exercise A Write **parallel** *in front of each sentence that contains parallel construction.* Write **nonparallel** *in front of each sentence that lacks parallel construction.*

Model: nonparallel We discussed deficit spending at home, at my club, and golfing.

1. ______________ Each office was staffed with one secretary, one receptionist, and two typists.
2. ______________ Manuel wanted not only clear thinking from his students but also for them to present their ideas forcefully.
3. ______________ The bread dough rose steadily, then dropping rapidly.
4. ______________ We had ants in the cupboard and the shelves.
5. ______________ A cell membrane resembles a slice of Swiss cheese and allows the passage of many substances into and out of the cell.

Exercise B Underline *parallel constructions and* circle *nonparallel constructions in the sentences below.*

Model: He likes to drive his car, to sail his boat, and racing his horse.

1. Max dislikes sanding and painting.

2. She is beautiful and arrogant.

3. He was pulled from the water coughing, choking, and with gasps.

4. Lenore talked about the accident with regret but without rancor.

5. Unfortunately, many home appliances are becoming expensive, unreliable, and costly to maintain.

6. They looked under the sofa, behind the drapes, and in the laundry basket, and they still could not find the lizard they had caught that afternoon.

7. Don Quixote wanted either to dream the impossible dream or to fight the impossible foe.

8. Mountain climbing, spelunking, and to back pack are popular activities.

9. Turn right at the first signal, follow the white line, driving to the end of the road.

10. Milt reported that the fire began suddenly, the fire fighters could not control the blaze,but that no one was hurt.

Exercise C Circle *the letter of the parallel sentence in each pair of sentences below.*

Model: (a) The baby learned to crawl, to sit, and to reach.
b. The baby learned crawling, to sit, and reaching.

1. a. As you already know, Agnes was dragged from the room screaming, kicking, and biting.
   b. As you already know, Agnes was dragged from the room with screams, kicking, and biting.

2. a. Although I have never seen an atom, molecule, or a pi meson, I believe they exist.
   b. Although I have never seen an atom, a molecule, or a pi meson, I believe they exist.

3. a. Napoleon was short, Caesar was bald, and Nelson was one-eyed.
   b. Napoleon was short, Caesar was bald, and one eye was all that Nelson had.

4. a. She is in the hospital because she liked singing in the rain and dancing in the shower.
   b. She is in the hospital because she liked to sing in the rain and dancing in the shower.

5. a. Not being able to write is a handicap; not being able to read is a tragedy.
   b. Not being able to write is a handicap; it is a tragedy not to be able to read.

Exercise D *In each sentence,* circle *the construction in parentheses that parallels the* **underlined** *construction.*

Model: Inez enjoys bowling, ((running), to run, ran), ((skating), to skate, skates), and ((playing tennis), to play tennis).

1. He coughed loudly and (repeatedly, with repetition).
2. Alex is looking for a book, (a pencil, pencil), and (an eraser, eraser).
3. The thieves took a red vase, (a good book, a book that was good), and (a bowl made of silver, a silver bowl).
4. Under the rock, (next to the tree, the tree is nearby), you will find a rare specimen.
5. He drove me almost mad drumming, (playing his harmonica, in playing his harmonica), and (with his song, singing).
6. To get to the island, he walked, (riding the bus, rode the bus, rides the bus), and (swimming, swims, swam).
7. I want either the money you owe me or (I want the collateral you put up, the collateral you put up).
8. He wrote that he was employed but (he was unhappy with the on-the-job training, that he was unhappy with the on-the-job training).
9. So far, they have agreed neither to accept the settlement (nor have they agreed to reject it, nor to reject it, and not to reject it either).
10. Roy hired the baby sitter, (he cancelled the milk delivery, cancelled the milk delivery, cancelling the milk delivery), and (he left on his vacation, left on his vacation, leaving on his vacation).

Exercise E *In each sentence below,* circle *the nonparallel part, and* rewrite *it in parallel form in the blank provided.*

Model: Although he didn't do it, Tex felt like beating him, kicking him, and to shake him. shaking him

1. When she got the money, Vera bought a tuner, amplifier, and four speakers. ______
2. Elena is neither a swimmer nor can she dive. ______
3. The Beatles', Bob Dylan's, and the recordings of Odetta have already become classics. ______
4. He tried explaining and to excuse what he had done. ______
5. Pierre knows well that entering the contest is foolhardy, that enduring it is difficult, and winning it is impossible. ______

Answers to Review and Practice are on pages 278–279.

CHAPTER TEST

In each sentence below, underline *the nonparallel part, then* write *it in parallel form in the space provided.*

Model: He wanted to write, to read, and cooking. to cook

1. My landlord owned a duplex, condominium, and a motel. ______

2. Stereo systems can be assembled from separate components, or they are purchaseable as preassembled units. ______

3. The operation was carried out with speed, finesse, and daringly. ______

4. Happily, with excitement, and without fear, she approached the empty house. ______

5. The accident was holding up traffic, making me nervous, and to force me to be late for dinner. ______

6. Andy seemed to believe neither in her own ability to control the situation nor that anyone was concerned for her welfare. ______

7. After surgery he had to relearn pitching, to catch, and fielding. ______

8. The retired hunter owned a camel, angora cat, and an ocelot. ______

9. Although it is one-celled, the amoeba can ingest food, respire, and reproduction. ______

10. He was paid to paint the house, to build the fence, and gardening. ______

Answers to Chapter Test are on page 279.

Answers: Chapter 11

Answers to Quick Quiz A

1. running 2. hunting 3. dinner 4. table 5. to eat dinner 6. fishing

Answers to Quick Quiz B

1. for socializing 2. with a jump 3. to make speeches 4. perch 5. running

Answers to Quick Quiz C

1. ~~the restoration of~~ to restore (our cities)
2. ~~to read~~ reading (my newspaper)
3. ~~roaring its motor~~ its motor roaring
4. ~~by infrequently resting~~ resting infrequently
5. ~~eating~~ foods rich in certain elements

Answers in Quick Quiz D

1. ~~his car he had tuned up~~ had his car turned up
2. (the job interview) ~~being held~~ had to be held
3. ~~in the basement the cat howled~~ the cat in the basement howled
4. (at home) ~~amusing~~ he amused (his friends with his adventures)

Answers to Review and Practice

Exercise A — Notice that ...

1. parallel
2. nonparallel — paired expressions like *not only* . . . *but also* must introduce parallel constructions. Parallel: Manuel wanted not only clear thinking but also forceful presentation of ideas from his students.
3. nonparallel — Parallel: . . . dropped rapidly.
4. nonparallel — Parallel: We had ants in the cupboard and on the shelves.
5. parallel

Exercise B

1. sanding, painting
2. beautiful, arrogant
3. coughing, choking, with gasps
4. with regret, without rancor
5. expensive, unreliable, costly
6. under the sofa, behind the drapes, in the laundry basket
7. to dream the impossible dream, to fight the impossible foe
8. mountain climbing, spelunking, and to back pack
9. Turn to the right at the first signal, follow the white line, driving to the end of the road
10. that the fire began suddenly, the firefighters could not control the blaze, that no one was hurt

Exercise C

1. (a) 2. (b) 3. (a) 4. (a) 5. (a)

Exercise D

1. repeatedly
2. a pencil, an eraser
3. a good book, a silver bowl
4. next to the tree.
5. playing his harmonica, singing
6. rode the bus, swam
7. the collateral you put up

8. that he was unhappy with the on-the-job training
9. nor to reject it
10. cancelled the milk delivery, left on his vacation

Exercise E

1. amplifier an amplifier
2. can she dive a diver
3. the recordings of Odetta Odetta's recordings
4. explaining to explain
   OR
   to excuse excusing
5. winning that winning

Answers to Chapter Test

1. condominium a condominium
2. they are purchaseable purchased
3. daringly daring
4. Happily with happiness
5. to force me (to be late for dinner) forcing me (to be late for dinner)
6. that anyone was concerned in anyone's concern
7. to catch catching
8. angora cat an angora cat
9. reproduction reproduce
10. for gardening to garden

CHAPTER 12

Awkward Sentences

- **The procedure for rewriting awkward sentences is on page 285.**

Chapter Contents

RULE: | Learn to recognize, revise, and avoid writing awkward sentences.

K/k/awk = awkwardness

When the errors in a sentence are not readily identifiable or when the sentence is simply poorly written, an instructor may use the marginal note *awkward.** Usually this is a signal to you to rewrite.

*awkward: *Awkward* sentences are sometimes labeled *confused, unclear, illogical,* or *obscure.* In general, no two sentences so marked are identical in structure.

A marginal notation of *awkward* may refer not only to the presence of errors in a passage so marked but also to a confused or blurred meaning that rereading does not clarify. *Awkward* often refers, also, to word order or sentence structure that interferes with smooth reading.

To achieve clarity of meaning, rewrite awkward sentences with simplicity and directness instead of trying to identify and correct individual errors separately. Try the following procedure first:

Step 1: Reread the sentence.

Step 2: Say what you mean to say out loud, the way you would in conversation.

Step 3: Write down the sentence the way you said it aloud.

Step 4: If you are not satisfied, rewrite the sentence again, starting with the *basic English word order*, which is subject* followed by verb.*

*subject: The *subject* of a sentence tells *who* or *what* the sentence is about.
*verb: The *verb* of a sentence tells what the subject *does*, what the subject *is*, or what action the subject *receives*.

Examples of basic word order

subj. vb.
a. *Jonathan built* a geodesic dome to live in.

subj. vb.
b. Her *research is progressing* rapidly.

subj. vb.
c. *Who claimed* the reward?

vb. subj. vb.
d. *Are you going*, too?
Notice that a question may differ—in word order—from other sentences.

Study the sentences below for help in revising your own awkward sentences. Notice that some parts of an awkward sentence may be both correct and easy to read when they stand alone. However, in combination with other parts of the sentence, they can cloud the meaning and/or can sound unharmonious.

In the process of rewriting an awkward sentence, you might consider the following questions:

1. *Who* or *what* is the sentence about?
The answer to this question is usually the *subject*.

2. *What* is the *subject doing*?
   The answer to this question usually includes the *verb.*

3. Answers to questions like *When? Where? Why? How?* should help you think clearly about what you really intend to say.

Rewriting Awkward Sentences

Examples **Awkward Sentence (1)** When my instructor writes *awkward* in the margin of my paper is because he says he is confused about it.

Rewriting this sentence might go something like this:

1. *Who* or *what* is the sentence about?
   Answer: *My instructor (subject)*
2. *What does my instructor do*?
   Answer: My instructor *writes (verb) awkward.*
3. *When? Where? Why? How?*

Where does my instructor do what he is doing?
Answer: My instructor writes awkward *in the margin.*
Why?
Answer: My instructor writes awkward in the margin of my paper *because he is confused by it* (the sentence).

Look over what you have written so far and finish the revision.
Sample revision (there is no single correct way to revise any sentence): *My instructor writes "awkward" in the margin of a paper when he is confused by a sentence.*

Awkward sentence (2) A law of any kind if it can be enforced, because there aren't that many law enforcement agents, should benefit many and maybe have been proven a burden to some.

Awkward	**Sample Revision**
A law of any kind if it can be enforced, because there aren't that many law enforcement agents	A law that can be enforced
should benefit many	should benefit many
and maybe has been proven a burden to some.	even though it proves to be a burden to some.

Revised sentence: A law that can be enforced should benefit many, even though it proves to be a burden to some.

Awkward sentence (3) In England, writing as he was about censorship, Piggott said (and I really didn't understand it) that you cannot say something on a stage in a play, but that the editor, however, would allow them to print where it could be read in privacy.

1. *Who* or *what* is the sentence about?
Answer: *Piggott*

2. *What did Piggott do?*
Answer: Piggott *wrote about censorship.*

3. *When? Where? Why? How?*
Where?
Answer: *In England*
Why?
Answer: Because he had something to say: *He said that some things that could not be said aloud on the stage could be printed.*

Sample revisions:

a. Piggott wrote about censorship in England; he said that things that could not be spoken on the stage could be printed.

b. Piggott was writing about censorship in England. He said that editors could publish things that could not be said on the stage.

c. In writing about censorship in England, Piggott said that there should not be as much freedom of speech on the stage as there is in print.

An error or combination of errors may be present in a sentence marked *awkward.* Below is a list of *errors common in awkward sentences.* References to explanations are in the right-hand column.

1. illogical or unnecessary shifts in
   a. point of view .... chapter 13
   b. tense .... chapter 3
   c. voice .... chapter 13

2. incorrect or unclear pronoun reference .... chapter 6

3. misplaced modifiers .... chapter 10

4. misuse of idiomatic expressions .... Glossary, dictionary

5. inaccurate parallelism .... chapter 11

6. repetitiousness .... chapter 14

7. stringiness .... chapter 16

8. unsuitable word choice or diction .... Appendix D

9. words out of harmony with general tone: See Dialect; Levels of English; Slang .... Glossary

10. inexact words .... dictionary

Procedure for Rewriting the Awkward Sentence

awk.

Step 1: Reread the sentence.

Step 2: Say what you mean to say out loud, the way you would in conversation.

Step 3: Write down the sentence the way you said it aloud.

Step 4: If you are not satisfied, rewrite the sentence again, starting with the basic English word order that puts *subject* + *verb* first.

CHAPTER 13

Voice

- **Items 197–203 in the Pretest are from this chapter.**
- **The procedure for identifying and changing the voice of verbs is on pages 290–291.**

Chapter Contents

RULE:	For stronger, more direct writing, use the active voice rather than the passive voice.

A Explanation of Voice

Every sentence must have a subject and a verb* (called a subject + verb unit). *Voice* is the form of the verb that tells whether the subject *does* the action or *receives* the action.

---

*subject and verb: The *subject* of a sentence names the person or thing that the sentence is about. The *verb* tells what the subject does, what the subject is, or what action the subject receives. (Also see chapters 1 and 2.)

subj. vb.
Kasper had eaten his lunch.

subj. vb.
Kasper's *lunch had been eaten.*

---

subj. vb.
Examples My nephew *works* hard. (active voice)

subj. vb.
This week he *will be given* a raise. (passive voice)

In the first example, the subject + verb unit is *nephew* + *works*. The subject *nephew* is the **doer** of the action *works*. In the second example, the subject + verb unit is *he* + *will be given*. The subject *he* is the **receiver** of the action *will be given*.

A-1 Active voice

When the subject is active—does the action—the verb is in the *active voice*. The subject is the *doer*.

A-2 Passive voice

When the subject is passive—receives the action—the verb is in the *passive voice*. The subject is not the doer; the subject is the *receiver*.

Read the sentences in the "Active Voice" column, then read the sentences in the "Passive Voice" column. Notice that sentences using the active voice are more direct and vigorous than sentences using the passive voice—perhaps because active voice shows an "actor" in "action." Passive voice, on the other hand, often seems vague and bland.

	Active Voice	*Passive Voice*
Examples	**a.** The earthquake *destroyed* the village (subj. / vb.) The active voice is more direct than the passive voice.	**a.** The village *was destroyed* by the earthquake. (subj. / vb.) The passive verb always includes a form of the verb be*, for example, *will be given, was* destroyed, *was* left.

*be: For forms of the verb be, see chapter 3, pages 64–65.

	Active Voice	*Passive Voice*
	b. Someone *left* a package in our mailbox. (subj. / vb.) Even when the doer is not known, the sentence can be in the active voice.	**b.** A package *was left* in our mailbox. (subj. / vb.)
	c. The city council *approved* the new medical plan. (subj. / vb.)	**c.** The new medical plan *was approved* by the city council. (subj. / vb.)

B Uses of Active and Passive Voices

The *active voice* emphasizes who (or what) performs an action.

Example **Active Voice** (emphasis on who performs the action)
The *trash collectors* finally picked up the garbage, which had been accumulating in the streets for two months.

The *passive voice* shifts emphasis away from the doer of an action and onto the receiver of an action. The passive voice can therefore be useful when it is more important to emphasize who (or what) received an action and less important to establish who performed the action.

Example **Passive Voice** (emphasis on what receives the action)
The *garbage*, which had been accumulating in the streets for two months, was finally picked up by the trash collectors.

Often when the passive voice is used, the doer of the action is not even specified.

Example The *garbage*, which had been accumulating in the streets for two months, was finally picked up.

NOTE: Both active voice and passive voice are correct, and both are useful. The active voice, however, results in less wordy, more vigorous writing. Therefore, you should use the active voice unless there is a definite reason for using the passive.

A sentence may contain both a passive verb and an active verb. Such a change (shift) in voice is correct when it is essential to the meaning or when it strengthens the writing.

Examples

a. subj. passive vb. subj. active vb.
Some people *have been thought* brave when, in reality, they *feared* running away.

subj. passive vb.
Some people *have been thought* brave. . .
(The subject *people* is *not the doer,* but the *receiver,* of *have been thought.*)

subj. vb.
. . . they *feared* running away.
(The subject *they* is *the doer* of the action.)

b. subj. act. vb. subj. pass. vb.
The hospital spokesperson *said* that the patient *had been given* a blood transfusion.

subj. vb.
The hospital spokesperson *said*. . .
(The subject is *the doer* of the action.)

subj. passive vb.
. . . that the patient *had been given* a blood transfusion.
(The subject is *not the doer,* but the *receiver,* of the action.)

Procedure for Identifying and Changing the Voice of Verbs

A marginal notation of *voice* usually refers to a passive voice verb that should be changed to an active voice verb.

Examples *voice*

a. The man was accused of dishonesty by the reporter.

Step 1: Find the subject + verb unit.
The subject + verb unit is *man* + *was accused.*

Step 2: Find the doer of the action.
The doer is the *reporter*. He did the accusing.

Step 3: If the subject is the *doer* of the action, the verb is in the active voice.

Step 4: If the doer is not the subject of the sentence, the verb is in the passive voice.
The doer (reporter) is not the subject of the sentence.

Rewrite the sentence making the doer the subject.

subject = doer

Rewritten: The *reporter accused* the man of dishonesty.

voice

b. The assistant ordered the tools, and the paper supplies were ordered by him also.

Step 1: Find the subject + verb unit.
This sentence has two subject + verb units.
1. *assistant + ordered*
2. *supplies + were ordered*

Step 2: Find the doer of the action.
The *assistant* is the doer.

Step 3: If the doer is the subject, the verb is in the active voice.
Assistant + ordered is in the active voice and does not need to be changed. If the subject is not the doer, the verb is in the passive voice.
Supplies + were ordered is in the passive voice.
Rewrite the sentence, making the doer the subject.
Since the shift from active to passive voice in the original sentence is not essential to the meaning, make the second verb active.
Rewritten: *The assistant ordered the tools and the paper supplies.*

REVIEW AND PRACTICE

Each of the sections of this Review and Practice is different. Do some exercises in each section, then check your answers and decide which sections—if any—you need to continue to work through. Answers are on page 294.

Exercise A *Below are pairs of sentences: one sentence is in the active voice and one in the passive voice.* Circle *each subject and* underline *each verb. If the subject is the doer of the action,* write doer *in the column marked subject. If the subject is the receiver of the action,* write receiver. Name *the voice by writing* active *or* passive *in the column marked voice.*

	Subject	Voice
Model: a. She offended him.	doer	active
b. He was offended by her.	receiver	passive
1a. The ball hit Lorenzo on the knee.	________	________
1b. Lorenzo was hit on the knee by the ball.	________	________
2a. The garage door was left unlocked.	________	________
2b. I left the garage door unlocked.	________	________
3a. The community elected him mayor twice.	________	________
3b. Roosevelt was elected president four times.	________	________
4a. My brother washed our car.	________	________

4b. Our windows were washed by my father. ________ ________

5a. No explanation was given by the company. ________ ________

5b. The repair technician gave no excuse. ________ ________

Exercise B Underline *the verbs in the following sentences. If a verb is in the active voice,* write active *in the blank; if a verb is in the passive voice,* write passive.

Voice

Model: Steel is produced by our company. passive

1. A service was rendered to the community by him. ________
2. Someone threatened to call the police. ________
3. The musicians, a bongo player and two violinists, were asked to play. ________
4. The operation was arranged by the surgeon. ________
5. One of the units encountered enemy action. ________

Exercise C *Rewrite sentences 1, 3, and 4 from Section B in the active voice.*

1. ________

3. ________

4. ________

Rewrite sentences 2 and 5 from Section B in the passive voice.

2. ________

5. ________

Answers to Review and Practice are on page 294.

CHAPTER TEST

In each sentence below underline *the verb and identify the voice of the verb by* circling active or passive *in parentheses.*

Model: The flood destroyed the field of cotton. (active passive)

1. Never before had young people been beset by so many conflicting ideas. (active passive)
2. The rapid transit bill was passed by a slim margin. (active passive)
3. Clement announced his candidacy at a press conference. (active passive)
4. Following the out-of-state car closely, Claudia barely could read the words "The Sunshine State" on its license plate. (active passive)
5. The leading man was known to have left town. (active passive)
6. As a consequence, the manager closed the theater for the summer. (active passive)
7. The men working on the canal were vaccinated against cholera. (active passive)
8. Someone threatened us with failure. (active passive)
9. In times of stress, we have been helped by friends. (active passive)
10. We're through. (active passive)

Answers to Chapter Test are on page 295.

Answers: Chapter 13

Answers to Review and Practice

Exercise A

		Subject	*Voice*
1a.	ball hit	doer	active
b.	Lorenzo was hit	receiver	passive
2a.	door was left	receiver	passive
b.	I left	doer	active
3a.	community elected	doer	active
b.	Roosevelt was elected	receiver	passive
4a.	brother washed	doer	active
b.	windows were washed	receiver	passive
5a.	explanation was given	receiver	passive
b.	repair technician gave	doer	active

Exercise B

1. was rendered, passive
2. threatened, active
3. were asked, passive
4. was arranged, passive
5. encountered, active

Exercise C

1. He rendered a service to the community. OR
   He rendered the community a service.

3. The committee asked the musicians, a bongo player and two violinists, to play for the dance. Notice that in changing a passive sentence into an active one, you may have to provide a subject. *Committee* is only one of a number of possible subjects for sentence 3.

4. The surgeon arranged for the operation.

2. A threat was made to call the police.

5. Enemy action was encountered by one of the units.

Answers to Chapter Test

1. had been beset (passive)
2. was passed (passive)
3. announced (active)
4. could read (active)
5. was known (passive)
6. closed (active)
7. were vaccinated (passive)
8. threatened (active)
9. have been helped (passive)
10. are (*we're* is a contraction of *we are*) (*active*)

CHAPTER 14

Wordiness

• **The procedure for revising wordy passages is on page 303.**

Chapter Contents

RULE: Learn to recognize, revise, and avoid wordiness in your writing.

wdy = wordiness

Wordiness is the use of more words than the meaning and style* of a piece of writing require. Unnecessary words cloud the meaning of a statement and weaken its impact. Aspects of wordiness travel under various names such as *repetitiousness, redundancy, padding, tautology.*

**style:* The individual way in which one expresses one's self. (See also Glossary, page 372.)

A Avoid Needless Repetition of Words or Phrases*

**phrase:* A group of words used as a unit. Example: I drove [to the theater] (phase).

Examples

	Repetitions	Sample revisions
a.	*Reading* the chapter on economic development was difficult *reading,* although I was interested in the subject. The use of *reading* a second time is repetitious.	Reading the chapter on economic development was difficult, although I was interested in the subject. OR The chapter on economic development was difficult reading, although the subject interested me.
b.	One problem *in this city* is that the people *in this city* have too few parks and playgrounds. The use of *in this city* a second time is repetitious.	One problem in this city is that the people have too few parks and playgrounds. OR One problem is that the people in this city have too few parks and playgrounds.
c.	The *football game* I found most interesting was the *football game* played January 1, 1971, in the Rose Bowl. The use of *football game* a second time is repetitious.	The football game I found most interesting was the one played in the 1971 Rose Bowl.

Repetitiousness can sometimes be avoided by substituting a *synonym* for the repeated element. (A *synonym* is a word that *means the same,* or almost the same, as another word. *Large* and *big, sad* and *unhappy, mute* and *speechless* are examples of synonyms.) Some changes in wording, punctuation, and capitalization may be necessary in the process of revision.

		Repetitions	Sample revisions
Examples	**a.**	They had two *automobiles,* a compact *automobile* and a station wagon.	They had two automobiles, a compact car and a station wagon. *Car* is a synonym for *automobile.*
	b.	He was in a *hurry* and *hurried* off before I could speak to him.	He was in a hurry and rushed off before I could speak to him.
	c.	This *substance* was formed from two other *substances.*	This substance was formed from two other elements.

Quick Quiz: A

In the following sentences, cross out *any repetitious words or phrases.*

Model: Letters to the editor are sometimes interesting ~~letters.~~

1. I think it is important to understand his analysis and, I think, his conclusions.
2. I wish I understood him, but I don't understand him.
3. They had two dogs, a collie dog and a shepherd dog.

Answers to Quick Quiz A are on page 307.

B Avoid Needless Repetition of Ideas

		Repetitions	Sample revisions
Examples	**a.**	The play's *final conclusion ended* with the death of Hamlet. *Final* means *conclusion* or *ending.* Needless repetition of the idea is redundant.	The play ended with the death of Hamlet.
	b.	*From the first, at the beginning* of the party I knew I would not like the honored guest. *From the first* means at *the beginning.*	At the beginning of the party, I knew I would not like the honored guest.
	c.	*In my opinion, I believe* the voting age should remain the same. *In my opinion* means *I believe.*	In my opinion, the voting age should remain the same.

Quick Quiz: B

In the following sentences, cross out *repetitious words and phrases.*

Model: ~~Right away~~ the whale surfaced immediately.

1. Some of the most advanced social thinkers lived during the nineteenth century, between 1800 and 1899.

2. Having nothing to eat for four days and being hungry, the men formulated an ingenious plan for getting food.

3. The intercommunication system that sends and receives messages is being misused.

Answers to Quick Quiz B are on page 307.

C Avoid Padding

Padding is the intentional inclusion of material that simply increases the length of a paragraph or paper without adding anything of importance to the meaning. Trying to produce a required number of words in a paper or report can result in padding. While padding may help the writer achieve length in his writing, it usually results in blurred meanings and uninteresting presentation of ideas. An alternative is a deeper treatment of a subject through additional points or examples.

One of the examples below is padded; one is not. Both use the same number of words, but because of excess verbiage the first sample manages to cover only a small part of the information present in the unpadded version.

Examples

Padded Version

According to one theory, and there are several others, the universe, which consists of everything we can detect with telescopes and other instruments, and more we cannot yet perceive, is the result of an enormously large explosion. That explosion is called the "Big Bang" by astronomers, those individuals who study stars, planets, and galaxies as well as other features of the sky. They estimate that the explosion occurred long ago, several billion years in the past to be more precise, although the event cannot be exactly dated. All the material of the universe—all gases, all solids, all molecules and atoms—was located in one place and formed a very dense object that included everything. The event that followed next was astonishing, unlike anything ever witnessed by man. Because all matter was packed so densely together in this one object, certain forces that typically come into effect when matter is . . .

Unpadded Version

According to one theory, the universe as we know it now is the result of a tremendous explosion, the so-called "Big Bang," which occurred several billion years ago. All matter present in today's universe was concentrated then in a single mass that simply blew apart because of normal physical forces that operate when matter is packed densely together. At first, for only moments, matter was transformed entirely into energy. Thereafter, as the energy of the explosion dissipated outward from the point of the event and the process slowed, energy began to convert into matter. Subsequently the matter in a given area was drawn together through the forces of gravity to form clouds of gases and eventually the solid stuff of the universe. That process, which began so long ago, has not yet completed itself, and the universe we witness is the still-changing result of that initial explosion.

Each sample is about one hundred and fifty words long. If the writer had been asked to write a two hundred and fifty word report on the Big Bang, he would need to fill out the unpadded version. More information would do it effectively; padding would not.

Quick Quiz: C

In the following sentences, cross out *padding.*

Model: I have always been impressed by ~~and stood in awe before~~ those who can understand the theory of relativity.

1. My uncle has a case of pneumonia.
2. No doubt, we are sure, spring has arrived.
3. People should safeguard birds and protect them from danger.
4. Galileo made radically new observations in the field of astronomy.
5. One of the signs that the local neighborhood is no longer, as it used to be, a place of what could be called genuine community is the unwanted and much deplored rise in the practice of what is known as vandalism.

Answers to Quick Quiz C are on page 307.

D Avoid Wordy Sentence Structures that Weaken Your Writing

D-1 "There is . . . ," "there are . . . ," "there was. . . ," "there were"

Avoiding these constructions will allow you to say what you have to say in fewer words. Compare the following:

Examples

a. There was a dispute among the allies about the partitioning of Germany. (12 words)
The allies disputed about the partitioning of Germany. (8 words)

b. There is a problem left, which must be solved by the next team of investigators. (15 words)
The next team of investigators must solve a remaining problem. (10 words)

c. There were several reasons why the meeting was moved to Cincinnati by the arrangers of the conference. (17 words)
The arrangers of the conference moved the meeting to Cincinnati for several reasons. (13 words)

D-2 The Passive Voice*

**Passive Voice*: In the *passive voice*, the doer of the action is not the subject of the sentence. In the *active voice*, on the other hand, the doer of the action is the subject of the sentence. See the examples below, and see also chapter 13.

The passive voice can be useful, but it requires more words than the active voice to say the same thing. Compare the following:

Examples

a. The *police* [subject] were called by the *victim*. [doer of action] (7 words)
(This sentence is in the *passive voice.*)

The *victim* [subject, doer of action] called the *police*. (5 words)
(This sentence is in the *active voice.)*

b. Our *intentions* were misunderstood by the *officials*. (7 words)
The *officials* misunderstood our *intentions*. (5 words)

c. If no errors are reported to our credit officers by you, it will be assumed by them that your statement is correct as it stands. (25 words)
If you do not report errors to our credit officers, they will assume that the statement is correct. (18 words)

E Avoid Words Added for Emphasis

Little words added for emphasis—*very, definitely, certainly, absolutely, really,* and so forth—rarely add emphasis. Instead, their first effect is to make sentences wordier.

Examples

a. **Wordy:** Josiah certainly knew very well what he was doing. Furthermore, he very definitely felt that he was absolutely securely within his rights. (22 words)
Revised: Josiah knew well what he was doing; furthermore, he felt securely within his rights. (14 words)

b. **Wordy:** I very sincerely mean it when I tell you I am quite certain this course of action absolutely will have very dire consequences. (23 words)
Revised: I mean it when I tell you I am certain this course of action will have dire consequences. (18 words)

F Avoid "I think," "I feel"

A reader assumes that you think what you write and that the opinions you express represent what you feel to be the case. Simply eliminate the "I think's," "I feel's," "I believe's," and "It is my opinion that's" from your papers.

Quick Quiz: D

In the following sentences, cross out the unnecessary words and phrases.

". . .But in a very much larger sense, it is my opinion that we cannot dedicate, we cannot consecrate, we certainly cannot hallow this ground. I believe that the very brave men, living and dead, who surely struggled here, have definitely consecrated it far above our poor power to add or to detract. I feel that the world surely will little note, nor very long remember, what we say here, but it definitely can never forget what they did here. I think it is for us, the living, rather to be entirely dedicated to the undoubtedly unfinished work which they who fought here have assuredly thus far so nobly advanced. Finally, I think that it is rather for us to be here dedicated to that enormously great task certainly remaining before us—that from these honored dead we take impressively increased devotion to that cause for which they absolutely gave the very last full measure of devotion; that we here very highly resolve that these dead certainly shall not have died in vain; that this nation, under God, absolutely shall have a quite new birth of freedom, and that government of the people, by the people, for the people shall not perish from the earth."

Answers to Quick Quiz D are on page 308.

Procedure for Revision of Wordy Passages

wdy Below is an example of a procedure for revising a wordy passage.

Like the other residents of the state, I have strong and firm feelings about how the residents of this state should finance the construction of highways. I believe, first of all, that the residents of this state should not have to pay more additional gasoline taxes to finance highway construction, and I believe that residents of the state should not be required to pay higher bridge tolls in order to finance highways.

Example **Step 1:** Look for repetition of words or phrases.
Find words or phrases that are repeated in the passage, and delete those that are unnecessary.
Find synonyms for frequently repeated—but essential—words or phrases.

Step 2: Look for repetition of ideas.
Find those ideas that are repeated in different ways, and delete those that are unnecessary.

Step 3: Look for padding.

Delete any words or sentences that increase the length of a passage but add nothing substantial to the meaning.

Step 4: Check to see that you have not overused constructions that lead to wordiness ("There is," "there are," and so forth; passive voice).

Step 5: Look for unnecessary words that have been added for emphasis or that mean the same as "I think," "I feel."

Like the other residents of this state, I have strong ~~and firm~~ feelings about how ~~the residents of this state~~ should finance the construction of highways. ~~I believe,~~ first ~~of all, that the residents of this state~~ should not have to pay ~~more~~ additional gasoline taxes ~~to finance highway construction,~~ and ~~I believe that residents of the state should not be required to pay~~ higher bridge tolls ~~in order to finance highways.~~

Step 6: Rewrite the passage in simple, smooth, concise form.
Sample revision:
Like other residents of the state, I feel strongly about how citizens should finance highway construction. First, I oppose additional gasoline taxes and bridge tolls.

(Notice that the meaning is clearer in the 25-word revision than in the 72-word original.)

CHAPTER REVIEW AND PRACTICE

Each of the sections of this Review and Practice is different. Do some exercises in each section, then decide which sections—if any—you need to continue to work through. Answers are on pages 308–309.

Exercise A *In each sentence below,* cross out *unnecessary words or groups of words.*

Model: ~~There are~~ only a few patients ~~who actually~~ know what services are available to them ~~as patients.~~

1. The lack of communication and the lack of involvement cause alienation among people.
2. Foremost in my mind is that I believe that this college is too impersonal.
3. There are three things that can be done to remedy the situation.
4. Much of the crop was ruined due to the fact of the flood.
5. I personally feel this is so.

Exercise B Rewrite *each sentence below, shortening the underlined passage.*

Model 1: Your shipment <u>was received by our firm</u> yesterday.
Revision: Our firm received your shipment yesterday.

Model 2: I have a liking for outdoor concerts.
Revision: I like outdoor concerts.

1. The office will be in need of a new air conditioner next summer.

2. England was invaded by the Normans in 1066.

3. His belief is that da Vinci was a better painter than Raphael.

4. Vitamin C deficiency is the cause of scurvy.

5. There are three specific changes that we feel should be made by the new administration next year.

Exercise C *Eliminate wordiness by* rewriting *each group of sentences.*

Model: Louis Pasteur devised a method of killing harmful bacteria in milk. He was also the discoverer of a rabies vaccine.
Sample revision: Louis Pasteur devised a method of killing harmful bacteria in milk and discovered a rabies vaccine.

1. One of the two major dangers to our environment is water pollution. The second imminent danger is that of air pollution.

2. Tchaikovsky composed ballet music for a ballet that was based on Shakespeare's *Romeo and Juliet*. Prokofieff also wrote music for a ballet based on *Romeo and Juliet*.

3. If any of the parts is structurally defective it will be replaced by us. We will also replace any parts that may have been damaged.

____

____

____

4. Auguste Renoir is regarded by some art historians as one of the most important of the impressionist painters. Other important painters known as impressionists are Claude Monet and Edgar Degas. These three men could be considered the most significant of the impressionist painters.

____

____

____

5. Many of the individuals in the community happened to hold a belief in witches. However, in reality in the majority of cases, even those people who believed in witches did not actually feel afraid of them.

____

____

____

Exercise D *Revise this passage, eliminating wordiness.*

Arthur Blanque insists and asserts that in order for there to be effective government there must be adequate and effective communication between each and every congressman, and those people that he represents in the Congress. He firmly and definitely believes that the incumbent seems to have failed in his duty and his responsibility of communicating effectively with the people in his (the incumbent's) congressional district. Arthur Blanque promises wholeheartedly that he will do his utmost intelligent best in order to change the situation if and when he is elected to the office of representative of the people in this district. If he is elected as a congressman (representative), Arthur Blanque will have sent to every registered voter in the district, regardless of his or her political party, a newsletter that will present his (Blanque's) voting record, the work and achievements of any committees that he may happen to belong to, and the trend of opinion in letters that have been received by him from his constituents in his district. In his opinion, he believes that such a newsletter would be very brief and short, and actually would be economical both to produce and also to mail.

Answers to Chapter Review and Practice are on pages 308–309.

ANSWERS: CHAPTER 14

Answers to Quick Quiz A

1. I think it is important to understand his analysis and, ~~I think,~~ his conclusions.
2. I wish I understood him, but I don't ~~understand him.~~
3. They had two dogs, a collie ~~dog~~ and a shepherd ~~dog.~~

Answers to Quick Quiz B

1. Some of the most advanced social thinkers lived during the nineteenth century, ~~between 1800 and 1899.~~

   OR

   Some of the most advanced social thinkers lived ~~during the nineteenth century~~, between 1800 and 1899.
2. Having nothing to eat for four days ~~and being hungry,~~ the men formulated an ingenious plan for getting food.

   OR

   ~~Having nothing to eat for four days and~~ Being hungry, the men formulated an ingenious plan for getting food.
3. The intercommunication system ~~that sends and receives messages~~ is being misused.

   OR

   The ~~intercommunication~~ system that sends and receives messages is being misused.

Sample Answers to Quick Quiz C

1. My uncle has ~~a case of~~ pneumonia.
2. No doubt, ~~we are sure,~~ spring has arrived.
3. People should safeguard birds ~~and protect them from danger~~.
4. Galileo made radically new observations in ~~the field of~~ astronomy.

5. One ~~of the~~ sign~~s~~ that the ~~local~~ neighborhood is no longer, ~~as it used to be,~~ a place of ~~what could be called~~ genuine community is the ~~unwanted and much deplored~~ rise in ~~the practice of what is known as~~ vandalism.
   (Unpadded: One sign that the neighborhood is no longer a place of genuine community is the rise in vandalism.)

Answers to Quick Quiz D

". . .But in a larger sense,we cannot dedicate, we cannot consecrate, we cannot hallow this ground. The brave men, living and dead, who struggled here, have consecrated it far above our poor power to add or detract. The world will little note, nor long remember, what we say here, but it can never forget what they did here. It is for us, the living, rather to be dedicated to the unfinished work which they who fought here have thus far so nobly advanced. It is rather for us to be here dedicated to that great task remaining before us—that from these honored dead we take increased devotion to that cause for which they gave the last full measure of devotion; that we here highly resolve that these dead shall not have died in vain; that this nation, under God, shall have a new birth of freedom, and that government of the people, by the people, for the people shall not perish from the earth."

Abraham Lincoln
—from *The Gettysburg Address*

Answers to Chapter Review and Practice

NOTE: Only one of several possible answers is given for each revision.

Exercise A

1. ~~The~~ lack of communication and ~~the lack~~ of involvement cause alienation among people.
2. ~~Foremost in my mind is that~~ I believe ~~that~~ this college is too impersonal.
3. ~~There are~~ three things ~~that~~ can be done to remedy the situation.
4. Much of the crop was ruined due to ~~the fact of~~ the flood.
5. ~~I personally feel~~ this is so.

Exercise B

1. The office will need a new air conditioner next summer.
2. The Normans invaded England in 1066.
3. He believes that da Vinci was a better painter than Raphael.
4. Vitamin C deficiency causes scurvy.
5. We feel that the new administration should make three specific changes next year.

Exercise C

1. The two major dangers to our environment are water and air pollution.
2. Tchaikovsky and Prokofieff each composed music for a ballet based on Shakespeare's *Romeo and Juliet.*
3. We will replace defective or damaged parts.
4. Some art historians regard Auguste Renoir, Claude Monet, and Edgar Degas as the most significant impressionist painters.
5. Many people in the community believed in witches but did not fear them.

Exercise D

Suggested revision in process. The completed revision follows.

Arthur Blanque insists ~~and asserts that in order for there to be~~ that effective government ~~there must be~~ requires adequate ~~and effective~~ communication between ~~each and every~~ a congressman and ~~those~~ the people ~~that~~ he represents ~~in the Congress.~~ He ~~firmly and definitely~~ believes that the incumbent ~~seems to have~~ has failed ~~in his duty and his~~ to inform the people ~~responsibility of communicating effectively with the people in his (the incumbent's) congressional district. Arthur~~ and Blanque promises ~~wholeheartedly that he will do his utmost intelligent best in order~~ to change the situation if ~~and when he is elected to the office of representative of the people in this district. If~~ he is elected ~~as a congressman (representative), Arthur Blanque~~ will ~~have sent to~~ send every registered voter in the district, ~~regardless of his or her political party~~, a newsletter ~~that will present~~ presenting his ~~(Blanque's)~~ voting record, the work ~~and achievements~~ of ~~any~~ committees ~~that~~ he ~~may happen to belong~~ belongs to, and the trend of opinion in letters ~~that have been received by him~~ from his constituents ~~in his district. In his opinion, he believes that~~ Such a newletter would be ~~very~~ brief ~~and short,~~ and ~~actually would be~~ economical both to produce and ~~also~~ to mail.

Sample revision

Arthur Blanque insists that effective government requires adequate communication between a congressman and the people he represents. He believes that the incumbent has failed to inform the people, and Blanque promises to change the situation. If he is elected, Blanque will send every registered voter in the district a newsletter presenting his voting record, the work of committees he belongs to, and the trend of opinion in letters from his constituents. Such a newsletter would be brief and economical to produce and mail.

(The original version consists of 196 words; the revised, of 83. To put it another way, the original version is 113 words too long. A mathematician might say it was 57.6% ineffective.)

CHAPTER 15

Choppy Sentences

- **The procedure for recognizing and revising choppy sentences is on pages 312–313.**

Chapter Contents

RULE: Learn to recognize and revise choppy sentences; avoid writing them except when their use strengthens what you are writing.

A Explanation of Choppy Sentences

Several short sentences following one another can cause abrupt stopping and starting, or choppiness.

Example (This entire passage is composed of choppy sentences that do not strengthen the writing.)
The hills were dry. No rain had occurred for several months. The temperature was near 90°. The average humidity was 9 percent. A tractor struck a rock. A spark flew into the brush. The Bel Air fire had started. It was 1961.

B Revision of Choppy Sentences

Combining two or more choppy sentences into a single sentence frequently eliminates choppiness. Some change in wording, punctuation, and capitalization may be necessary.

		Choppy sentences	**Sample revisions**
Examples	**a.**	The hills were dry. No rain had occurred for several months.	The hills were dry since no rain had occurred for several months.
	b.	The temperature was near 90°. The average humidity was 9 percent.	The temperature was near 90°, and the average humidity was 9 percent.
	c.	A tractor struck a rock. A spark flew into the brush. The Bel Air fire had started. It was 1961.	A spark, caused by a tractor striking a rock, flew into the brush, and the 1961 Bel Air fire had started.

Procedure for Recognizing and Correcting Choppy Sentences

chop. *It was noon. I heard the dog bark. Then, I heard the doorbell. I saw three friends. They were my best friends. They were Alicia, Bernard, and Craig.*

Step 1: Look for short sentences.

Step 2: If you find several following one another, decide if their shortness strengthens what you are writing. If it does not, then

Step 3: combine them into longer sentences, changing wording, punctuation, and capitalization as necessary.

Sample revision: About noon, I heard the dog, then the doorbell. I went to the door and saw my three best friends—Alicia, Bernard, and Craig.

CHAPTER REVIEW AND PRACTICE

Combine each group of choppy sentences into a single clear sentence.

Model: Choppy: Mark sat down. The chair broke.
Some possible revisions: (a) Mark sat down, and the chair broke. (b) As Mark sat down, the chair broke. (c) Upon sitting down, Mark broke the chair. (d) The chair broke as Mark sat down.

1. The game started. Miller popped up. Gomez caught the ball.

2. Dave played bongo drums. Ann played guitar.

3. The window opened. The rain dripped in.

4. The spark fell. The rug ignited. The house caught fire.

5. Queen Elizabeth loved Robert Devereux. She had him executed.

6. I went to the opera. I fell asleep. A high C wakened me.

7. Bach was a prolific composer. He influenced modern jazz.

8. I went to the polling place. I signed my name. I received a ballot.

Answers to Chapter Review and Practice are on page 314.

ANSWERS: CHAPTER 15

Answers to Chapter Review and Practice

NOTE: Only one of several possible revisions of each item is given.

1. The game started, Miller popped up, and Gomez caught the ball.
2. Dave played bongo drums, while Ann played guitar.
3. The window opened, and the rain dripped in.
4. After the spark fell, the rug ignited, and the house caught fire.
5. Although Queen Elizabeth loved Robert Devereux, she had him executed.
6. I fell asleep at the opera, only to be awakened by a high C.
7. Bach was a prolific composer who influenced modern jazz.
8. I went to the polling place, signed my name, and received a ballot.

CHAPTER 16

Stringy Sentences

- **The procedure for correcting stringy sentences is on page 316.**

Chapter Contents

RULE: Learn to recognize, revise, and avoid writing stringy sentences.

A Explanation of Stringy Sentences

When a writer ignores logical stopping places and ties together ideas that should be expressed in separate sentences, the result is a stringy sentence.

NOTE: Passages marked "stringy" may include run-on sentences. (See also chapter 8 for run-ons.)

Example Yesterday, the Air Safety Board's investigation of the midair collision of a commercial passenger plane and a twin-engine private plane, which resulted in the deaths of 56 people, was completed, and the investigation showed that, immediately before impact, the private plane had made a 360 degree roll, and that both planes had been in an air corridor that was restricted to incoming commercial flights, and the board concluded that, in all probability, the accident was the result of pilot error.

B Revision of Stringy Sentences

Stringiness can generally be eliminated by dividing the stringy sentence into two or more sentences. Changes in wording, punctuation, and capitalization may be necessary.

Example Yesterday, the Air Safety Board's investigation of the midair collision of a commercial passenger plane and a twin-engine private plane, which resulted in the deaths of 56 people, was completed.// The investigation showed that, immediately before impact, the private plane had made a 360 degree roll.// The report stated that both planes had been in an air corridor restricted to incoming commercial flights.// The board concluded that, in all probability, the accident was a result of pilot error.

Procedure for Recognizing and Correcting Stringy Sentences

Step 1: Find any sentence that ignores logical stopping places and, therefore, has become rambling or stringy.
Step 2: Divide the sentence at logical stopping places, and reword as necessary.

CHAPTER REVIEW AND PRACTICE

Revise these sentences to eliminate stringiness.

Model: Stringy: The senator has, for many years, been a watchdog for the consumer, and he said that deceptive labeling and packaging are forms of theft, and that the public is being manipulated, defrauded, and exploited by manufacturers and distributors; he predicted that until consumers become aware, articulate, and active on their own behalf, the situation would steadily worsen.

Revised: The senator has, for many years, been a watchdog for the consumer.//He said that deceptive labeling and packaging are forms of theft, and that the public is being manipulated, defrauded, and exploited by manufacturers and distributors.//He predicted that until consumers become aware, articulate, and active on their own behalf, the situation would steadily worsen.

1. Until scientific investigations were carried out, zoologists believed that the rat and the rabbit belonged to the same biological group, but those studies revealed that the animals differed so much in their embryonic structure that they could no longer be classified together, but had to be assigned to two orders: *rodentia* for the rat and *lagomorpha* for the rabbit.

____

____

____

____

____

2. Before the Second World War, it was common practice to pay certain European writers by the word, and these writers became experts on long, involved sentences, since these individuals wished to earn as much money as possible for each article, and therefore, many of their sentences covered more than a page, even when the writers had little of interest to say.

____

____

____

____

____

3. One hundred years ago, a scientist could be competent in several fields of learning, such as chemistry, physics, and mathematics, but today, few scientists are fully competent in any single field, since there is too much information in each for any one person to grasp, and this multiplication of knowledge has led to a great increase of experts in narrow, but deep, areas of science.

Answers to Chapter Review and Practice are on page 319.

ANSWERS: CHAPTER 16

Answers to Chapter Review and Practice

NOTE: Only one of a number of possible revisions for each item appears below.

1. Until scientific investigations were carried out, zoologists believed that the rat and the rabbit belonged to the same biological group.// Those studies revealed that the animals differed so much in their embryonic structure that they could not be classified together.// They had to be assigned to two orders: *rodentia* for the rat and *lagomorpha* for the rabbit.
2. Before the Second World War, it was common practice to pay certain European writers by the word.// Some of these writers became experts on long, involved sentences, since the writers wished to earn as much money as possible for each article.// Therefore, many of their sentences covered more than a page, even when the writers had little of interest to say.
3. One hundred years ago, a scientist could be competent in several fields of learning, such as chemistry, physics, and mathematics.// Today, few scientists are fully competent in any single field, since there is too much information in each for any one person to grasp.// The multiplication of knowledge has led to a great increase of experts in narrow, but deep, areas of science.

CHAPTER 17

The Paragraph and the Paper

Chapter Contents

RULE:	1. See that the topic sentence of a paragraph clearly labels the contents of that paragraph. 2. See that the discussion sentences provide sufficient evidence to support the topic statement. 3. Use a transition to introduce each new topic.

A The Paragraph and Its Structure

A paragraph is a group of sentences that work together to explain or explore a single, fairly narrow topic. In general, college papers contain three types of paragraphs: *introductory* paragraphs, *discussion* paragraphs, and *closing* paragraphs.

Because they form the major part—the body—of a paper, discussion paragraphs will be explained first. It is through discussion paragraphs that the writer conveys most of the essential material in support of his or her thesis. Introductory, or opening, paragraphs will be explained next, and closing, or ending, paragraphs last.

A-1 The discussion paragraph

The discussion paragraph is usually made up of

(1) a *topic sentence*, which is a single sentence, or a *topic statement*, which is more than one sentence;
(2) some *discussion sentences that explain the topic sentence; and,*
(3) *a transitional element* of one or more words.

The Structure of the Discussion Paragraph

A diagram of a discussion paragraph:

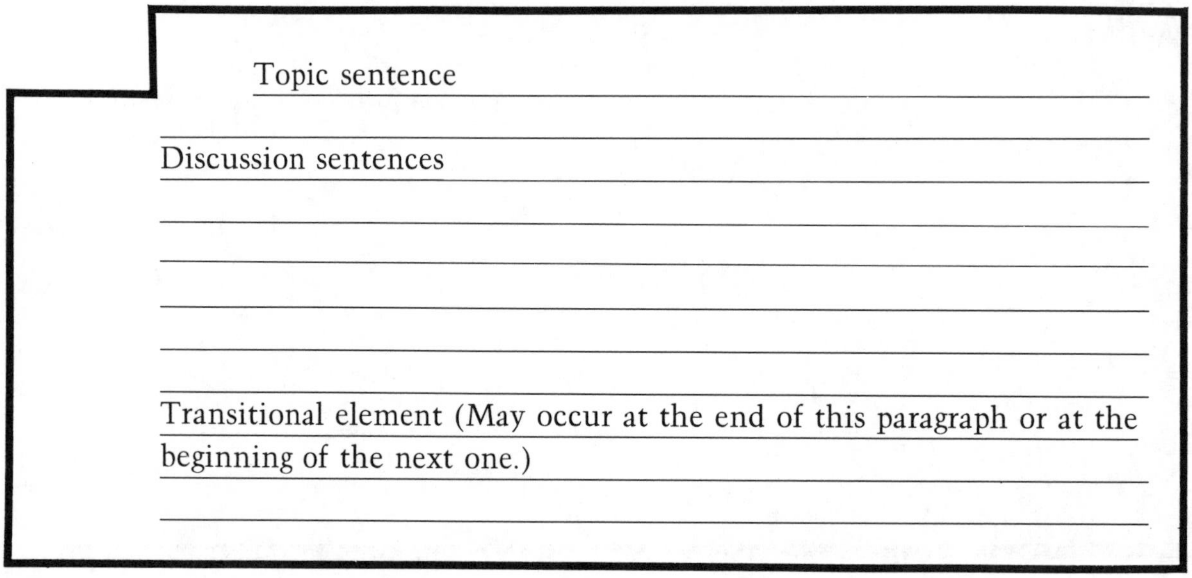

Topic sentence
Discussion sentences
Transitional element (May occur at the end of this paragraph or at the beginning of the next one.)

It may help you to think of the discussion paragraph as a package of information: The topic sentence is the label; the discussion sentences are the contents. Transitions are added to provide continuity of thought when the writer is ready to move on to a new discussion paragraph.

1. *The Topic Sentence or Topic Statement*

RULE: See that the topic sentence of a discussion paragraph clearly labels the contents of that paragraph.

• The topic sentence tells the reader in a brief, clear manner what will be discussed in the paragraph.

• The topic sentence serves as a guide to the most important points of the discussion.

• Without a clear topic sentence, the reader is often not sure what point a discussion paragraph is trying to illustrate.

The topic sentence generally raises unanswered questions in the reader's mind. For example, someone reading the topic sentence *In recent years, some critics have spoken out against the cost of space exploration* might ask: Who are the critics? What have they said? Are all complaints directed toward the same—or different—problems?

Examples of Topic Sentences

a. *The Democrats and the Republicans held different points of view regarding government aid to returning veterans.*

For practice, think of the major questions that result from sentence **a**.

____

____

____

____

____

b. *Some vegetarians omit essential nutrients from their diets.*
For practice, think of the major questions that result from sentence **b**.

____

____

____

c. *Many scholars have disagreed with the view of history presented by Arnold Toynbee.*
Think about what you, as a *reader*, would have to be presented with in the discussion sentences in order to understand topic sentence **c**.

d. *Finding employment is more difficult for some college students than for others.*
What questions arise from this topic sentence? Following this topic sentence, you might discuss the differences in job availability for men and women, for upper and lower division students, for certain ethnic groups, for urban and rural populations, and so forth.

Having raised questions in your reader's mind, you need to think—and to plan—to provide discussion sentences that will answer those questions effectively. No matter which problems are taken up, the writer needs to discuss them in enough detail to help a reader understand why the writer believes that the topic sentence is true.

2. *Discussion Sentences*

RULE:	See that the discussion sentences provide sufficient evidence to support the topic sentence.

The purpose of discussion sentences is to let the reader know, in effect, *why* the writer believes the topic statement to be true. The substance of the discussion sentences—the contents of the paragraph—must fit the package label as expressed in the topic sentence.

Discussion sentences may offer information, may present opinions of authorities in the field, and/or may present your own thinking about the concept expressed in the topic sentence.

Examples of Discussion Sentences

a. Topic Sentence: *In recent years, some critics have spoken out against the cost of space exploration programs.* Some of the critics—from the field of social welfare—have pointed to the shortage of tax money available for helping the poor and the disabled. Others—from the health sciences—have complained that inadequate budgets have held up vital research that could allow us, in the foreseeable future, to relieve human suffering. Still others—taxpayers themselves—have objected that the economic burden of taxes has prevented them from enjoying the standard of living they have earned through their labors. Although none of these groups is necessarily opposed to the idea of man's exploration of space, all of them agree that money to be used for the study of outer space could be better used here on earth.

In the paragraph above, the label fits the contents of the paragraph. The discussion sentences let the reader know why the writer thinks the topic statement is true.

b. Topic Sentence: *In addition to the inaccuracies previously cited, television advertising teaches us anatomy and physiology lessons never found in textbooks.* We are shown stomachs made of transparent plastics, heads equipped with pounding hammers and vibrating springs, and skin resembling electric hot plates. We learn that Brand X acts to stop the bubbling in our see-through stomachs, that Brand Y is capable of removing the assorted hardware from our heads, and that Brand Z can uncoil our filamentous skin. Distortions such as these might be fairly humorous were it not for the residue of confusion and undue concern they leave in the minds of many, particularly children, and the inaccuracies they teach us all.

c. Topic Sentence: *Secondly, newspapers permit readers to review information and to test both memory and perception.* I sometimes do not hear, or remember, important words in a news broadcast on radio or television. On one occasion, I argued for a whole evening with my wife over whether a certain city parking building was to cost thirty thousand or three hundred thousand dollars. We had no way of repeating the broadcast or of checking our facts. This was a minor incident, but the truth is that a person can reread any part of a newspaper account to refresh his memory or to compare one paper's account of the facts with some other source of information.

d. Topic Sentence: *In the matter of setting and scenery, however, the film seems a more flexible medium than the stage.* The camera can focus on an area only inches in size and then move to a panorama of many miles, while the size of the stage is fixed, and an indoor stage can represent outdoor settings only by means of obviously artificial devices. Furthermore, a film can show one place immediately after another, while a play must provide breaks in the action to allow for the movement of props.

e. Topic Sentence: *Ancient Egyptian agricultural rites, intended to assure the growth of a plentiful crop, represented the death of the old year and the birth of the new.* In these ceremonies, participants divided into teams and in some unknown way used a round object, the ancestor of the modern ball. Authorities speculate that this object symbolized both the head of the god of agriculture and the sun. The ancient Egyptian culture strongly influenced all neighboring peoples, and eventually the rite involving the round object spread over the entire Mediterranean basin. With the Moorish invasions of Spain during the Middle Ages, this ancestor of many ball games became established in Western Europe where, in medieval France, agricultural and religious rites merged.

(This example is the first discussion paragraph of the essay on lacrosse, page 335.)

Often students' papers are "thin." They lack detail sufficient to let a reader know why the writer thinks what he or she asserts in the topic sentences of the paper. Insufficiently developed paragraphs often cause such "thinness." By asking yourself what a reader will **need** to know in order to understand why you are making a major statement (topic sentence), you can usually decide what information to include in any discussion paragraph.

3. *Transitional Elements*

RULE:	Use a transitional word, group of words, or sentence to introduce each new point of view.

A transition may consist of one or more words—often of a whole sentence—and it prepares the reader for what is to come next. Transitions are meant to keep the reader on track in following your discussions. A transition may occur at the end of one paragraph or at the beginning of the next one.
Notice the transitional sentence underlined at the end of the following paragraph:

In recent years, some critics have spoken out against the cost of space exploration programs. Some of the critics—from the field of social welfare—have pointed to the shortage of tax money available for helping the poor and disabled. Others—from the health sciences—have complained that inadequate budgets

> have held up vital research that could allow us, in the foreseeable future, to relieve human suffering. Still others—taxpayers themselves—have objected that the economic burden of taxes has prevented them from enjoying the standard of living they have earned through their labor. Although none of these groups is necessarily opposed to the idea of man's exploration of space, all of them agree that money to be used for the study of outer space could better be used here on earth. But space scientists find these arguments shortsighted.
>
> Mankind will benefit enormously from space exploration, say the supporters of extraterrestrial research. To strenghten their point, they remind their critics of the "spin-off" products that have already resulted from the space program: improved ceramic products, sensitive equipment to check human physical responses. . . .

Notice that the *transitional sentence* signals the reader that a new package of information is coming. The transition suggests that the new paragraph will describe arguments counter to those of the social welfare workers, the health scientists, and the taxpayers.

The transition could, instead, appear in the topic sentence of the new paragraph:

> While none of these groups is necessarily opposed to the idea of man's exploration of space, all of them agree that money to be used for the study of outer space could better be used here on earth.
>
> The space scientists, *on the other hand,* argue that mankind will indeed benefit enormously from space exploration. To strengthen their point. . . .

Thus, the reader is ready to receive the arguments from the space scientists saying that the expense is worthwhile because of benefits on earth.

Notice that in the sentence *The space scientists, on the other hand, argue that mankind will indeed benefit enormously from space exploration,* the single phrase, *on the other hand,* signals the shift in discussion.

The reader focuses attention on a topic as it is being discussed, and he or she needs to be prepared for a change. Unless you signal the reader, through transitions, the reader's attention will remain on the topic you have been discussing.

It may help you to think of transitions as road signs to the reader. Through transitions you let the reader know which turns to take in order to follow your thoughts. Make your transitions clear and brief, saying just enough to let the reader know that you are shifting to a new point.

The following underlined transitions are from the paragraphs on pages 340–342.

- In addition to the inaccuracies previously cited, television advertising teaches us anatomy and physiology lessons never found in textbooks.
- Secondly, newspapers permit readers to review information and test for both memory and perception.
- In the matter of setting and scenery, however, the film seems a more flexible medium than the stage.
- With the Moorish invasion of Spain during the Middle Ages, this ancestor of many ball games became established in Western Europe where, in medieval France, agricultural and religious rites merged. (This is the last sentence of the first discussion paragraph of the essay on lacrosse, page 335—and it previews the second discussion paragraph of that essay.)

4. *Paragraph Length*

How long should a paragraph be?

In general, avoid single-sentence paragraphs (such as the one on the preceding page!).

A paragraph must be long enough—developed enough—to (1) present its topic clearly and (2) do justice in discussing that topic. Your reader must have enough time to take in the meaning of your topic statement, enough to feel convinced that you know your subject, and enough to relate the substance of the discussion to the main idea in your topic sentence. Short paragraphs often fail to provide enough information or evidence to support the topic statement.

Details that give substance to a discussion may include examples that show your reader what you mean, quotations from authorities in the field, and *your own analytical thinking* on the topic under discussion.

A paragraph can be *too long.* Frequently students include more information in a paragraph than a reader can take in easily.* Paragraphs that are too long tend to burden the reader with information without giving time to absorb meanings and relationships. In this case, the writer should learn to recognize the start of a new topic and should shift to a separate paragraph.

*For another problem—that of unrelated material in the paragraph—see *Example of Irrelevance,* page 333.

The following material, all included in one paragraph, really should be presented in two. Where can it best be divided?

> The nineteenth century breakdown in values that came about in part because of the effects of Europe's rapid change to an industrial economy was experienced by many people, but among the first to express the breakdown were the poets and artists. All of the arts had been orderly and, in some sense, ordinary during the eighteenth century. In the new age, however, poets arose who wanted to speak, through their poetry, of what their society had lost: a sense of meaning in nature, a sense of magic in the universe, a sense of depth within the individual. Suddenly, in poetry, writers were describing the innocence of the child, storms raging on Mont Blanc, a walk through fields of daffodils, and a moody, lonely hero. Wordsworth, Coleridge, and Blake started the new movement in poetry, and others learned from them that poetry could say more and hint at more than had been believed earlier. In the eighteenth century, visual artists had painted tame scenes and portraits in which all was sweetness and light, but this began to give way to a more dramatic style of art. Blake, not only a poet but also an artist, drew figures never seen in this world, which seemed to express some mighty existence beyond the earthly one. Later, Turner experimented with color in ways that showed that one could paint surface reality and also the inner reality that the human eye never actually sees but that the spirit senses. As the century progressed, movements such as these increased, with a growing attempt on the part of some painters to express the inner condition of human beings and the pain they were coming to suffer at seeing their world of values changing swiftly and with little sense of direction.

Here the reader is being asked to hold his attention too long on what the writer is saying, since information is all handled as one paragraph. Where might this long paragraph be divided? The paragraph does, in fact, talk about two things: (1) the response of poets and (2) the response of artists. Two paragraphs, one dealing with the poets and one with the artists, would be easier for a reader to understand. When the paragraph has been divided, will the addition of a transition help the reader shift attention to the new area?

The sentence that begins the second section is <u>In the eighteenth century, visual artists had painted tame scenes and portraits in which all was sweetness and light, but this began to give way to a more dramatic style of art.</u> If the writer does break the paragraph in two, it would be helpful to add a topic sentence with some transitional element in it to prepare the reader for what is to come.

Example The same spirit of adventure and seeking expressed by the poets also appeared in the visual arts, but more slowly. In the eighteenth century artists had painted tame scenes and portraits in which all was sweetness and light, but this began to give way. . . .

Notice that the new sentence serves both as a topic sentence for the new paragraph and as a transition to show how the new material is related to what has just been discussed. Transitional elements are underlined with one line; the new topic sentence information is underlined with two:

> The same spirit of adventure and seeking expressed by the poets also appeared in the visual arts, but more slowly.

In summary, make each paragraph long enough for a reader to come to understand why you made the statement you did in the topic sentence, and short enough to deal with just one major point.

A-2 The introductory paragraph

The purpose of an introductory paragraph is to make three things clear. These three things are related to a reader's need to know—from the start—what the writer intends to say. The reader needs to know

(1) the topic
(2) what the writer intends to say about the topic
(3) how the writer plans to present his material.

The introductory paragraph tells the reader these things through a *thesis sentence* and an *essay format.*

1. Thesis sentence

The *thesis sentence,* or *thesis statement,* expresses exactly the idea the writer intends to support through the discussion paragraphs. Everything in the paper should work together to demonstrate that the writer was justified in making the thesis statement. For a paper to make sense, a reader needs a thesis statement clearly presented in the introduction.

2. Essay format

Once your readers learn—through the thesis—the idea the paper will explore, they need to know what steps you plan to take to justify your thesis statement. The *essay format* lays out those steps. In it you name each of the main points to be discussed and *the order in which you will present them.* The reader is thus equipped with three essentials for traveling the path of the paper with you:

(1) the subject to be explored—the thesis
(2) the steps through which the writer will present supporting evidence
(3) the order in which those steps will be taken.

At the beginning of this chapter, an example of a discussion paragraph dealt with disagreements about the cost of space exploration. The *introductory* paragraph leading into the discussion paragraphs might have been the following:

> As the public has become aware of the huge cost of the National Aeronautics and Space Agency's (NASA's) plans to send flights to explore outer space, a debate has been growing. On one side are those who think the project wasteful; on the other are those who say the benefits outweigh the costs.

The first sentence is the *thesis* since it states the main idea the paper will examine. The second sentence is the *essay format* since it names the main points to be discussed and the order of discussion.

In the examples of brief introductory paragraphs below, the **thesis statements** are written in **dark type** and the *essay formats* in *italics*.

Examples of Introductory Paragraphs

a. **Filling San Francisco Bay will upset a delicately balanced ecology.** *A recent report by the Bay Authority points out how the migration of the white heron, the nesting of the bay shrimp, and the mating of the striped bass will be disturbed if the present filling program continues.*

b. **Few socially acceptable activities satisfy human needs more than does the process of breadmaking.** *Breadmaking satisfies, among other things, the need to receive tactile stimulation, the need to express aggression, the need to satisfy hunger, the need to create.*

c. **In their search for the basic building blocks of matter, modern physicists have begun to investigate particles that are smaller by far than atoms themselves.** *Hadrons, leptons, and quarks are three kinds of particles that earlier physicists never described, and perhaps did not envision.*

d. **The modern game of lacrosse, anthropologists tell us, developed from ancient and medieval ceremonials.** *Its ancestors came from three cultures: the ancient Egyptian, the medieval French, and the pre-Columbian Indian.*

e. Three controversial but nonviolent plans for the permanent reduction of unemployment have been suggested: *price control, wage control, and the guaranteed annual income.* **The problem of unemployment in the United States must be solved. The alternative, some say, is civil war.**

Notice that the thesis statement need not be limited to a single sentence, nor need it be the first sentence in the paragraph.

f. I prefer the "take-off" to the "put-on": I prefer exaggeration to deception, imitation to affectation, and criticism to belittlement.

Notice that the thesis sentence and the essay format may both be in a single sentence.

Many students have been taught that an introductory paragraph serves mainly to catch a reader's attention. While there is nothing wrong with catching a reader's attention, this in itself does not meet the reader's need to catch your meaning. You may certainly entice or entertain your reader, but be sure that the thesis and essay format are clear.

It is not necessary to use a transitional element between the introductory paragraph and the first discussion paragraph, for the reader still has your essay format clearly in mind and knows where you will begin your discussion. At the end of the first discussion section, however, you do need to remind the reader what your second discussion topic is. If you use simple, clear *transitions* as you move from one discussion section to the next, the whole essay should come together, and your reader will eventually be able to say, "Now I know what you meant by your thesis sentence."

Often it is more effective to write a final version of an introductory paragraph *after* you have written the body of the essay. Since, "Thoughts summon words, and words bring thoughts in turn," what you find you *have written* is often other (and often better) than what you planned to write. Studying your essay, then, can guide you to rethinking (and rewriting) your introductory paragraph.

A-3 The closing paragraph

The ending of a paper is often called the *end*, the *closing*, or the *conclusion*. Whatever its name, its purpose is to be let the reader know that the discussion is over. The writer does this through a closing paragraph that (1) *summarizes* the essay by rephrasing its thesis and essay format, or that (2) *presents* conclusions drawn from facts, observations, or concepts set forth in the essay.

Examples: Summaries

a. A mountain cabin of native wood was easier to keep warm than was one of brick; but in the desert, native stone was superior to wood because stone walls were thicker and retained cooling moisture. In the tropics, native palm-leaf thatch was cooler than tin and equally protective against rain. In each of these cases, building materials native to the region were better than those imported from different climates.

NOTE: The structure of this closing paragraph is a restatement of the thesis sentence: Native building materials are superior to imported ones. A summary of major points of the discussion:

In the mountains, wood is superior to brick.
In the desert, stone is superior to wood.
In the tropics, palm-thatch is superior to tin.

b. In modern lacrosse, then, ancient and medieval ceremonials are mixed. One form of the Egyptian agricultural rite became a French Easter game during the Middle Ages. Explorers brought a secularized form of that game to the New World, where Indians were already participating in a similar ceremony. Out of a fusion of those two games evolved what is known today as lacrosse.

(This is the closing paragraph of the essay on lacrosse, page 336.)

Examples: Conclusions

a. Our family's investigations of soaps A and B were decisive. Since soap A left no scum, removed dirt, and was harmless to skin, while soap B produced scum, was harmless to dirt, and removed skin, we concluded that soap A was a better cleaning agent than soap B.

b. The new budget, which includes appropriations for the National Aeronautics and Space Agency, will be voted on in Congress within the next few weeks. After seeing how that vote goes, we should be able to judge whose arguments have been more effective, those of the space scientists or those of the individuals who want our wealth limited to use on earth.

B The Paper, or Essay, and Its Structure

Before studying the structure of the essay, it is important that you know that no two essays are identical in form, and that many essays are decidedly different in form from the structure described here. However, the material about the paragraph and the paper is meant to initiate you into the task of writing your first essays, a task that may be unfamiliar to many of you.

There is an old bit of widsom about the structure of an essay, which has helped many in their writing:

(1) Tell people what you're going to tell them. (Introduction)
(2) Tell them. (Discussion)
(3) Then tell them what you've told them! (Conclusion)

And that's close to what you'll be doing in your essays.

The three types of paragraphs described in the first part of this chapter are the building blocks of essays. An *introductory paragraph* introduces your reader to your subject and what you intend to say about it through a *thesis sentence.* It also describes, through an *essay format,* how you intend to present your material. It may include additional sentences to help your reader become acquainted with your topic.

Discussion paragraphs follow, each of them dealing with a major aspect of your topic and appearing **in the order in which** you have promised to take them up in the essay format of the introduction. *Transitions* that show the relationships between the various major parts of your paper help guide the reader from one major point to the next.

Finally, a *closing* summarizes your paper or presents conclusions you have arrived at. The paper is finished, and you have made a serious effort to communicate with your reader.

B-1 Guidelines

1: The subject should be narrow enough

- to make it manageable within the writer's planned essay length and
- to allow for some fullness of treatment.

One way for a writer to narrow a subject is to work out an essay format, since the format, by definition, expresses the limitations he is putting on the subject.

2: The paper should be long enough

- to allow for a significant thesis sentence and essay format
- to permit an effective discussion of the substance that the thesis and essay format lead the reader to expect

- to include a fairly thorough examination of each of the major points and
- to allow clear and accurate communication of the writer's ideas.

3: The paper should be consistent in point of view.
In discussions about writing, *point of view* refers to *person.*
First person refers to the person *speaking: I, we.*
Second person refers to the person *spoken to: you.*
Third person refers to the person or thing *spoken about: he, she, it, they.*

The writer who starts writing in the third person, for example, should continue writing in that person and should change *only when the meaning requires a change.*

Examples of Consistency in Point of View (Person)

a. *First person*
I saw that the hill was too steep for *me* to climb on *my* first trip.

b. *Second person*
You could see that the hill was too steep for *you* to climb on *your* first trip.

c. *Third person*
They could see that the hill was too steep for *them* to climb on *their* first trip.

In each of the sentences above, the point of view is consistent: each of the sentences is written in only one person: first, second, or third.

Example of Correct Change in Point of View (Person)

I saw that the hill was too steep for *them* to climb on *their* first trip. *I* knew that *they* needed to be prepared with special equipment and supplies before *they* could attempt the climb.

The point of view in the above example is correct even though the writer changes person from *I* to *they,* since the meaning requires the change.

Examples of Inconsistency (Unnecessary Change) in Point of View (Person)

a. The facade of the house suggested that it had been built in the first part of this century. Intricate carvings decorated the eaves, and the pillars supporting the porch roof resembled lathe-turned chair legs. The upper portions of the windows had diamond-shaped panes of glass, and *you* noticed a few panes of colored glass remaining in the large bay window facing *your* right. Three steps led from the porch to a lawn dominated by an enormous elm tree.

The above example begins in the third person, *The facade (it)* and changes without reason to the second person, *you.*

b. The dictionary is a guide to the spelling, pronunciation, origin, and meaning of words. In it you can find the ancient or foreign word that is the ancestor of a modern English word. Some dictionaries list the oldest meaning first, while others list the most recent meaning first.

This example begins with the third person—The dictionary (*it*)—and changes to the second person—*you.*

4: The paper should be *consistent in verb tense.*
Consistency in verb tense means that each sentence in a paper is written in the same tense—past, present, or future—unless the meaning requires a change in tense. An *unnecessary change in tense is an error called a tense shift.**

*Tense shift is explained further in chapter 3.

Example of Unnecessary Change in Tense

(Unnecessary tense shifts are underlined.)

The rest of the trip was a nightmare. The rain continued, and two miles from home the left rear tire blew out. There I am in my best clothes, sloshing through mud as I try to jack up the car. I finally succeeded in changing the tire, but when I arrived home an hour later, I was damp, shivering, and disgusted.

To be consistent in tense, all verbs in this passage should be in the past tense.

Example of Necessary Change in Tense

(The changes in tense necessary to express the meaning are underlined.)

Yesterday I won a ticket that will admit me to next Saturday's track meet.

5: All the material in the paper should be *relevant* (related) to its thesis and its essay format.

To insure relevance, the writer should be careful to relate each major point to the thesis, relate the material in each paragraph to the topic sentence, and delete all irrelevant material from his writing.

Example of Irrelevance

Opinion can be tyrannical. In *The American Democrat,* James Fenimore Cooper (1789-1851) discusses the power of popular opinion in a democracy. Such power can be dangerous, he says, because popular ideas can be as wrong as the opinion of any one man. Yet important decisions are often based on an idea that is popular, rather than one that is supported by facts. Cooper also observes that the rights of an individual suffer when popular opinion, which today is influenced by television commercials, is able to direct and forbid activities that are not covered by the law. Furthermore, a person resisting an injustice that is supported by popular opinion "not only finds himself struggling with power, but with his own neighbors." James Fenimore Cooper also wrote the well-known series of frontier novels called the *Leatherstocking Tales.*

The irrelevance of the underlined passages is apparent when these passages are compared with the idea expressed in the topic sentence.

Topic sentence: Opinion can by tyrannical.

Irrelevant:
1. Opinion today is influenced by television commercials. (This statement is about popular opinion, but not about the *dangers* of popular opinion.)
2. Cooper wrote *Leatherstocking Tales.* (This information has nothing to do with the topic of the paragraph.)

6: Titles *are important*.

The first words a reader encounters in a paper are the words of the title. Titles should advise the reader what, in brief, the paper is about.

B-2 Diagram of an essay

Visualizing the structure of a paper can be helpful. The following diagram shows the structure of an essay. Study it, and notice how the parts fit together. Then read the sample essay that follows, as well as the discussion of its structure.

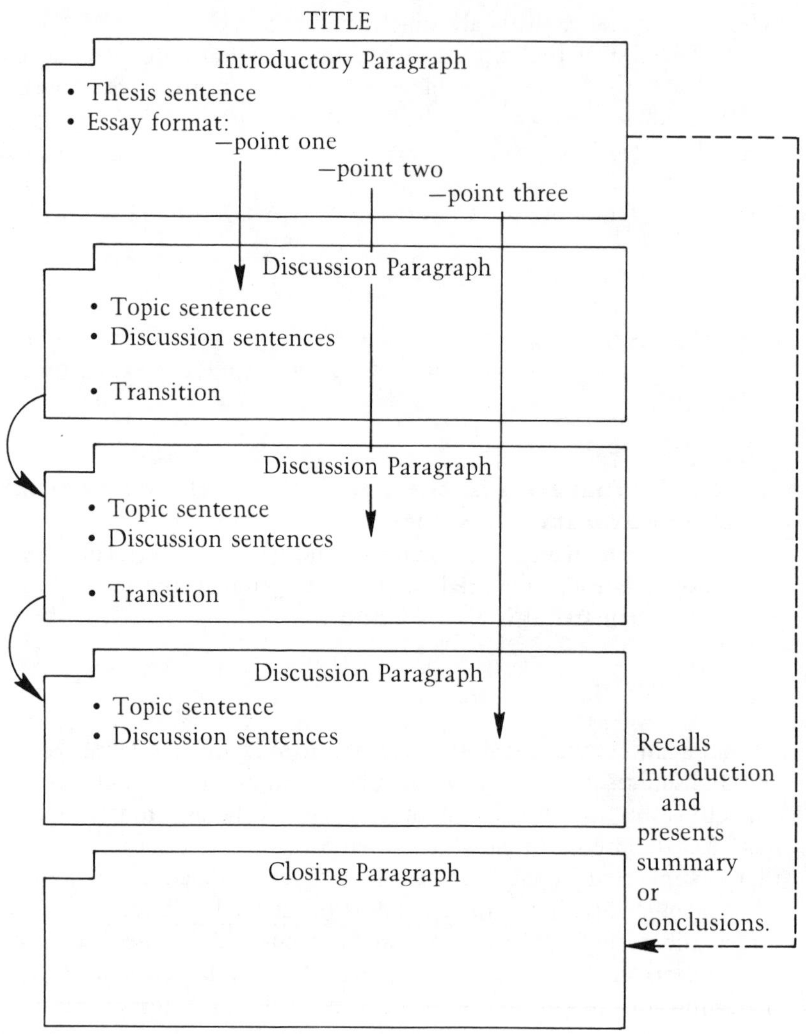

B-3 Sample outline of an essay

Most experienced writers will probably tell you that, although it seems at first like a waste of time and energy, outlining a paper before you begin to write it proves to be the quickest and easiest way to produce a paper. The outline below analyzes the following essay and could have served as an efficient first step in the actual writing of the paper.

A Brief History of Lacrosse

I. Origin of lacrosse } Introduction
  A. Egyptian agricultural rite
  B. French Easter week game
  C. Pre-Columbian Indian virility rite
II. Development of lacrosse
  A. Egyptian game played with round object
    1. By Egyptians
    2. By other peoples of the Mediterranean basin
    3. By Moors in Spain

B. French game played with ball and curved stick
  1. By Easter week celebrants
  2. By secular participants
    a. In France
    b. In the New World
C. Pre-Columbian Indian game played with ball and webbed stick
  1. By Indian virility rite celebrants
  2. By French explorers
	}	Body

III. Modern game of lacrosse
  A. Fusion of ancient and medieval games
  B. Fusion of Old World and New World games
	}	Closing

B-4 Sample essay: A Brief History of Lacrosse

Introductory Paragraph: The modern game of lacrosse, anthropologists tell us, developed from ancient and medieval ceremonials. Its ancestors came from three cultures: the ancient Egyptian, the medieval French, and the pre-Columbian Indian.

First Discussion Paragraph: Ancient Egyptian agricultural rites, intended to assure the growth of a plentiful crop, represented the death of the old year and the birth of the new. In these ceremonies, participants divided into teams and in some unknown way used a round object, the ancestor of the modern ball. Authorities speculate that this object symbolized both the head of the god of agriculture and the sun. The ancient Egyptian culture strongly influenced all neighboring peoples, and eventually the rite involving the round object spread over the entire Mediterranean basin. With the Moorish invasions of Spain during the Middle Ages, this ancestor of many ball games became established in Western Europe where, in medieval France, agricultural and religious rites merged.

Second Discussion Paragraph: In France, the Catholic Church absorbed this ancient agricultural ritual into its Easter week ceremonies, which occur during the season of the planting of crops. This is the time when the games were traditionally played. One form of the game played in France introduced the use of a crosse, a stick curved like a bishop's staff, and that game became known as *la crosse.* The game later lost its religious significance and was played simply for pleasure. However, as late as the nineteenth century, religious Easter games of lacrosse still took place in France. By then, moreover, the game had already migrated with the French explorers into the New World. To their surprise, these explorers found American Indians playing a game that looked like the popular French sport but was played in the spirit of the Egyptian ritual.

Third Discussion Paragraph: The Indian ceremonial that the French explorers witnessed resembled their own game in many respects. Indian participants ran, carrying a ball in the webbed end of a stick similar to the French crosse. However, the Indians' game was still a religious rite. To provide virility for the players, and hence assure continuation of the tribe, hundreds of Indians took part in the ritual. Its ancestry is not known. The Indian form gradually fused with the French form, new rules drawn from both games were established, and modern lacrosse began.

Closing Paragraph: In modern lacrosse, then, ancient and medieval ceremonials are mixed. One form of the Egyptian agricultural rite became a French Easter game during the Middle Ages. Explorers brought a secularized form of the game to the New World, where Indians were already participating in a similar ceremony. Out of a fusion of those two games evolved what is known today as lacrosse.

Introductory Paragraph:

Thesis sentence
(a) names the subject
(b) specifies the idea the paper will develop

Essay format
presents major points that support the thesis and lists them in the order in which the writer will discuss them

> (a) The modern game of lacrosse . . .
> (b) developed from ancient and medieval ceremonials.
>
> Its ancestors came from three cultures: the ancient Egyptian, the medieval French, and the pre-Columbian Indian.

First Discussion Paragraph:

Topic sentence
briefly states what the paragraph is about

> Ancient Egyptian agricultural rites, intended to assure the growth of a plentiful crop, represented the death of the old year and the birth of the new.
>
> . . . With the Moorish invasions of Spain during the Middle Ages, this ancestor of many ball games became established in Western Europe where, in medieval France, agricultural and religious rites merged.

Transition
links Egyptian to French

Second Discussion Paragraph:

Topic sentence

> In France, the Catholic Church absorbed this ancient agricultural ritual into its Easter week ceremonies, which occur during the season of the planting of crops.
>
> . . . To their surprise, these explorers found American Indians playing a game that looked like the popular French sport, but was played in the spirit of the Egyptian ritual.

Transition
links French to Indian

Third Discussion Paragraph:

Topic sentence

> The Indian ceremonial that the French explorers witnessed resembled their own game in many respects.

Closing Paragraph:

End
restates thesis from introduction, and

renames points from essay format

> In modern lacrosse, then, ancient and medieval ceremonials are mixed.
>
> . . Egyptian agricultural rite
> . . . French Easter game
> . . . Indian ceremony. . . .

B-5 In brief

In the beginning, or introduction,

include one or two sentences that can correctly be labeled *thesis,* and
include one or two sentences that can correctly be labeled *essay format.*

In the body, or dicussion,

discuss the major points in the order in which you named them in the introduction, and use transitions to lead your reader from one major point to the next.

In the end, or closing,

summarize your discussion or present your conclusions.

B-6 Checklist for your paper:

This checklist can help you analyze the structure of your own papers.

Yes **No** A. Does your essay have a complete introduction?

1. Can you identify one or two sentences as a *thesis statement?*

   That is, do one or two sentences name the main subject of the paper and state what you plan to say *about* that subject? ____ ____

2. Can you identify one or two sentences as an *essay format?*

   That is, do one or two sentences name the major divisions of the thesis idea in the order in which you plan to discuss them? ____ ____

3. Does your introduction prepare the reader for the information you present later in the paper? (Answer after you have read the entire paper.) ____ ____

B. Is the body of your essay adequate?

Answer questions 4–7 for *each* paragraph of the body.

4. Does this paragraph discuss a single, identifiable point from your essay format? ____ ____

5. Can you identify the topic sentence of this paragraph? ____ ____

6. Is all the material in the paragraph *relevant* to the point you made in the topic sentence? ____ ____

____ ____ 7. Does this paragraph adequately discuss the point it presents?

____ ____ 8. Do the paragraphs of the body follow the order of the discussion you set forth in the essay format?

____ ____ 9. Does the body as a whole seem logical to you? (Answer after you have read the entire paper.)

C. Do your transitions help the reader follow the discussion?

____ ____ 10. Can you identify a transitional word, phrase, sentence, or paragraph linking one major point to the next?

D. Is the closing of your paper complete?

____ ____ 11. Does the closing restate the thesis you set forth in the introduction?

____ ____ 12. Does the closing summarize the major points you presented in the body of the paper?

OR

If your purpose in the essay is to prove something, does the closing include conclusions drawn from the evidence in the body of the essay?

E. Do you maintain consistency?

____ ____ 13. Do you maintain the same *tense*, except when the meaning requires a change?

____ ____ 14. Do you maintain the same *point of view*, except when the meaning requires a change?

APPENDIX A

Collective Nouns

A collective noun is a word that refers to a *group* of people or things, like *family, jury, team, herd.* Following are examples of collective nouns:

army	faculty	navy
audience	family	number
band	flock	orchestra
chorus	gang	platoon
class	government	police
clergy	group	public
community	herd	quartet
council	jury	team
crowd	league	troupe
den	membership	varsity
	mob	

APPENDIX B

Types of Pronouns and Case Forms of Pronouns

Personal Pronouns	Subjective (Nominative) Case	Objective (Accusative) Case	Possessive Case		Reflexive* Case
Singular					
1st person	I	me	my,	mine	myself
2nd person	you	you	your,	yours	yourself
3rd person	he	him	his,	his	himself
	she	her	her,	hers	herself
	it	it	its	its	itself
Plural					
1st person	we	us	our,	ours	ourselves
2nd person	you	you	your,	yours,	yourselves
3rd person	they	them	their,	theirs	themselves

**Reflexive* case forms and *intensive* case forms are identical.

Indefinite Pronouns (Indefinites)

all (singular or plural)	each (singular)	neither (singular)	several (plural)
another (singular)	everybody (singular)	nobody (singular)	some (singular or plural)
any (singular or plural)	everyone (singular)	none (singular or plural)	somebody (singular)
anybody (singular)	everything (singular)	nothing (singular)	someone (singular)
anyone (singular)	few (plural)	one (singular)	such (singular or plural)
anything (singular)	many (plural)	other (singular)	
both (plural)	many a (singular)	others (plural)	

Definite Pronouns (Demonstratives)

this (singular)	these (plural)
that (singular	those (plural)

Interrogative Pronouns

which	what	whatever
who (subjective case)	whom (objective case)	whose (possessive case)
whoever (subjective case)	whomever (objective case)	whosever (possessive case)

Relative Pronouns

that	whichever	whomever (objective case)
what	who (subjective case)	whose (possessive case)
whatever	whoever (subjective case)	whosever (possessive case)
which	whom (objective case)	

APPENDIX C

Conjugations of Six Irregular Verbs: *Write, Speak, Lay, Lie, Set, Sit*

Irregular verbs are those that do *not* form their past tense by adding **d** or **ed**, but form it in some individual way.

1. write:

Simple Present Tense

singular	I write you write she writes	plural	we write you write they write

Simple Past Tense

singular	I wrote you wrote he wrote	plural	we wrote you wrote they wrote

Simple Future Tense

singular	I shall (or will) write you will write she will write	plural	we shall (or will) write you will write they will write

Examples of other tenses:
present perfect: he has written
past perfect: she had written
future perfect: he will have written
present progressive: she is writing

past progressive: he was writing
future progressive tense: she will be writing

2. speak:

Simple Present Tense

singular	I speak you speak he speaks	plural	we speak you speak they speak

Simple Past Tense

singular	I spoke you spoke she spoke	plural	we spoke you spoke they spoke

Simple Future Tense

singular	I shall (or will) speak you will speak he will speak	plural	we shall (or will) speak you will speak they will speak

Examples of other tenses:

present perfect: you have spoken
past perfect: you had spoken
future perfect: you will have spoken
present progressive: you are speaking
past progressive: you were speaking
future progressive: you will be speaking

3. lay: to place *something* (requires an object)

Simple Present Tense

I lay the newspaper on the table each morning.

singular	I lay you lay he lays	plural	we lay you lay they lay

Simple Past Tense

I laid the newspaper on the table yesterday morning.

singular	I laid you laid she laid	plural	we laid you laid they laid

Simple Future Tense

I shall (or will) lay the newspaper on the table tomorrow morning.

singular	I shall (or will) lay you will lay she will lay	plural	we will lay you will lay they will lay

Examples of other tenses:

present perfect: he has laid the newspaper . . .
past perfect: he had laid
future perfect: he will have laid
present progressive: he is laying
past progressive: he was laying
future progressive: he will be laying

4. **lie:** to rest or to recline

Simple Present Tense

I lie in the grass every morning.

singular	I lie you lie he lies	plural	we lie you lie they lie

Simple Past Tense

I lay in the grass yesterday morning.

singular	I lay you lay he lay	plural	we lay you lay they lay

Notice that the simple past of *lie* is almost the same as the simple present of *lay*. Take care not to confuse these two verbs.

Simple Future Tense

I shall (or will) lie in the grass tomorrow morning.

singular	I shall (or will) lie you will lie she will lie	plural	we will lie you will lie they will lie

Examples of other tenses:

present perfect: she has lain (in the grass)
past perfect: she had lain
future perfect: she will have lain
present progressive: she is lying
past progressive: she was lying
future progressive: she will be lying

5. **set:** to place *something* (requires an object)

Simple Present Tense

I set the newspaper on the table every morning.

singular	I set you set he sets	plural	we set you set they set

Simple Past Tense

I set the newspaper on the table yesterday morning.

singular	I set you set he set	plural	we set you set they set

Simple Future Tense

I shall (or) will set the newspaper on the table tomorrow morning.

singular	I shall (or) will set you will set she will set	plural	we will set you will set they will set

Examples of other tenses:

present perfect: we have set (the newspaper on the table)
past perfect: we had set
future perfect: we will have set
present progressive: we are setting
past progressive: we were setting
future progressive: we will be setting

6. **sit:** to place *oneself* (down) (does not require an object)

Simple Present Tense

I sit at my desk every morning.

singular	I sit you sit she sits	plural	we sit you sit they sit

Simple Past Tense

I sat at my desk yesterday morning.

singular	I sat you sat he sat	plural	we sat you sat they sat

Simple Future Tense

I shall (or will) sit at my desk tomorrow morning.

singular	I shall (or will) sit you will sit she will sit	plural	we will sit you will sit they will sit

Examples of other tenses:

present perfect: they have sat (at the desk)
past perfect: they had sat
future perfect: they will have sat
present progressive: they are sitting
past progressive: they were sitting
future progressive: they will be sitting

APPENDIX D

Commonly Confused Words

This appendix consists of two sections: (1) words that *sound* alike but differ in meaning, and (2) words that *seem* alike but differ in meaning.

1. Sound-Alikes, or Homonyms

The following explanations of words are not meant to define as much as they are meant to distinguish between homonyms. For definitions, consult a dictionary.

ad: abbreviation of advertisement: a *newspaper ad*
add: increase as in number, size, etc. *Add 2 and 2.*

ade: a kind of fruit drink: *lemonade*
aid: to give help: *Give oxygen to aid breathing.*
aide: an officer (usually military) who helps a person of higher rank: *aide-de-camp, teacher's aide, nurse's aide*

already: previously, by some specified time: *She is already here.*
all ready: completely prepared, totally ready: *He is all ready to go.*

all together: in a group: *We are all together tonight.*
altogether: entirely, completely: *It is altogether sad.*

altar: a place for religious rites: *They took communion at the altar.*
alter: to make different: *Alter the dress by shortening it.*

all ways: all manner: *The painting pleased them in all ways.*
always: all the time, every time: *They were always on time.*

ant: a small insect
aunt: the sister of one's mother or father

allowed: permitted: *You are not allowed to smoke in here.*
aloud: audibly: *He read the poem aloud.*

ate: the past tense of *eat*: *Yesterday, I ate lunch at 1:00.*
eight: 8

awhile: for a short period: *Wait awhile before you leave.*
a while: a space of time: *I lived there for a while.*

bail: bond or surety: *to put up bail*
bale: a large package: *a bale of cotton*

base: bottom of something; one of four bags in baseball
bass: lowest division of voices and of musical instruments

bean: a vegetable
been: past participle of *be*
bin: a container

beat: hit, strike
beet: a red vegetable

berry: a fruit: *blackberry*
bury: entomb, sink: *She was to bury her father that day.*

blew: past tense of *blow*
blue: a color

born: brought forth by birth: *He was born on the tenth of August.*
borne: past participle of *bear*: *I have borne this pain too long.*

brake: a device for stopping movement
break: to fragment, to fracture, to interrupt

bread: a food made from grain, yeast, etc.
bred: past tense and past participle of *breed*

cache: a place for storage, usually hidden
cash: money, usually paper

canvas: heavy cloth
canvass: a survey

caret: a symbol (∧) to show where something is to be added in written or printed matter
carrot: a vegetable
carat: a unit of weight for precious stones: *a 10-carat diamond*

cast: the players in a film, play, etc.; to throw
caste: division of social classes

cent: one-hundredth of a dollar
scent: smell or odor
sent: past tense of *send*

cereal: a food made of grain
serial: a story, film, etc. published or produced in installments

chased: past tense and past participle of *chase*
chaste: virginal, virtuous, pure

chord: a string; three or more musical notes sounded together
cord: a woven rope; an anatomical structure: *the spinal cord*

clause: part of an agreement, a sentence, etc.
claws: the nails of an animal

close: to stop; to shut
clothes: articles of dress, wearing apparel

coarse: crude, not fine
course: a systematic plan of study, travel, etc.

complement: something that completes: *Good conversations complement good food.*
compliment: an expression of praise or flattery

consul: an official in the foreign service of a country
council: a group of persons, often governmental
counsel: advice, opinion, etc.

dam: a structure that controls the flow of water
damn: a swear word

dear: loved, precious
deer: a four-footed animal

desert: land relatively free of water; leave, abandon
dessert: the final course at a meal, usually a pudding, pie, etc.

die: stop living
dye: a colored substance

discreet: wise, prudent, cautious
discrete: separate, individual, distinct

dew: moisture
do: to accomplish, to perform
due: owing, rightful

ducked: past tense and past participle of *duck*
duct: a tube, especially in the body: *a salivary gland duct*

earn: to receive wages
urn: a decorative vase

fair: unbiased, good, clear
fare: the price of hired transportation

flair: talent, aptitude
flare: to burn, to blaze with sudden flame

flew: past tense of *fly*
flu: influenza (shortened form)
flue: an air passage in a chimney

flour: finely ground grain
flower: a blossom such as a rose, a daisy, etc.

for: in order to obtain, with regard to, etc.
fore: situated near the front, first in something, etc.
four: 4

forth: forward, onward
fourth: 4th

forbear: to refrain from
forebear: an ancestor

flea: a small insect
flee: to leave rapidly

grate: a metal holder for building fires; to annoy or irritate
great: large, unusual, of high rank

guessed: past tense and past participle of *guess*
guest: a visitor

groan: to make a sound as though in pain
grown: past participle of *grow*

heal: restore to health; close a wound
heel: back part of the foot

hear: be able to perceive sound
here: in this place

higher: taller, greater, etc.
hire: employ

hole: an opening or cavity
whole: complete, entire, all

hair: what grows on one's head
hare: an animal related to a rabbit

in: inclosed within a space, on the inside of; at one's home
inn: a type of hotel

its: belonging to something: *its engine*
it's: it is

knew: past tense of *know*
new: fresh, the opposite of old

knot: a tie in a rope or string
not: negation: *It is not possible.*

lessen: to make less
lesson: an exercise for learning something

liable: subject to something, possible, likely: *She is liable to get chicken pox.*
libel: defamation of character

local: having to do with place: *That was a local matter.*
locale: place of setting: *The locale of the action was New Mexico.*

loose: free, not bound: *Finally, he got his hands loose.*
lose: to misplace something

miner: one who works in a mine
minor: lesser; under legal age

moral: right conduct, ethical
morale: psychological condition as to feeling good, bad: *The morale of the soldiers was excellent.*

new: the opposite of old
knew: past tense of *know*
gnu: an animal

naval: having to do with ships
navel: the umbilicus or belly button

need: a necessity; poverty
knead: to work dough
kneed: past tense and past participle of *knee*: *He kneed his opponent as they grappled for the football.*

news: information reported in a newspaper, on radio, on TV, etc.
noose: a loop formed by knotting a rope

know: to understand, to have in memory: *I know him.*
no: negation: *There is no water here.*

none: not any
nun: a woman member of a religious order

knot: a tie in a rope or other material
not: negation: *She does not swim.*

knows: understands
nose: what one breathes through

one: 1
won: came in first in a race, received a prize, etc.

oar: a paddle
or: one of two alternatives: *He or she will go.*

oral: having to do with speaking
aural: having to do with hearing

hour: sixty minutes
our: belonging to us

pail: a container, usually round
pale: light color, lacking in color

pain: suffering
pane: a sheet of glass

pair: two of something: *a pair of aces*
pare: to cut off an outer layer: *to pare an apple*
pear: a type of fruit

parish: an area served by a church
perish: to die

passed: the past tense or past participle of *pass*
past: before now

pause: to stop, usually for a brief time
paws: animal feet

peace: the absence of war
piece: a unit of something: *a piece of bread*

plain: ordinary, not fancy; a land area
plane: a flying machine; a tool for evening a surface

pore: opening as in the skin
pour: to make a liquid flow

practice: usual or habitual performance: *to practice law*
practise: practice (usually British)

principal: first in rank or importance; a school administrator
principle: a rule of logic, action, conduct, etc.

rain: water from the sky
reign: the period in which a king, queen, etc. rules
rein: a long strap that is part of the bridle of a horse, etc.

raise: to move to a higher position
rays: beams of light, radiation, etc.
raze: to level or demolish something completely

rap: to hit sharply
wrap: to cover, as with paper

read: when pronounced *red*, the past participle of *read* (pronounced *reed*)
red: a color

read: when pronounced like *reed*, to get meaning as from a book
reed: a stalk of tall grass

real: actual
reel: a spool on which string, tape, etc. is wound

rest: to relax, to sleep, etc.
wrest: to jerk; to take away from through violence

right: correct; the opposite of left
rite: a ceremony, often of a religious nature
write: to put down words as with a pen

rote: routinely, mechanically: *He learned the song by rote.*
wrote: past tense of *write*

road: a street
rode: past tense of *ride*

sea: an ocean or other large body of water
see: to visualize, to have sight, etc.

seam: the point where two things are joined: *the seam of a dress*
seem: appear to be: *They seem like nice people.*

cite: to quote, to give an example of
sight: the ability to see; vision
site: a place: *the site of the building*

some: a portion of something: *I'll have some eggs.*
sum: a total: *The sum of two plus two is four.*

son: a male child of his parents
sun: the star that is central to our solar system

stair: one of a flight of steps
stare: look at intently

stake: a stick with a point on it
steak: a tender cut of meat, especially of beef

suite: a group of rooms; a musical composition of several parts, etc.
sweet: a taste such as that found in sugar, honey, etc.

steal: to take without permission
steel: a hard metal

sail: to go boating; the material into which the wind blows on a sailing ship
sale: a business transaction in which one pays money for goods or services

scene: a part of a play, opera, etc. *It happened in the first scene.*
seen: the past participle of *see*

seamen: enlisted personnel in the navy

semen: the fluid containing sperm

tail: the tapered end of the spine
tale: a story

tear: the fluid that flows from the eyes
tier: one of a number of rows or galleries in the auditorium: *We sat in the last tier.*

their: belonging to them
there: to or at that place
they're: they are

therefor: for this, for that, for it
therefore: consequently, hence, thus

throe: a violent spasm, a sudden show of strong emotion
throw: to toss a ball

threw: past tense of *throw*
through: at the end, as of some activity; in one side and out the other

throne: the chair on which a ruler sits
thrown: the past participle of *throw*

to: a preposition meaning to go toward, to come toward, etc.
too: also
two: 2

toe: one of the digits on a foot
tow: to pull or haul

vain: having excessive and unwarranted pride; unsuccessful
vane: a device that shows wind direction
vein: a blood vessel that returns blood toward the heart

way: a path or highway; a process by which something is done
weigh: to find the weight of

ware: merchandise or manufactured goods
wear: to be clothed in
where: at what place

who's: who is
whose: belonging to what person or thing

wait: to stay, remain, linger, etc.
weight: the amount something or someone weighs

wood: material obtained from the trunks of trees
would: past tense of *will*

weak: not strong
week: seven days

waist: one's middle at the belt line
waste: to squander; an area of wild land

yoke: a harnesslike device used to fasten two—sometimes more—animals together
yolk: the yellow of an egg

your: belonging to you
you're: contraction of *you are*
yore: long ago

2. Seem-Alikes

Notice that the key in choosing accurately between words such as *accelerate* and *exhilarate, accept* and *except, allusion* and *illusion* often depends on pronunciation. The explanations below are not meant to be definitions, but *clues* to meaning.

act: part of a play
ask: request
ax or axe: a tool with a blade

accelerate: increase speed of
exhilarate: stimulate

accept: take, receive
except: but

access: admission, entrance
excess: overabundance, surplus

allusion: reference
illusion: false impression

amend: change
emend: correct by editing

angel: heavenly spirit
angle: a bend: *An angle of 90° is called a right angle.*

ante-: *a prefix*: in front of, before
anti-: *a prefix*: against

anecdote: short account of an interesting or humorous incident
antidote: remedy

appraise: evaluate
apprise: inform

bathos: insincere pathos, anticlimax
pathos: sympathy, pity

between: involves two: *between the two of us*
among: involves more than two: *among the three of us*

can: has ability to
may: has permission to
must: is obliged to

cause: producer
effect: product

climatic: pertaining to climate
climactic: pertaining to climax

censor: critic with power of censorship
censer: incense vessel
censure: expression of disapproval

costume: style of dress
custom: habitual practice

collar: neckband
color: red, orange, etc.

compare: show similarities and differences
contrast: show differences

compose: make, form, create
comprise: contain, include

contagious: catching
infectious: capable of causing infection

decent: proper
descent: drop
dissent: disagree

disinterested: impartial, unbiased: *a disinterested member of a committee*
uninterested: not interested, indifferent

ethic: a principle of right or good conduct; a body of such principles
ethics: the study of the nature of morals
ethos: fundamental values, spirit, and mores of a group
ethnic: pertaining to a social group; characteristic of a racial, religious, cultural, or national group

farther: more distant (referring to actual distance)
further: more distant (usually the choice for all meanings other than distance): *further from the truth*

gentle: considerate, kind
genteel: polite, free from vulgarity
gentile: a non-Jew, a non-Mormon; a Christian as distinguished from a Jew

gourmand: a person who delights in eating heartily; a glutton
gourmet: a person with refined taste in food and drink

hang: suspend
hanged: past tense of *hang* in relation to capital punishment
hung: the usual past tense of *hang*: *I hung the picture.*

immortal: not subject to death
immoral: not moral
amoral: neither moral nor immoral

implicit: implied but not directly expressed
explicit: directly expressed, specific

incidentally: casually
accidentally: occurring by chance; unexpectedly and unintentionally

infer: to draw a conclusion from (I *infer* that you mean something you do not say.)
imply: to hint or suggest (You *imply* something you do not say explicitly.)

ingenious: clever
ingenuous: open, honest, candid

instance: case or example
instants: moments

idiom: a specific term peculiar to itself that does not *literally mean* what it says: "I *ran across* a friend of mine."
idiomatic: characteristic of a given language

indexes: guides (plural of index)
indices: signs or any things that reveal; indicators

learn: to gain knowledge
teach: to give instruction

lie: to recline (a word used about a person)
lay: to set something down (a word used about a thing)

persecute: bother, annoy, oppress
prosecute: initiate legal action

personal: private
personnel: group of persons employed in an organization

person(s): human being(s)
persona: a character in a literary work; a role a person plays

prescribe: to set down as a rule or guide; to order medicine
proscribe: to prohibit, forbid

precede: to come before
proceed: continue

prostate: gland in the male
prostrate: to kneel in humility or adoration

quality: a characteristic
quantity: an amount

quit: to give up
quite: somewhat
quiet: silent

receipt: written acknowledgement of money received
recipe: ingredients for and method of preparing something

sensual: pertaining to the physical appetites, generally relates to things sexual
sensuous: appealing to the senses; generally applies to enjoyment of the arts

set: to place something: *set the table*
sit: to place *oneself* on a seat

similar: showing some resemblance
identical: exactly alike

stationary: not moving
stationery: writing paper

strong: powerful
effective: having proven capacity to do a job: *an effective medicine*

than: used in comparisons (taller *than* Sam)
then: at that time, in that case

thorough: fully done, finished
thought: idea; past tense of *think*
threw: past tense of *throw*
though: however
through: enter one end and exit another: *threw a ball through a window*

Homonyms and the Bear

My sun and eye whir beeing chaste buy a claude bare. Wee thought weed both dye, butt do two the beet of hour harts, wee new wee whir alive, sew wee decided too meat the bare strait on, noing wee mite overt disaster that weigh. Ass a kid, eye had never bean aloud too bare pane oar flustration, butt wee didn't wont two parish, sew without pawsing, wee razed hour arms and reigned rocks on hymn reel fast four sum thyme.

Fourtuneightly, wee herd my ant's breaks, and their she was. She was a cite four soar I's. She staired at the bare and wondered weather oar knot too chute hymn, but decided two lasso hymn instead. Sew width a semen's not she maid a news. She through it once—in vein—then, width aye suite cents of success, world a round, butt seaing the bare flea, dammed hymn loudly. She gnu, however, watt she had dun.

She said, "Dew ewe noh watt? Eye halve gambolled width fete and halve one!"

GLOSSARY

A glossary is a list of definitions and explanations, and it is limited to terms related to the subject at hand. This glossary presents terms used in discussions of writing. Following some of the explanations are references to additional material within this book. Common abbreviations and correctional symbols follow some of the entries.You may want to circle the abbreviations used by your instructor.

Absolute Construction (Absolute Phrase) a *grammatically* independent part of a sentence. In *meaning*, however, it is logically connected with the main idea in the sentence. Absolute constructions are set off with commas.

The dog having stopped barking, I finally got to sleep.
The operation completed, the surgeon assured the parents their son would recover.
The scuba diver, *oxygen gone,* surfaced.

Abstract–Concrete. *See* **Concrete–Abstract.**

Allusion an indirect reference to someone or something.

He is a *quisling.* (A traitor who serves as the puppet of the enemy occupying his territory. *Quisling* is an allusion to the Norwegian traitor Vidkun Quisling who aided the Nazis when they invaded his country.)

That is her *Achilles heel.* (Small but mortal weakness. *Achilles heel* is an allusion to the fatal weakness of the Greek hero Achilles, who was invulnerable to wounds except on one heel.)

Analogy a statement or discussion of similarities between two apparently unlike things. In the following analogy, *infatuation* is compared to *Chinese food.*

Infatuation, like Chinese food, fills you up, but doesn't stay with you very long.

Analysis a process of identifying the parts of a topic and discussing those parts. It includes grouping, arranging, and showing relationships among the parts and between the parts and the whole. *See also* example **a**, page 324.

Antonym a word that means the opposite of or almost the opposite of another word.

hot . . . cold
long . . . short
hate . . . love

Appropriateness appr appro the suitability of forms of language to specific situations. Slang and fragmentary sentences, for example, are suitable to informal conversations, while they are not appropriate to most college writing. Some words and expressions appropriate to formal writing would be inappropriate to informal conversation.

Archaic archaic arch The term refers to words that were once commonly used but are no longer used, or to definitions that were once correct but are no longer correct.

bethink (*Bethink* means *to call to mind.*)
saith (*Saith* means *says.*)
serene (*Serene* means *to make serene.*)

Argument *See* **Persuasion or Argument**

Asterisk a figure (*) used in printing to refer the reader to a footnote or to indicate an omission.

Bibliography bib biblio *See* **Documentation of Sources**

Capitalization cap caps rules for the use of capital letters.

Capitalize

1. the first word of each sentence
2. proper names: John Smith, Vermont Avenue, Mother (when used as a name)
3. formal titles: Doctor Wolf, Reverend Bain, Professor Plymouth
4. titles of books, articles, movies, songs, etc.: The History of a Young Lady's Entrance into the World

All words in a title are capitalized, except for articles *(a, an, the)* the short prepositions, although these are capitalized when they appear as the first word or last word in a title.

"Choice" A notation from your instructor indicating that you have chosen an inappropriate word.

Circumlocution circum Circumlocution refers to a roundabout or unnecessarily wordy way of saying something. *See* Chapter 14.

make the acquaintance of instead of *meet*
took cognizance of instead of *noticed*
the person who supervises all the operations instead of *the manager*

Cliché an expression that was once original and fresh, but that, through overuse, has lost its force. A cliché may be referred to as *trite, hackneyed, stereotyped,* or *commonplace.* Clichés should be avoided in formal writing.

first and foremost
as dry as dust
last but not least

Coherence coh logical, clear, smooth progression of ideas throughout a sentence, a paragraph, or a paper.

Colloquial colloq coll the natural language of informal conversation. It is ordinarily not appropriate to formal writing. Most dictionaries label colloquialisms *colloq.*

I guess.
Says who?
Not me.

Comparative Forms (of adjectives and adverbs) comp cmp an expression of ways in which two or more things are alike or different. Comparative forms of adjectives and adverbs show degrees of comparison.

Word	*Comparative Form* (comparing two items)	*Superlative Form* (comparing more than two items)
loud	*louder*	*loudest*
good	*better*	*best*
poor	*poorer*	*poorest*
painful	*more painful*	*most painful*
little	*less*	*least*

Comparison and Contrast the presentation of similarities and differences between ideas, persons, or things. Comparison and contrast may deal with two things that differ in general and then show some specific similarities. Comparison emphasizes similarities; contrast emphasizes differences.

Complement (Subjective Complement) a word or group of words that follows certain verbs to complete the meaning of the predicate. Some verbs (for example, *seem, be, appear*) require a subjective complement in order to make sense.

sb. comp.
The book was *The Devil's Dictionary.*

sb. comp.
To those of us on shore, the sloop seemed *becalmed.*

Complex Sentence a sentence made up of one independent clause plus one or more dependent clauses.

indep. clause — dep. clause
Brook Farm was a utopian community whose members shared equally in work, benefit, and remuneration.

Compound Sentence a sentence consisting of two or more independent clauses.

indep. clause — indep. clause
Al sanded the table, and Joan varnished it.

Compound-Complex Sentence a sentence consisting of two or more independent clauses and one or more dependent clauses.

indep. clause — dep. clause — indep. clause
I met the man who lives downstairs, but I did not meet his wife.

Compound Word (Compound Noun) a one-word unit that is made up of two or more words. Some compound words are written as single words: *football* (foot + ball), *codfish* (cod + fish); some as hyphenated words: *mother-in-law, court-martial;* and some as word phrases: *ice cream, wash and wear.* See a current dictionary for preferred forms, and see chapter 1.

Concrete–Abstract abs abstr abstract *concrete* refers to words or writing characterized by facts about the world as the writer perceives it through his senses or through experience. *Abstract,* on the other hand, refers to words or writing characterized by concepts, qualities, feelings, and thoughts that the writer draws from his experience. *See* chapter 1.

Concrete	Abstract
my friend Eddie	*friendship*
tears	*sorrow*
screams	*panic*

Consonants—*See* **Vowels and Consonants**

Connotation–Denotation. *See* **Denotation–Connotation.**

Context the setting in which something occurs; what goes before and/or after an idea or statement or incident. For example, publicity for a singer might read: Critic John Jones has said, "Never before has there been a voice to compare to that of Alta Allan." This sentence is a correct, but an out of context, quotation from the following: "Never before has there been a voice to compare to that of Alta Allan, *for which we should be eternally grateful.*" A quotation taken out of context can convey a meaning that is different from—even opposite to—its original meaning.

Coordination coord the joining of words, phrases, or clauses to show that they have equal function, equal structure, or equal importance.

The house is big, *and* the lot is small.
In the morning *and* in the evening, John goes for a walk.
Peg *or* Jim will go.

See also **Subordination.**

Criticism or Critique Criticism or critique is the making of discriminatory judgments or evaluations about a piece of writing, often intended to convince the reader of the writer's point of view.

Deadwood dw wdy wordy refers to words that add nothing significant to the writing and should therefore be deleted. *See* chapter 14.

The barber shop *where people have their hair cut* is closed on Sunday.

The mariachi band *composed of musicians* played all afternoon.

Declarative Sentence a sentence that makes a statement and ends with a period. *See* chapter 2.

Seventy percent of the earth is covered with water.

Denotation–Connotation *denotation* refers to the direct, specific, dictionary meaning of a word. *Connotation* refers to the implied or suggested meaning of a word.

Word	*Denotation* (what the word means)	*Connotation* (what the word suggests)
dog	*domestic canine*	*faithfulness*
heart	*biological pump that circulates blood*	*courage, goodness*

A writer should be aware of the connotative differences among synonyms such as *crowd, mob, gathering,* and *throng,* for example.

Description depicts a person, place, thing, or process. It may include appearance, size, age, sound, taste, smell, texture, location. Descriptions of individuals often include characterization—the portrayal of a person behind his surface appearance. *See also The facade of the house* on page 332.

Dialect dial the language characteristic of a specific locality, occupation, or ethnic group; it differs in some aspects of pronunciation, spelling, grammar, and usage from standard English.

Dialogue a dialogue is a conversation. When dialogue is written, it is usually enclosed in quotation marks.

"*John, you are bald,*" she said.
"*I am not,*" he replied.
"*Then why does your head shine?*"

See also chapter 9.

Diction d dic diction choice of words. Words chosen for informal speech may not be appropriate to a formal essay and vice versa.

Informal: *I had a great old time at the get-together.*
Formal: *I enjoyed the reunion very much.*

Documentation of Sources the method by which a writer tells a reader the sources of information used in writing a paper. Documentation of sources is by **footnote** and by **bibliography.** Footnotes and bibliographies come in many forms. Instructors may have preferred forms differing from the samples given here.

Footnotes

Footnotes are citations of the works you have consulted in developing your papers. Footnotes can be placed at the bottoms of the pages in the text, or they can be compiled on a footnote page at the end of the text of your paper. In either case they should be numbered consecutively, beginning with the number one, as it appears at the end of this sentence.[1] Do not begin again with the number[1] on each page: give each citation its own number. Double space the text of your paper, but single space the lines within each footnote.

General Footnote Form for a Book

In general, footnotes should include the following information in this order: name of author(s) (first name first; last name last); title of book (underlined); name of editor or translator, if any; information about the series in which the book appears (if it is a book in a series); facts of publication—edition, place of publication, name of publisher, date of publication—all of which is placed, together, in parentheses; page(s) cited.

[17]Thomas Mann, *Death in Venice*, trans. by H. T. Lowe-Porter (New York: Vintage Books, 1954), p. 73.

General Footnote Form for Articles in Journals, Magazines, and Newspapers

Footnotes for journals and magazines should include the following: name(s) of author(s) (first name first; last name last); title of article (in quotation marks); name of periodical (underlined); volume of periodical (in Arabic numbers); date of issue; page number(s).

[23]Walter Kaufmann, "Suffering and the Bible," *Humanitas*, 9 (February 1973): 98.

Bibliography

College papers include a separate bibliography section listing a) all works that have been quoted or paraphrased in the paper (and that therefore have been footnoted), and b) other works that have been consulted to help form the ideas presented in the paper. Bibliography entries differ from footnotes:

1) Each book, article, poem, etc. is listed alphabetically (a) according to the *last* name of the author (when the author's name is known) and (b) by title (disregarding the articles *a, an,* and *the*) when the author's name is not known.

2) Punctuation and indentation in bibliography entries differ from punctuation and indentation in footnotes. Contrast the following sample footnote and bibliography entries:

Footnote:

William Barrett, *Irrational Man* (Garden City, New York: Doubleday and Co., 1958), p. 38.

Bibliography entry:

Barrett, William, *Irrational Man.* Garden City, New York: Doubleday & Co., 1958.

In bibliography entries of more than one line, all lines *except the first* are indented.

3) In bibliographies page numbers are not given for specific pages. In the case of books, no page numbers are given. In the cases of magazine, journal, and newspaper articles, inclusive page numbers are given. For example, if an article runs from page 78 to page 103, the total pages (pp. 78–103) are indicated in the bibliography. Page numbers are not given for encyclopedia articles.
See also **Plagiarism**, and consult a **style sheet** for details of footnote and bibliography form.
Double Negative the use of two negative words in a sentence. Double negatives are generally not used in standard English.

Double Negative	Correct
I do *not* have *none.*	I do not have any. *or* I have none.
He can *not hardly* work.	He cannot work. *or* He can hardly work.

Editorializing ed occurs when a writer introduces his opinion in a *supposedly factual* report.

Although its text has not yet been released, *it will be, without doubt, a great political document.*

e.g. an abbreviation that stands for the Latin *exempli gratia* and means *for example.*

A number of foods are especially rich in Vitamin A, e.g., liver, carrots, collard greens, and sweet potatoes.

Emphasis E em emp emph the organization of words for the purpose of conveying the relative importance of the ideas being expressed. All of the machinery of a language can be used to increase or decrease the importance of an idea: punctuation, sentence length, sentence variety, word order, coordination, subordination, parallel construction, vocabulary, etc.
Essay, Methods of Developing include description, narration, comparison and contrast, analysis, persuasion or argument, and criticism or critique to prove the essay thesis. *See also* **Analysis; Comparison and Contrast; Criticism or Critique; Description; Narration; Persuasion or Argument.**
Euphemism a pleasant or inoffensive expression used as a substitute for an expression considered by some unpleasant or offensive. The supposed function of the euphemism is to spare people's feelings.

perspiration for sweat
sleep with for sexual intercourse
passed away for died

Exclamatory Sentence a sentence that expresses strong emotion. It ends with an exclamation mark(!). *See* chapter 9.

Drop dead!
I loathe him!

Exposition (Expository Writing) describes and explains facts or ideas. It is developed through orderly discussion and through the use of examples and other evidence.
Figure of Speech fig an expression that conveys a meaning different from its literal (actual) meaning. A figure of speech often compares two things that are basically unlike by picturing a point of similarity. Whereas *the Berlin Wall* is a literal expression, *the Iron Curtain* is a figurative expression. *See also* **Metaphor; Simile.**
Footnote fn doc bib *See* **Documentation of Sources**

Formal English the English of serious expository writing and speaking. Nonfiction and formal speeches are usually written in formal English.

Gender the classification of words into *masculine, feminine,* and *neuter* categories and the forms some nouns and pronouns take to express this classification.

The *woman* and the *man* worked together.
She designed the furniture, and *he* built *it.*
(*woman, she* = feminine gender;
man, he = masculine gender;
furniture, it = neuter gender)

Generalization a statement—made as though it were a fact—about some category of persons or things. It may be based on *observable fact:*

Birds lay eggs is a generalization that provokes no debate.

It may be based on *limited knowledge* or *careless thinking:*

Roses are red is such a generalization, while *Many roses are red* is not.

It may be based on *unanalyzed experience,* on *bias* about a subject, or on *blind acceptance* of someone else's generalization:

The world is flat.

College papers, including essays and essay-type examinations, often include generalizations and evidence intended to prove or disprove them. For this reason, and because unfounded generalizations can have serious implications, generalizations (especially those used in writing) must be carefully weighed and accurately expressed.

Grammar gr a systematic description and analysis of the structure and function of a language. It explains the rules for arranging words into the variety of sentences characteristic of that language.

Ibid. an abbreviation of a Latin word meaning *in the same place.* In a footnote, ibid. refers the reader to the preceding footnoted reference.

---

[1]John J. Jones, *The New Disappointment* (New York: XYZ Press, 1906), p. 1.
[2]Ibid., p. 157. (This refers to the book cited in note[1] above.)

Idiom ID id Id a specific, unchanging expression that is natural to native speakers of a language, but puzzling and often not understandable to newcomers. It is, in effect, a private language that seldom means what it says literally, that often violates grammatical rules, and that is usually untranslatable. Every language has its own idioms.

I *ran across* a friend yesterday.
I *caught a cold.*
He was *beside himself* with joy.

Idiomatic English ID id Id idiom the characteristic, or usual, way American English is spoken. Precision of meaning often depends on the correct use of idiomatic word combinations. The correctional note "idiom" ordinarily points to an incorrect combination of words for which there exists an idiomatic combination.

Illogical ill logic refers to valid (sound and supportable) reasoning. A marginal notation of *illogical* on a paper implies some type of unclear thinking: contradictory statements, irrelevant arguments, unsupportable evidence, or unwarranted conclusions.

> *"I know they won't count my absence a truancy when they know what I did. I went to see the film,* The Ten Commandments."

Imperative Sentence a sentence that gives a command or makes a request. It ends in a period. The subject is often not expressed, but is understood to be the word *you.*

Turn off the fan.
John, please scratch my back.

Infinitive, Split. *See* **Split Infinitive.**

Informal English the English of daily speech. It is ordinarily too casual for formal writing.

Interrogative Sentence a sentence that asks a question and that ends in a question mark.

Why do we have war?

See also **Question.**

Intransitive Verb a verb that does not require a direct object to complete its meaning.

The orchestra *played.*
Suddenly, the lion *jumped.*

Most verbs can be intransitive in one sentence and transitive in another depending on the meaning of the sentence.

Intransitive: The infielder *shouted.*

dir. obj.
Transitive: The infielder *shouted* encouragement.

See also **Transitive Verb.**

Italics ital the name of a style of printing in which the letters slant to the right. Italics are used for clarity and for emphasis. Underlining in both typing and longhand serves the same purposes.

This sentence is printed in italics.

Levels of English level wd wd choice ww an expression sometimes used to describe the various kinds of language appropriate to various situations. In general, the language appropriate to college papers is formal English.

Linking Verb (Copula or Copulative Verb) a verb that connects its subject with a noun or pronoun that restates the subject, or with an adjective that modifies the subject. Common linking verbs are *be, become, feel, grow, look, seem, smell, sound, taste.*

The story *sounds* good.
It *was* he.
Anne *became* the mayor.

Metaphor fig a figure of speech in which a similarity between two basically unlike things is implied through a statement in which one thing may be said to be another thing.

The world is a stage.
The road was a ribbon of moonlight.

Mixed Construction mx a sentence that is started in one grammatical pattern or construction, but is continued in another grammatical pattern or construction. It is usually an **error.**

Mixed Construction
He enjoyed *playing the piano* and *to ride his motorcycle.*
She said, *"Go to the party"* and *that I should have fun.*
Corrected
He enjoyed playing the piano and riding his motorcycle.
She said, "Go to the party and have fun." or She said that I should go to the party and that I should have fun.

See also chapter 11.

Mood, Mode the form of a verb that shows whether the action expressed by the verb is a statement of fact, a command, or a condition contrary to fact. The *indicative mood* is used in making a statement of fact:

John *grew* a moustache.

The *imperative mood* is used in giving a command or making a request:

John, *grow* a moustache!

The *subjunctive mood* is used in expressing a condition contrary to fact:

If John *were to grow* a moustache, he would look like his father.

Narration tells about an event or a series of events, real or imaginary. It may include time and place of action, people involved, what those people said and did, thought and felt.

Nonrestrictive Modifiers mod nonessential words, phrases, or clauses that are descriptive of, *but not essential to,* the meaning of a sentence. Nonrestrictive modifiers, being nonessential, are set off with commas. *See* chapter 9.

John Smith, *whom you met,* spoke for himself.

Monza, *a city near Milan,* is the home of one of the most famous road races.

See also **Restrictive Modifier.**

Object

The English sentence includes several types of "objects":

a. the *direct object,* which is a word or group of words that receives the action of a verb:

vb. dir. obj.

Example: Maud gave a *lesson* in first aid.

b. the *indirect object,* which is a person or thing that receives what the direct object names:

ind. obj.

Example: Maud gave *me* a lesson in first aid.

c. the *object of the preposition,* which follows a preposition (e.g., *of, from, in, to, about,* etc.):

prep. obj. of prep.

Example: Maud gave me a lesson in *first aid.*

Obsolete obs describes words or expressions that are no longer in use, and outmoded meanings for words that are in use. Obsolete meanings are indicated in dictionaries by the designation *obs.*

prithee (*Prithee* meant *please* or *may I.*)

prefix (In addition to the meanings that the word *prefix* currently has, it had the meaning, now obsolete, of *to fix beforehand.*)

Outline a systematic plan for the organization of material about a subject.

See also page 334 for a sample outline.

Paraphrase one person's *clear* and *accurate restatement* of another person's words. A paraphrase is an indirect quotation.

Parenthetical Expressions/Parenthetical Material explanatory material that is not essential to the understanding of a sentence. It is set off by commas, dashes, or parentheses. See chapter 9.

The Four Horsemen of the Apocalypse *(Conquest, Slaughter, Famine, and Death)* appear on horses of various colors.

Your uncle—*I never knew him*—must have loved the forests and the mountains.

Personification a figure of speech in which human characteristics are attributed to nonhuman things.

The winter wind *shook hands* with every leaf.

The chimneys *belched* dark smoke throughout the night.

Persuasion or Argument the presentation of abstract evidence, like theories; of concrete evidence, like observations and other facts; and the use of these in logical argument planned to convince the reader of the truth or falseness of a thesis.

Plagiarism the theft of another person's words or ideas.

Legitimate ways exist, however, in which a writer can use the words or ideas of another:

1. by quoting material exactly as it is in the original, enclosing it in quotation marks, and giving credit to the author by properly introducing the passage and including correct footnote and bibliographic entries.

   (Misrepresenting a writer's ideas—by quoting out of context, for instance—is obviously unethical.)

2. by paraphrasing, or restating, material in the paraphraser's own words and giving credit to the originator.

Precis a brief abstract or summary of the essential points of a book, play, movie, or other work.

Predicate pred one of two basic parts of a sentence. The subject tells who or what the sentence is about. The predicate tells something about the subject. The predicate must contain a verb.

subj. pred.
The engineers *work*.
The engineers *have* tools.
The engineers *are* here.
The engineers *are paving* the road.

Prefix a word element placed before a word to change the meaning of that word. Learning the meaning of prefixes is a basic part of building a vocabulary.

Prefix	Meaning	Examples of Use
anti	against	*anti*social, *anti*pathy, *anti*body, *anti*aircraft
ex	out of	*ex*tract, *ex*clude, *ex*pel
inter	between	*inter*cept, *inter*com
re	again	*re*peat, *re*bound, *re*cognize *re*open, *re*order

See also **Root; Suffix.**

Pun a play on words, or a playing with words, in a light and humorous way. In a pun, a word is presented as having two meanings simultaneously, or one word is substituted for another, similar-sounding word.

People who pun a great deal are sentenced to *punitentiaries.*
The kitten chewed a hole in my sweater. It was a *catastrophe.*
The marine biologist knew what his *porpoise* in life was.
Arnold Palmer follows the *golf stream*.

Question (Interrogative Sentence or Direct Question) a sentence that asks something and that ends with a question mark.

How do you get to Carnegie Hall?
Will you get my tools?

An indirect question is a question reworded as a statement in the speaker's or writer's own words. An indirect question ends with a period.

He asked *how to get to Carnegie Hall.* "Practice, practice!" she said.
The mechanic asked *if I would get him his tools.*

Quotation the repetition by one person of the words of another person. A quotation may be direct or indirect. A **direct quotation** is the word-for-word reproduction of something heard or read. A direct quotation is enclosed in quotation marks. It must be exactly like the original in wording, spelling, and punctuation when it is quoted from written or printed material.

He said, *"It is unlikely to happen before the year 2000."*
She screamed, *"Get out!"*
"Can this really be what is happening?" he asked.

An indirect quotation is the rewording of a direct quotation—the expression of the idea in words other than those of the person being quoted. Quotation marks are not used.

He said that it was unlikely to happen before the year 2000.
She told me to get out.
He asked if this was really what was happening.

See chapter 9.

Reflexive (or Intensive) Case Forms *myself, yourself, himself, herself, itself, ourselves, yourselves, themselves.* Reflexive forms are used in two ways:

1. to reflect back to the subject.

Adriana washed *herself.*
They shouted *themselves* hoarse.

2. for emphasis (called intensive)

Cuthbert did it *himself.*
We didn't send anyone else; we *ourselves* went.

Relative Clause a dependent clause that functions as an adjective, modifying a noun or pronoun. It is called a relative clause because it starts with a *relative pronoun (who, which, that)* or a *relative adverb (where, when, why).* Generally, *who* refers to persons; *which,* to things; and *that* to either persons or things. *That* usually introduces restrictive (essential) clauses.

The fire *that was just put out* had been started by a careless smoker. (The relative clause *that was just put out* refers to and modifies fire.)
The car struck Jim, *who was running across the street.* (The relative clause *who was running across the street* refers to and modifies Jim.)
The reason *why he went* is obscure. (The relative clause *why he went* refers to and modifies reason.)

Restrictive Modifier words, phrases, and clauses that are essential to the identification of the noun or noun equivalent they modify. A restrictive modifier is not set off by commas. *See* chapter 9.

The painter *Rembrandt* was born in Holland.
Mountains *that are subject to forest fires* should be off-limits to campers.
Animals *that have bitten people* should be quarantined.

Revision the process of careful rereading, correcting, and rewriting (when necessary) for the improvement of the entire work.

Rhetorical Question a question asked for an effect rather than for an answer. An answer is not expected because the answer is presumably obvious.

Is there any decent person who does not love his fellow man?
Is anything more destructive than nuclear holocaust?

Root a basic word element to which prefixes and suffixes can be added for variations in meaning. The root carries its meaning into every word in which it plays a part. Notice the common thread of meaning running through the following words containing the root *scribe*:

a*scribe,* de*scribe,* in*scribe,* pre*scribe,* sub*scribe,* *scrib*ble, *script,* con*script,* tran*script.*

See also **Prefix and Suffix.**

Sentence a group of words that contains at least one subject+verb unit and that communicates a sense of completeness. *See also* chapter 2; and **Complex Sentence; Compound Sentence; Compound-Complex Sentence; Declarative Sentence; Exclamatory Sentence; Imperative Sentence; Interrogative Sentence; Question; Simple Sentence** in this Glossary.

Sic a term that appears in brackets [*sic*] within a quotation to point to something questionable (perhaps a spelling error) in the word or words immediately preceding it. [*Sic*] shows that the quoter recognizes the error but is being true to the original quotation by reproducing that quotation with exactness.

The author begins, "With the sounding of the vesper bell Easter Moday [*sic*], 1282, the massacre, ironically called the Sicilian Vespers, began."

Simile fig a figure of speech presenting a point of similarity between two basically unlike things. In a simile something is generally said to be *as* or *like* something else.

The marble was as cold as ice.
The escalator, like an endless caterpillar, came and went, came and went.

See also **Figure of Speech; Metaphor.**

Simple Sentence a sentence that contains only one subject + verb unit. *See* also chapter 2.

subj. vb.
The Mississippi River flooded the Delta.

Slang sl dict informal words and expressions usually originated by various age, occupational, cultural, and interest groups. New words and expressions are continually being created. When a great many people understand the meaning of a new expression, it generally comes to be known as slang. Slang is an aspect of a living language. Some formerly slang expressions have become part of standard English; other slang expressions are short-lived, like fads in clothes. Because of its informality, slang is seldom appropriate to formal writing.

Split Infinitive INF inf placing an adverb within the infinitive form (*to* + verb: *to read, to walk)* of a verb. As a general rule, *to* and the *verb* should be separated only when the separation avoids awkwardness or increases clarity, or when the split is part of an idiom. The adverb usually fits more smoothly after the infinitive than within it.

Split	Not Split
to accurately *shoot* baskets	to shoot baskets accurately
to rapidly *run*	to run rapidly
to completely *read*	to read completely

Standard English the predominant English dialect, spoken and written by educated people. It may be either formal or informal, depending on the occasion of its use. *See also* **Levels of English.**

Style the unique way in which one writes—one's choice of words and the ways in which one puts those words together—as differentiated from what one writes about (although this, too, influences style). Style reflects many things about the writer, among them knowledge, experience, talent, learned and innate skill in communication, patterns of thinking, discipline, concepts of wrong and right, views of the world, and attitudes toward readers.

Subordination the structuring of sentence elements for the purpose of conveying their relative importance. Subordination is easily expressed by placing the more important of two ideas in an independent clause and the less important (subordinate) idea in a dependent clause. *See also* chapter 2.

dep. (subordinate) clause indep. clause
When I was hiking yesterday, a rattlesnake bit me.

Substandard English dict level slang language that is inappropriate to formal writing because of elements such as grammatical errors or informal vocabulary.

Substantive sb subst any sentence element that can function as a noun.

The *house* is big.
To err is human.
Playing football is hard *work.*

Suffix a word element that is attached to the end of a word to change the meaning of that word. Learning the meaning of suffixes is a basic part of vocabulary building.

tact*less* (without tact)
fool*ish* (like a fool)

See also **Prefix; Root.**

Superlative Forms (of adjectives and adverbs) comp cmp. *See* **Comparative Forms.**

Synonyms words having similar meanings. Since words that are synonyms seldom convey exactly the same meaning, a knowledge of synonyms and their distinctive shades of meaning is a major element in clear and accurate thinking and writing. (A dictionary of synonyms can be helpful in building a vocabulary.)

burning, feverish, hot

beautiful, handsome, aesthetic
baby, weakling, coward

See also **Antonym.**

Tautology rep wdy wordy the needless repetition of an idea in different words.

They all stood up simultaneously *at the same time.*

See also chapter 14.

Tone the attitude or feeling a writer conveys throughout any particular piece of writing. It is comparable to tone of voice in speaking. Tone may be, for example, *warm, cold, amused, reverent, detached, sarcastic, angry, friendly, excited, concerned, sad, happy.* However, the tone the writer adopts toward a topic should be maintained consistently unless there is good reason for changing the tone.

Transitive Verb vb verb a verb that requires an object to complete its meaning. A verb that does not require an object is called an intransitive verb. The same verb (*work,* for example) can be transitive in one sentence and intransitive in another, although not all verbs can be both transitive and intransitive.

Transitive	Intransitive
The farmer *worked* his land. (obj.)	The farmer *worked* continuously.

See also **Intransitive Verb.**

Trite a word used to describe expressions that are outworn and stale. They may be figures of speech, quotations, idioms, slang, or other words or word combinations. A trite expression is too familiar to add substance to a piece of writing.

Underlining corresponds to *italicizing* in printed material. In typed or handwritten matter, titles of books or magazines, and other material or expressions that need to be emphasized, can be underlined. Since practices in underlining vary, some instructors recommend their preferred methods to their students.

<u>The Saturday Review</u>
<u>Mad Magazine</u>
She is the <u>only</u> person who understands the situation.
He is the <u>real</u> John Jones.

Unity U un coh writing in which each part contributes clearly and directly to the central idea of the whole so that the reader feels a oneness in the work.

Usage Us dict the customary ways in which words and expressions are actually used under various circumstances. Some language, like some clothes, may be appropriate on one occasion and not on another. Most dictionaries categorize usage on a scale from informality through formality with labels like *slang, colloquial,* and *dialect.*

Formal Usage
He displayed anxiety and tension.
It has been shown that this conclusion is unwarranted.
She played the piano.

Informal Usage
He was "up tight."
His idea is no good.
She banged on the keys.

Verbals are formed from verbs but function as some other part of speech. *Infinitives* (to + verb) function as nouns, adjectives, and adverbs; *gerunds* (verb + ing) function as nouns; *participles* (verb+ ing or past form of verb), function as adjectives. See chapter 1.

Variety in Sentence Structure Var contributes to the effectiveness of writing. Sentence elements—words, phrases, and clauses—can be combined to form many kinds of sentences. Writing that limits itself to simple sentences, for example, tends to be monotonous.

Vowels and Consonants classification of letters of the alphabet. The letters *a, e, i, o, u,* and sometimes *y* are *vowels.* All other letters are consonants.

Word Choice See "**Choice.**"

Word Order wo The basic word order in English sentences is subject + verb. Other sentence elements may precede or follow the subject and/or the verb. *In questions, the verb may precede the subject; in commands or requests, the subject may be unexpressed. See also* chapter 12.

subj. vb.
Peace came.

subj. vb.
The *building remained* unfinished.

subj. vb.
After a long climb up the mountain, *we saw* the valley far below.

vb. subj. vb.
Have they understood? (question)

vb.
Remember this number! (command)

Index

Commonly Misspelled Words

1. absence
2. absolutely
3. abundance
4. accept
5. accommodate
6. accompanied
7. accurate
8. accuse
9. achieve
10. acquaintance
11. acquire
12. adolescent
13. advantageous
14. advisable
15. ancient
16. apparatus
17. apparent
18. apparently
19. appearance
20. applies
21. applying
22. appreciated
23. approximate
24. approximately
25. argument
26. arrangements
27. article
28. assistance
29. assistant
30. association
31. athlete
32. attacked
33. attendant
34. attitude
35. available
36. bargain
37. belief
38. believe
39. benefit
40. bureau
41. businesses
42. calendar
43. candidate
44. capital
45. capitol
46. challenge
47. changeable
48. characteristic
49. chief
50. circumstances
51. civilization
52. commercial
53. commission
54. commitment
55. committed
56. committee
57. comparatively
58. complement
59. compliment
60. conceive
61. condemn
62. confidential
63. conscience
64. conscientious
65. conscious
66. consequently
67. convenience
68. correspondence
69. council
70. counsel
71. courteous
72. criticism
73. deceive
74. decision
75. defense
76. deficient
77. definite
78. definitely
79. definition
80. descend
81. description
82. determined
83. develop
84. disappear
85. disastrous
86. discipline
87. discussed
88. disgusted
89. distinctly
90. dropped
91. duplicate
92. earliest
93. effect
94. efficient
95. eligible
96. elimination
97. embarrass
98. emphasize
99. employees
100. enclosure
101. encouraging
102. endeavor
103. enormous
104. environment
105. equipment
106. equipped
107. especially
108. essential
109. eventually
110. examination
111. excitement
112. executive
113. exhibition
114. existence
115. expense
116. experience
117. extremely
118. February
119. financial
120. flourish
121. foreign
122. forfeit
123. fortunately
124. freight
125. generally
126. genuine
127. glimpse
128. gratitude
129. happiness
130. height
131. heir
132. hoping
133. ignorance
134. ignorant
135. illustration
136. immediate
137. immediately
138. immense
139. inconvenienced
140. indefinite
141. independence
142. industrial
143. inevitable
144. inquiries
145. inquiry
146. installation
147. intelligence
148. intelligent
149. interfere
150. investigate
151. journal
152. knowledge
153. laboratory
154. licenses
155. literature
156. maintenance